A Publication Distributed by Heron Books

100
GREAT THINKERS

100
GREAT THINKERS

Volume 2

Distributed by
HERON BOOKS

CONTENTS
Volume 2

——Immanuel Kant——

[1724–1804]

THIS EXTRAORDINARY PHILOSOPHER led a very ordinary life. So ordinary, that every biographer is compelled to quote the great German poet Heinrich Heine about Kant:

> . . . he had neither life nor history, for he lived a mechanically ordered and abstract old bachelor life in a quiet retired street in Koenigsberg, an old town on the northeast border of Germany. I do not believe that the great clock of the cathedral there did its daily work more dispassionately and regularly than its compatriot Immanuel Kant. Rising, coffee drinking, writing, reading college lectures, eating, walking, all had their fixed time, and the neighbors knew that it was exactly half past three when Immanuel Kant . . . left his house door and went to the Lime Tree Avenue, which is still called, in memory of him, the Philosopher's Walk. . . .

Kant rarely left the Prussian city of Königsberg and in his eighty years of life never traveled more than seventy miles from its medieval walls. He was short, barely five feet two inches tall. His body was misshapen and he was, in his earlier years, a hypochondriac. He abstained from the pleasures of wine, women, and song. He allowed himself one pipeful of tobacco a day. To avoid head colds, he breathed through his nostrils. For this reason, so legend tells us, he took his long daily walks alone. Were he with someone, he would have to open his mouth to speak. Daily, he went to bed at ten and rose at five. Twice, Kant contemplated marriage. His contemplations were so lengthy that the first lady married someone else; the second lady left town before Kant had concluded his deliberations.

Kant's father, a maker of saddles, practiced religious pietism. Both father and mother were quiet people who led the kind of devotional life that is so expressive of the best in religious conduct. Of his mother, Kant said that he had derived his desire for good conduct from her. She died when Immanuel was thirteen, dying in an act of Christian charity. A friend of hers had fallen ill after having been deserted by her fiancé. She would not take the prescribed foul-tasting medicine. Unsuccessful at persuasion, Kant's mother attempted to set an example by taking the medicine. She was seized with nausea, developed a high fever, and died a few days later.

Kant attended the University of Königsberg, and supplemented his meager income by tutoring in the houses of the Prussian nobility. He liked to teach the youngsters of average ability. The geniuses, he said, would learn by themselves, and the stupid would never learn at all. He was a good teacher, and many of the political leaders who fought for the abolition of serfdom were his former pupils.

Kant came to his philosophic probings late in life. At first he was primarily interested in the physical sciences. In 1775, Kant proposed in *Theory of the Heavens* that the solar system developed out of a gaseous atmosphere. This exposition of the nebular theory anticipated Laplace's work of forty years later.

Two intellectual experiences changed the course of Kant's life. In his forties, he read Rousseau; and in his fifties, he read Hume.

Of Rousseau's impact, he wrote:

> I am myself by inclination a seeker after truth. I feel a consuming thirst for knowledge and a restless passion to advance in it. . . . There was a time when I thought that this alone could constitute the honor of mankind, and I despised the common man who knows nothing. Rousseau set me right. . . . I learned to respect human nature, and I should consider myself far more useless than the ordinary workingman if I did not believe that this view could give worth to all others to establish the rights of man.

It is no wonder that a picture of Rousseau was the only piece of art in his simple study.

Of David Hume's impact, Kant wrote that he had been awakened from his dogmatic slumbers by the fierce onslaught of the Scottish philosopher upon the principles that were the indispensable basis of the traditional rationalistic philosophy.

Hume had written, "If I must be a fool, as all who reason or believe anything *certainly* are, my follies shall at least be natural and agreeable." To the Scot, mind and matter do not exist. Our experience is a subjective one; the mind is only a "heap of perceptions." In the last days of the Age of Enlightenment, Hume had brought a devastating light to the world. God does not exist; scientific law does not exist; and man as a moral and purposeful human being does not exist. All that is left is for man to live by his instincts.

It was Immanuel Kant who fashioned a positive and all-embracing philosophy in the face of Hume's negative ideas. It was this structuring of a philosophic system out of the debris of the philosophic ruins that stamps Kant's contribution as one of the greatest in modern Western thought.

In 1781, Kant, at fifty-seven, presented *The Critique of Pure Reason* to a world that was well on its way to denying religion and doubting science.

Kant described his efforts as the Copernican revolution in philosophy. Copernicus had changed the course of astronomical inquiry by asserting the motion of the earth about the sun rather than by accepting the accepted view of a stationary earth as the center of the motion of the heavenly bodies. Similarly, Kant turned away from the traditional philosophic method of looking first at the objects of experience and then at the effect these sensory impressions had upon the mind. Kant made the assumption that it is the operating mind that determines the objects of knowledge it will know and understand.

Physics and mathematics had proved to Kant's satisfaction that the mind does exist and does operate on fixed principles; he saw in these sciences acknowledged universal propositions and principles. From these, conclusions are drawn that are true of experience. Supporting evidence is neither necessary nor always available. In our time, Albert Einstein waited forty years for experience to show the truth of his findings.

Thus, for Kant, Man is not a *tabula rasa*, a passive, clean slate upon which experience is written. Kant wrote:

Experience is by no means the only field to which our understanding can be confined. Experience tells us what is, but not that it must be necessarily what it is and not otherwise. It therefore never gives us any really general truths; and our reason, which is particularly anxious for that class of knowledge, is roused by it rather than satisfied. General truths, which at the same time, bear the character of an inward necessity, must be independent of experience—clear and certain in themselves.

To determine these "general truths," Kant formulated a yardstick by which the experiences could be measured. He called these yardstick measurements "a priori intuitions and concepts." These known-beforehand and prior-to-experience concepts, vital to the understanding of any experience, are the holders into which we pour our experiences. There are twelve such categories, as well as the elements of space and time.

For example, Kant said that time and space do not exist by themselves. Our mind forges these tools in order to be receptive to the impressions of experience. We know that time exists because we recognize the passage of time in a sequence of events. Similarly, a perceived object in space gives us the possibility of organizing objects into a framework that we call "space." Therefore, we do not experience "space" or "time" as sensory reactions to physical phenomena. Rather, we place our sensory experiences into this a priori developed frame-of-reference structure.

The Kantian categories are divided into four sets of three: (1) of quantity: unity, plurality, totality; (2) of quality: reality, negation, limitation; (3) of relation: substance-and-accident, cause-and-effect, reciprocity; (4) of modality: possibility, existence, necessity.

These are the a priori concepts that function as containers; these containers receive the human being's sensory perceptions. Within the containers, the sensory impressions are related and molded into coherent thought. Thus, the mind acts as the umpire of an athletic contest in regulating the game, and the categories act as the procedural rules by which the umpire views and judges the events of the game.

The sensations come to the mind in droves—unorganized and unrelated. It is man's being, his mind, if you will, whose sense of purpose organizes a logical and coherent thought pattern out of this mass of unrelated empirical observations.

So, Kant wrote, "Perceptions without conceptions are blind."

Inherent in Kant's philosophy is man's inability to gain full knowledge of the world, for his understanding is limited to the mind's categorizing sensory perceptions within the framework of time, space, and the twelve categories. What we know through this method are phenomena—things-as-they-appear-to-us. We do not know objects as they exist apart from us. The latter things Kant called "noumena"—"things-in-themselves."

Philosophic fallacies emerge from associating the categories with things that are not experienced. These, Kant called "antinomies"—statements that carry mutually contradictory propositions. In one antinomy, the thesis says: "The world has a beginning in time, and is also limited as regards space." The antithesis says: "The world has no beginning in time, and no limits in space; it is infinite as regards both time and space." Similarly, the fourth antinomy shows that there is, and is not, an absolutely necessary Being.

Kant, according to Heine, killed God, for Kant's conclusion was that we could only know things-as-they-appear-to-us. "Since metaphysics pretends to be the science of the suprasensible and since only the sensible can ever be an object of knowledge, a metaphysics of pure reason is impossible."

He served science no better. His conclusions limited the scope of science; it could know only the world as it appeared to us.

The sage of Königsberg struck valiant blows for the freedom and dignity of the individual. He had not forgotten Rousseau, who had taught him to honor man. So the concept of freedom stands at the heart of Kant's ethical works: *Groundwork of the Metaphysic of Morals* (1785) and *Critique of Practical Reason* (1788).

Man is free because he is not morally molded by outside forces or experiences. It is his inner reasoning that dictates his moral actions. These actions, motivated by the mind's reasoning, are free actions. And it is this freedom that he must accord his fellow man regardless of status, color, or creed. Kant called this universal rule of action a "categorical imperative." This rule must be followed absolutely without any regard to wants and desires. "Act only on that maxim whereby thou canst at the same time will that it should become a universal law."

That maxim enunciates the principle of respect for humanity. Kant stated the categorical imperative in another way: "So act as to treat humanity, whether in thine own person or in that of any other, in every case as an end withal, never as a means only."

Man is not a cog in a machine. Neither is he a statistic. He is an end in himself and must treat his fellow human as an agent of complete freedom. Kant admonished us "not to put our own interests or those of our favorites first." To use our inner reasoning is to form a pattern of conduct which is equally valid for all.

It has been correctly noted that Kant's categorical imperative is very similar to Christianity's golden rule.

In 1795, Kant published a treatise on war, *Perpetual Peace*. In this work, Kant condemned war and called for a federation of free states. Only an international government bound together by a covenant forbidding war could prevent these man-made holocausts. In addition, he called for the separation of the executive and legislative branches. Since a ruler might go to war "as if it were but a hunting expedition," war could be declared only "by a plebiscite of all the citizens." Furthermore, the state, far from imposing dictatorial power upon its people, must assist in the moral and ethical development of the human race. Too often, ". . . our rulers have no money to spend on public education . . . because all their resources are already placed to the account of the next war." Again, Kant reiterated the best that is in democratic thought: "Every man is to be respected as an absolute end in himself; and it is a crime against the dignity that belongs to him as a human being to use him as a mere means for some external purpose."

In 1794, when he was sixty-nine, Kant wrote *Religion within the Bounds of Mere Reason*. In this work, he proposed that Christianity is the historical form of an ethical concept. The true church is composed of people who willingly execute the categorical imperative. These people are devoted to Kant's universal moral law. The existing church has value when it helps man in his quest for full moral development. When ritual and ceremony, when creed and practice, become primary activities of the church, then religion has nothing to offer.

So, as it came to Socrates, Copernicus, and Galileo, official displeasure fell upon the venerable seventy-year-old sage of

Königsberg. The Prussian King, Friedrich Wilhelm II, forbade him to publish or discuss this work. Kant argued that every thinker should have the freedom to pursue and formulate truths, but he agreed to be silent during Wilhelm's reign. When Wilhelm died, Kant published this work.

In his last years, Kant lost his memory. He could not sleep; his days were plagued with mental unrest. Theory has it that he suffered from a brain condition. Finally, after a long illness, Kant died in 1804. The categorical imperative to do one's moral duty was strong in him. Ten days before his death, the withered old man got to his feet when his doctor visited. When the doctor protested this act of courtesy, Kant replied, "The sense of humanity has not yet left me."

Kant's influence ranged through the thought patterns of nineteench-century Europe. Schopenhauer and Nietzsche developed the concept of the inner freedom of man. Bergson developed the thesis of intuitions. William James carried Kant's empiricism into the doctrine of pragmatism. Hegel and Marx developed complete systems of philosophy by employing the idea of categories. Finally, in our time, Sartre and de Beauvoir worked out an existential ethics that draws heavily on Kant's philosophy. Since all men are free, men must treat each other as what they are: free! And this freedom must be used to further man's individuality. The categorical imperative is still in force.

FURTHER READING

Cassirer, Ernst. *Rousseau, Kant and Goethe.*
Gran, M. *Kant.*
Klinke, Willibald. *Kant for Everyman.*
Smith, T. V., and Grene, Marjorie, eds. *Philosophers Speak for Themselves: Berkeley, Hume, and Kant.*
Whitney, G. T., and Bowers, D. F., eds. *The Heritage of Kant.*

——Thomas Paine——
[1737–1809]

THE AMERICAN REVOLUTION had begun with high hopes and an inspiring stand on Bunker Hill in June of 1775. By the end of the next year, however, the situation had changed drastically. General Washington had suffered a series of defeats on Long Island, Manhattan, and New Jersey. His troops had dwindled to about thirty-five hundred, against thirty-five thousand British regulars. Ammunition, clothing, food, and money were scarce and the morale of the American patriots was at a low ebb as he was about to lead them to winter encampment at Valley Forge. It was at this time that a young volunteer aide-de-camp of General Nathanael Greene, who had been in the country for only two years, began publishing a series of pamphlets called *The Crisis*, beginning with the lines: "These are the times that try men's souls. The summer soldier and the sunshine patriot will, in this crisis, shrink from the service of their country."

In his pamphlets he proclaimed, in clear, dynamic prose, the value of the American struggle and the price that had to be paid for freedom. His essays were circulated widely and played an important part in maintaining morale through the critical times.

Paine had known hardships and plain living from his early life. He was born in Thetford, England, and at age thirteen, after grammar school, had been apprenticed to his Quaker father's trade of corsetmaking. The life of an apprentice was a difficult one, and he left it. Thereafter he was a sailor, grocer, and exciseman. He entered a youthful marriage, which ended in tragedy when his wife died.

One of the early beginnings of his work on behalf of the

300

lowly was his appeal to Parliament to raise the pay of excisemen, an appeal that led to the loss of his job.

In 1774, on the advice of Benjamin Franklin, he left England for America, where he became editor of the successful *Pennsylvania Magazine*. These were times of controversy in America: many were dissatisfied with the unfair treatment by the British, who, under a policy of mercantilism, sought to exploit their colonies. Most of the American leaders talked of redressing their grievances as Englishmen. Very few wanted independence from England, even at the beginning of hostilities in 1776.

One of the few was Thomas Paine, who, in 1776, wrote a brilliant pamphlet, *Common Sense*, which argued that independence was the only possible goal that would make America unified and strong. He urged that it was America's obligation to the world to rid the new continent of a monarchy and create a federal republic. Some half a million copies of this pamphlet were sold. It influenced Thomas Jefferson and others who wrote and signed the Declaration of Independence.

As secretary of the Continental Congress during the war he became embroiled with the French representatives and was dismissed. Though Paine's tactlessness and occasional excessive use of liquor were to get him into difficulties many times in his life, after the war New York granted him a farm in New Rochelle, and Pennsylvania offered the sum of £ 500 for his services.

In an article called "Public Good" Paine was one of the first, in 1780, to issue a call for a national convention to replace the ineffectual Articles of Confederation with a strong constitutional government. It is interesting that his views later changed. In *The Rights of Man* he later advocated a sort of oversimplified anarchism with a minimum of government.

Paine was in England and France from 1787 to 1802. He had initially gone to England to sell his idea of a pierless iron bridge, but he inevitably became involved as a propagandist in the political struggles of both countries. In 1791 and 1792 he published *The Rights of Man*, which defended the principles of the French Revolution, founded on individual rights to liberty, security, republicanism, and freedom from oppression. He also advocated the overthrow of the monarchy and the formation of a republican government in England, for which Prime Minister Pitt had him indicted for treason. Paine escaped by fleeing to France. Although Paine was regarded as an extreme radical, many of the views he expressed in *The Rights of Man* are accepted policy now. He said, "Every age and generation must be free to act for itself in all cases as the ages and generations which preceded it. . . . I am contending for the rights of the living." He wanted the government to be a humanitarian agent, to provide for the needy and helpless. He even advocated a progressive income tax. Such views, of course, were anathema to the French Bourbon rulers, as well as to the English ruling group.

On July 1, 1791, Tom Paine and his friend, Condorcet, distributed leaflets in Paris urging the formation of a French republic. Although Paine could speak no French, he was elected to the French Convention. However, he incurred the wrath of Robespierre when he urged the exile rather than execution of King Louis XVI. As a result of his views, he was imprisoned from December 1793 to November 1794 and almost lost his life.

Living in Paris, he published his philosophical and religious beliefs in the *Age of Reason* (1794, 1796); this is an exposition of his belief in God, but he refused to accept the dogma or traditional teachings of the Church. He based his religious beliefs upon reason, not faith. He accepted a mechanistic or materialistic design of the cosmos; he recognized the necessity of man living in society, but like Godwin and Rousseau he had faith in the natural goodness of man that would guide him to a better life through his use of reason. His *Age of Reason* provoked the wrath of ecclesiastics and led to accusations of atheism, although he really was professing deism. Paine was a spokesman for the ideals of the Age of Enlightenment which followed the unveiling of scientific truths about the universe. He believed in freedom of speech, the dignity of the individual, religious freedom, and humanitarianism. He surely influenced Thomas Jefferson, who admitted professing many of Paine's principles, and indirectly his influence helped bring about the Reform Bill of 1832, which extended suffrage and human rights in England.

Thomas Paine's tactlessness, as shown in his open letter to George Washington accusing the latter of helping to have him imprisoned in France, caused him to be unpopular during the last few years of his life in America. He died in New York City, but his body was later removed for burial in England.

Paine proved that "the pen is mightier than the sword," for his influence achieved more enduring changes than the strategy of the generals who were his contemporaries.

FURTHER READING

Clark, Harry Hayden, ed. *Thomas Paine, Representative Selections.*

Foner, Philip S., ed. *Life and Major Writings of Thomas Paine.*

Woodward, William E. *Tom Paine: America's Godfather.*

——Thomas Jefferson——
[1743–1826]

WOODROW WILSON said of him, "The immortality of Thomas Jefferson does not lie in any one of his achievements but in his attitude toward mankind." John Adams—with whom Jefferson had had personal and political differences—as he lay dying, said hopefully for the new nation: "Jefferson still lives." Ironically, Jefferson was dying, too, the same day, July 4, 1826.

Jefferson has been characterized as a liberal. Although the English Tories and some of his enemies who were Federalists regarded him as a dangerous radical, he was surely no violent revolutionary at odds with his times. His chief concern was a liberty in which the freedom of the mind was an absolute.

Thomas Jefferson was a tall, thin redheaded man. His curiosity was insatiable, a quality it was said he inherited from his father, Peter Jefferson. Heir to the Tidewater and the Piedmont estates, he was close to the problems of the slave owner, the tobacco raiser, the plantation owner, and the trials of the frontiersman.

Jefferson's education played a tremendous part in his thinking. He went to English school in Tuckahoe at the age of five, and to Latin school at the age of nine. At sixteen he entered William and Mary. He was "eager after information," a phrase that Jefferson used to describe his own father.

The times were those when scholars felt the reaction against revelation. These scholars sought truth in objective things and nature. William Small, professor of mathematics at William and Mary, and a nonclerical faculty member, not only opened Jefferson's mind to a liberal point of view but also opened the doors of George Wyeth's law office to the young Jefferson, so that from 1762 to 1765 he was engaged in private study under Wyeth. He was not an apprentice as such but a student. It is interesting that this thorough scholar mastered English, Roman, French, and Saxon law.

These same years, living at Williamsburg much of the time, Jefferson formed friendships with Governor Farquier, Peyton Randolph, and Dabny Carr. Jefferson was a notetaker; his *Commonplace Book* is a storehouse of thoughts, and one learns from it that he had a creative mind in things as well as ideas. His study program was, in modern terms, staggering: from eight in the morning to noon, law; from noon to one, politics; and from three to seven, history and literature. He also learned to play the violin. He had social interests, and we find letters to an unknown Belinda. Years later he was to set an equally ambitious schedule for his daughter, one that on the surface provided no time for rest, recreation, or eating but set forth hours for drawing, letter writing, and music. He said, "It is wonderful how much may be done if we are always doing."

By 1776 he was a member of the bar, a member of the House of Burgesses of Virginia, and a married man. He had married a widow, Martha Wayles Skelton; they had six children, of whom only two daughters survived. When his home on his father's estate at Shadwell was destroyed by fire, he moved to Monticello in Virginia. His married life was affectionate and happy. When his wife died in 1782, Jefferson never remarried.

Now we begin to see in his activities the truth of the slogan, "Coming events cast their shadows ahead." In 1770 he took the case of Samuel Howell, a slave suing for his freedom—

his servitude having arisen from a penalty inflicted on his grandmother in 1706. Although Jefferson lost the case, we read in his argument: "It will not be pretended that the mother being a servant the child would be a servant under the law of nature, because under the law of nature all men are born free." In 1774 he wrote that the king is no more than a chief officer, that the British Parliament has no right to authority, that God gives life and liberty at the same time. Thus, there had been preparation for the task of writing the Declaration of Independence, a task that took him eighteen days. It sprang from a fertile and prepared mind that was influenced by such liberal thinkers as the English philosopher John Locke (1632–1704).

In the period prior to the American Revolution, he opposed the Townshend Acts, which restricted the commerce and growth of the colonies, and he presented to the Virginia Convention (the House of Burgesses having been dissolved) a *Summary View of the Rights of British America* (1774). In this he declared that the British had no special rights in the colonies at all. Although these views were too radical to be adopted, they had great influence and won for Jefferson a leading role in the American Revolution. His draft of the later declaration drew on this document.

Jefferson traveled to Philadelphia to the First Continental Congress. It was on this and subsequent trips that he was struck by the multiplicity and variety of coins that were used —the British shilling, the Spanish dollar, the Portuguese crown. It was to eliminate this confusion that ten years later he introduced the idea of a uniform decimal coinage system in his "Notes on Establishment of a Money Unit and of a Coinage System for the United States" (1784).

From 1776 to 1779 Jefferson was a legislator, a member of the Virginia house of delegates to the Continental Congress. There he led an attack on entail and primogeniture, the traditional method of inheritance, which unfairly gave the estate of a deceased to his eldest son and left the others as dependents. He also led the attack, started earlier, on taxation that forced people to support religions other than their own. In 1779 he produced the clearly reasoned *Ordinance for Establishment of Religious Freedom.* He believed that God created the mind free, that civil rights were not dependent on religious opinions, that religious opinions are not the object of civil government, that no man should suffer legally for his religious opinions, and that ideas cease to be dangerous when freely circulated. He stood for freedom in government, thought, and speech.

In 1779, too, we find Jefferson's interest in education resulting in his effort to stimulate an interest in public-supported education for all, a prophecy perhaps of some provisions of the Northwest Ordinance. In Virginia, free public education failed to pass but he formulated a bill for the diffusion of knowledge which would provide elementary education for all, college for the middle group, and provisions for the teaching of science. Years later in 1809 he said, "I always hear with pleasure of institutions for the promotion of knowledge among my country men. The people of every country are the only safe guardians of their own rights and are the only instruments which can be used for their destruction. . . . To avoid this [being deceived] they should be instructed to a certain degree."

In 1784, as a member of the Congress under the Articles of Confederation, he headed a committee regarding the plan for governing the western Territories (later included in the Northwest Ordinance). Then, in 1784, his plan included a provision for the exclusion of slavery in that area after 1800. This was, again, a forecast of his growing antislavery views.

While he was envoy to France, first with Benjamin Franklin and later alone, his interests were as diversified as ever. Architecture, the decimal system, and the education of his children all were reflected in his letters.

His return to the United States and his position as Secretary of State under Washington brought to him years of controversy and conflict. His conflict with Alexander Hamilton stemmed from fundamental differences in political philosophy and background. Hamilton was the champion of a strong central government, Jefferson the supporter of an American democracy close to the people. The former was interested in the growth of manufacture; Jefferson stayed close to the agrarian point of view. Their views became the pivots around which the Federalists and the Anti-Federalists revolved. Hamilton's sympathies were with Great Britain, Jefferson's with France. Yet Jefferson favored a policy of neutrality toward France and a separation from European politics—a view later embodied in the Monroe Doctrine.

He left all the conflicts, with a sense of relief, when he was able to return to scientific and architectural pursuits at Monticello. Yet, in 1790, we find him conferring with George Nicholas and Wilson Carey, preparing a sketch of resolutions that clearly delineate his concept of the role of the federal government.

He thought that the Constitution was a compact that did not require unlimited submission by the states to the central government. Rather, the states had delegated to that government definite powers; he opposed the elastic-clause concept. He held that a government created by a compact could not be the sole judge of its own powers. Whenever a central government assumed undelegated powers, those acts should be void. When Jefferson was President, he disagreed completely with Supreme Court Chief Justice John Marshall, a Federalist who favored expansion of the powers of the national government. Basically, Jefferson feared the tyranny of a strong central government. He was unwilling to cast off the yoke of British autocracy only to assume a new autocracy here.

Jefferson was elected President in 1800. His inauguration and his practices as President were revolutionary for those days. His inauguration ceremonies were simple. He sent written messages to Congress instead of appearing personally. He sought to avoid all titles and privileges. His belief in a republican form of government was reflected in his political and social life. In 1803, he faced the dilemma of squaring his own political philosophy with practical politics. The purchase of Louisiana was at issue. Jefferson knew that his position about the constitutionality of this purchase was in question. In his view there was no authority in the Constitution for such a purchase. Twice he suggested an amendment to the Constitution to legalize it. Twice his cabinet held him off. Finally, he authorized the purchase, but his words betray his sense of guilt: "It is the case of the guardian investing the money of his ward. I did this for your good . . . you may disavow me. . . . I thought it my duty to risk myself for you."

From his youth, Jefferson's pursuit of scientific knowledge was phenomenal. His *Commonplace Notebook* and his *Notes on Virginia* all are replete with scientific observations. In his instructions to the Lewis and Clark expedition we see the proof of his all-encompassing mind. He instructed the explorers to investigate the natural history of the soil, the rocks, the animals, and the waterfalls of the great expanse in which they were to venture. His soil experiments, his compass in the ceiling at Monticello, and his horticultural experiments are proofs of his insatiable curiosity and of his advanced thinking.

Jefferson's agrarian background influenced all his thinking. He was interested in the wide distribution of land and in the small landowners. He took a position that was reflected in the Homestead Act decades later, when he said: "It is too soon yet . . . to say that every man who cannot find employment, but who can find uncultivated land shall be at liberty to cultivate it, paying a moderate rent."

In his position as President, Jefferson had other serious decisions to make. Foreign policy was a serious problem. It is interesting to read his words: "I consider Europe at present as a world apart from us. We consider interests of Cuba, Mexico and ours are the same; the object of both must be to exclude all European influence from this hemisphere." Here was the Monroe Doctrine in embryo.

In his retired years he devoted himself not only to Monticello but to the University of Virginia at Charlottesville. The planning, the construction, the faculty, and the curriculum were all his great concern. His views on curriculum and administration would be called by some "twentieth-century."

Was Thomas Jefferson a liberal, moderate, or radical? Regarding Shays's Rebellion he wrote to John Adams, "I like a little rebellion now and then. It is like a storm in the atmosphere." Later to Colonel Smith he wrote, "The tree of liberty must be refreshed with the blood of patriots and tyrants. It is its natural manure!"

As one considers Jefferson's contributions, there is his own evaluation of his work as described by the epitaph he composed for himself: "Here was buried Thomas Jefferson, author of the Declaration of Independence, of the Statute of Virginia for Religious Freedom and father of the University of Virginia."

One can agree with Abraham Lincoln, "Every party in this country today reckons Jefferson as its patron Saint." His own seal carries his motto, "Rebellion to tyrants is Obedience to God."

FURTHER READING

Bowers, Claude. *Jefferson in Power.*
Dos Passos, John. *The Shackles of Power.*
Malone, Dumas. *Jefferson the Virginian.*

————Jeremy Bentham————
[1748–1832]

IN THE YEAR 1760, Jeremiah Bentham decided to
send his son, Jeremy, then twelve, to Oxford University. The
lad, timid but intelligent, had read much, and his father
thought that a few years at Oxford would prepare him for a
career at the bar. At that time one of the formalities connected
with admission—a formality somewhat analogous to loyalty
oaths in twentieth-century America—was the signing of the
Thirty-nine Articles, which, since the sixteenth century, had
expressed the official doctrine of the Church of England.
Young Bentham had reservations, but he was prevailed upon
to sign in spite of them. He never forgot that experience. One
is tempted to think—though it would probably be an oversimplification to believe—that from this small incident Jeremy
Bentham's career as a reformer in law, in government, and in
philosophy began.

It would perhaps be more precise to say that Bentham was
a great theorist of reform, rather than a reformer. He was
an acute critic of existing institutions, and he had a fertile
imagination that was busily engaged during his long life in
conceiving of efficient and reasonable ways of doing things
that were being done poorly or not at all.

After leaving Oxford, he had a brief and unspectacular
career as a lawyer. His experience taught him that the laws
and the legal procedures of England were a collection of
superstitions, fallacies, confusions, and devices to enrich

lawyers and judicial officers at the expense of those who came
before the bar of justice. He set out to right these wrongs
with his mind and his pen.

His life as a reformer may be divided into two parts. In
his initial efforts, he was working on the assumption that all
that was necessary for the reformer to succeed was to show
that existing practices were wrong and to suggest better ones.
As he himself said later, "I was a great reformist, but never
suspected that 'the people in power' were against reform. I
supposed that they only wanted to know what was good in
order to embrace it." This sanguine approach to the problems
of men and society survived many setbacks and never really
left him.

An eccentric as an individual, Bentham was unique as a
reformer. He rejected most of the currently progressive
principles, such as the doctrine of natural rights of man and
the theory of the social contract, referring to them as unnecessary fictions. He was more interested in dealing with the
specific facts of how things worked in practice and how they
could be made to work better. He was continually asking
"Why?" He would accept no vague answer that referred to
precedent, tradition, or custom. This made him a devastating
critic of the hypocrisy of his day.

In place of the vague generalizations and pious platitudes
that satisfied his contemporaries, tories and reformers alike,
Bentham honored one principle which he called "the greatest
happiness principle," or "the principle of utility." This
principle declares that "the greatest happiness of the greatest
number is the measure of right and wrong." Happiness is
defined in terms of pleasure and pain, by the presence of the
former and the absence of the latter. This utilitarian doctrine
antedated Bentham; however, he made it famous, devised a
means for its application, and through his disciples influenced
the entire world with it.

His approach was simple. In considering any practice or
institution, he would inquire about how it worked and what
its actual effects were. Did the particular practice he was
investigating produce happiness or did it produce the reverse?
If the former, could it be made to produce a greater quantity
of happiness? If it produced unhappiness, could it be eliminated or changed? It is easy to see that this method required
that pleasures and pains be analyzed; they had to be meas-

ured, or quantified. The crucial question to be answered was: How much pleasure and how much pain are consequent on particular courses of action?

For this purpose, Bentham devised "the felicific calculus," the calculus of pleasures and pains. The value of a pleasure to an individual will be greater or less according to the following circumstances: (1) its intensity, (2) its duration, (3) its certainty or uncertainty, (4) its proximity or remoteness, (5) its fecundity (its chance of being followed by similar sensations), and (6) its purity. If a number of persons are affected, one must also consider (7) its extent (the number of persons who are affected by it). Bentham devised a mnemonic jingle to summarize the felicific calculus:

> *Intense, long, certain, speedy, fruitful, pure—*
> Such marks in *pleasures* and in *pains* endure.
> Such pleasures seek if *private* be thy end:
> If it be *public*, wide let them *extend*.
> Such *pains* avoid, whichever be thy view:
> If pains *must* come, let them *extend* to few.

Bentham envisioned legislators, confronted with alternative policies, calculating the pleasures and pains that would flow from each and determining a course of action in the direction of the policy that would produce "the greatest happiness of the greatest number." Thus he was a democrat in the sense that he believed that government ought to act in the interest of the people, but he was not a democrat in the sense of believing that government ought to be carried on by the people. The best government was government by the experts for the people.

The relation of government to the economic life of the country also concerned Bentham. He extended Smith's thesis of *laissez faire* with the premise that each individual knows his own interest best. He claimed that government interference was both needless and pernicious, pernicious because it always requires restrictions, which diminish happiness. His successor, John Stuart Mill, took the view that government interference is desirable in some areas of the economy.

The second phase of Bentham's career as a reformer came when he realized that those in power were not interested in reform. They were not really concerned with the welfare of

the people, but only with their own power and welfare.
Bentham then came to feel that only through a reform of
government itself, only with the introduction of a system of
government in which the rulers' interest was identical with
that of the ruled, could reform and good government be
achieved.

The utilitarian theory on this matter, the elaboration of
Bentham's doctrine, was formulated by James Mill in his *Essay
on Government* (1820). The solution to the problem of securing an identity of interest between the rulers and the ruled lies
in an adequate system of representation. Parliament as con-
stituted did not correctly represent the interest of the people.
Disenfranchisement by property requirements for voting and
corruption interfered with the expression of the popular
interest. Sinister (partial) interests dominated its councils. The
solution was the reform of Parliament. It is to this end that
Bentham devoted the last years of his life. The culmination
was the passage of the Reform Bill of 1832, which contained many of the reforms that the utilitarians had advocated.
Bentham died in that year and did not live to learn that the
reformed Parliament did not achieve what he had hoped
from it. His disciple John Stuart Mill saw this outcome, and
was led to further reflections on the problems of government.

The central criticism that has been leveled against Bentham's theory is that it oversimplifies human experience, in that
it conceives of pleasures and pains as entities that can be
measured and compared. Bentham's critics, both the sympathetic ones, like J. S. Mill, and the hostile ones, have pointed
out that qualitative differences among pleasures are usually of
crucial importance in making decisions and that the character
of a life cannot be determined by adding and subtracting
pleasures and pains.

In Bentham's defense it may be said that he was neither a
psychologist nor a philosopher, but rather a reforming lawyer
who used certain congenial philosophical and psychological
ideas to help him in the great task of providing a scientific
basis for a system of law and government. That he was not
completely successful does not detract from the fact that he
provided the impetus to lead others to carry on the work. The
reforms that have been accomplished in England and elsewhere all rest partly on his work.

FURTHER READING

Everett, Charles W., ed. *Jeremy Bentham.*
Ogden, C. K. *Bentham's Theory of Fictions.*
Stephen, Leslie. *The English Utilitarians.*

——John Marshall——
[1755–1835]

THE AMERICAN REVOLUTION was almost over and young John Marshall returned to his native Virginia. Several years had passed since he and his father, Tom, both crackshot backwoodsmen from the Blue Ridge Mountains of Virginia, had enlisted to fight for freedom. Side by side they had endured the hardships of Valley Forge and numerous other campaigns, and John had risen to the rank of captain.

Now there was a new challenge before him, the challenge of making a career. During his years of military service he had revealed a keen mind and ability to analyze problems, so that his fellow soldiers found themselves going to him for advice. His pioneer parents, Mary and Tom, had wrested a hard living from the soil and forests, but John had reasons to aim higher. He had fallen in love with one of the daughters of the treasurer of Virginia—Mary Ambler, a slim vivacious girl, whose family traced its origin to the ruling clans of Scotland. Tall and gangling in his homespun clothes, John went courting, and there was a charm about his straightforward manner and clear mind that won Mary's family to him.

He decided upon a career in law, hoping that success in this honorable profession would equalize the gap between him and Mary's family. One of the few books that John had perused as a boy in his father's cabin had been Blackstone's *Commentaries on the Law.* He enrolled in the College of William and Mary, where he stayed for some six weeks,

studying the theory of law. Then, in need of money and
impatient to earn a living, Marshall left William and Mary
and, in 1781, obtained admission to the bar (at this time it
was not necessary to have a law degree or formal training to
be a lawyer).

Marshall began the practice of law in his native Fauquier
County in Virginia, and his personality was such that success
came to him from the beginning. In 1782 he married Mary
Ambler and was elected to the Virginia Assembly the same
year. In 1783, he moved to Richmond, where his practice
increased considerably with the assistance of his wife's family
but chiefly because of his own talents and genius.

In 1788 the proposed Constitution of the United States came
before Virginia for ratification. There was considerable opposition to the new Constitution by men who feared that a
strong central government would endanger the very freedom
they had wrested from England. John Marshall, realizing the
necessity of a strong government to protect their hard-won
independence and to promote the general welfare, took his
stand with Madison, Jefferson, and Washington in strong support of ratification, and used his eloquence to persuade the
delegates to accept it. The vote of Virginia, with its high
prestige among the colonies, was crucial. When the Constitution was ratified by a ten-vote majority, due in part to the
efforts of Marshall, his reputation became a national one.

In 1795 President Washington offered him the attorney-
generalship and in 1796 the position of Ambassador to France
that had just been vacated by James Monroe. Marshall
declined these appointments because of the pressure of his
own legal work. However, when the independence of his
country seemed threatened by the new revolutionary government of France, he accepted an appointment by President
Adams as special envoy to the directorate of France. In 1797
and 1798 he was in France, seeking to work out an honorable
solution. However, when the French Directory, in effect,
demanded a huge bribe (the X.Y.Z. Affair) to cease interfering with our shipping, Marshall broke off the discussions
and returned home.

His statesmanship and refusal to compromise the honor of
his country won the acclaim of his countrymen. It was on
this occasion that the famous words "Millions for defense but
not one cent for tribute" were uttered in Congress. In 1799

Marshall was elected to the House of Representatives, one of the few members of the Federalist party to be elected in a time of ascendency of the Republican party under Thomas Jefferson, a distant cousin of Marshall. In 1800, he was appointed Secretary of State by President Adams and in 1801, he was offered the post of Chief Justice of the Supreme Court of the United States.

John Marshall now had a difficult decision to make. His law practice was lucrative; he now possessed a substantial fortune, and his prestige was high. On the other hand, as a Supreme Court justice, he would have to give up his private practice—and for what? The Court had neither authority nor prestige. John Jay had recently resigned the position of Chief Justice, saying that the Court would never amount to anything. Moreover, Thomas Jefferson, the incoming President, was a Republican who was regarded as a radical and even a threat to property owners. How could Marshall, a Federalist and a conservative, hope to influence the government, or even to work in harmony with it? The temptation to decline was great, but John Marshall decided that the government for which he had risked his life in war had a prime claim upon his talents and energy. He accepted the appointment.

The first problem that he had to solve was disunity of purpose among the six justices. The practice of each judge setting forth his own opinion had a weakening effect upon the judgment rendered, and Chief Justice Marshall persuaded the other judges to debate in private and to issue one decision with himself as spokesman. This new procedure of the Court speaking in a single voice, the eloquent, logical voice of John Marshall, soon gave its decisions a new dignity and acceptance.

His next effort was to establish in theory and practice the functions and powers of the U.S. Supreme Court and, even more important, to interpret the powers of the new federal government in the light of the Constitution. These formative years were among the most critical ones in the history of the nation. There were many patriots who had fought for freedom and who opposed the new Constitution and a strong federal government. There was mistrust between the members of the two major parties, the Republicans and the Federalists. There were wide differences between the merchants and industrialists of New England, the plantation owners of the South, and the independent farmers and backwoodsmen of the West. Would the Constitution, which had barely been ratified, be accepted as a working document? How should disputants be satisfied when there were basic differences in interpretation?

Two years after Marshall took office, the first major case came before the Court, *Marbury* v. *Madison* (1803). The case was a difficult one. Marbury had been legally appointed a judge by Adams, but his appointment had been voided by the next Congress. Marbury appealed to the Supreme Court for a writ of mandamus to secure his position. The temper of the new Republican Congress was such that, if the Federalist Marshall had issued the mandamus, it would have been disregarded, and the authority of the Supreme Court would have suffered a fatal blow. In this situation, the Chief Justice decided upon a bold but canny course. He denied the mandamus as not within the jurisdiction of his court, but in an *obiter dictum,* he held the law that voided the appointment unconstitutional. Thus he established, without overt challenge, the right of the U.S. Supreme Court to review any law of Congress or of a state legislature and to declare it unconstitutional.

In *McCulloch* v. *Maryland* (1819), Marshall conceded that the powers of the federal government were *delegated powers,* but he argued that the exercise of the *delegated powers* implied that Congress must have latitude and discretion in passing laws to carry out these powers. Thus he held that Congress had the implied power to create a United States Bank in order to achieve its delegated fiscal powers. His reasoning was expressed thus: "Let the end be legitimate, and all the means which are appropriate . . . which are not prohibited . . . are constitutional." The Supreme Court ruled that Maryland had no right to tax the United States Bank, for "the right to tax is the right to destroy" and no state has authority to destroy that which is created by the national government in its legitimate purposes.

In *Gibbons* v. *Ogden* (1821), he further strengthened the authority of the national government by declaring that the *delegated power* to regulate commerce included not only the regulation of the exchange of goods but also the means by which such exchange was carried on, including the use of waterways. On the ground that the regulation of shipping was a federal matter, the Supreme Court under Marshall struck down a New York State law giving a monopoly to one ship company to operate on the rivers of the state.

In *Cohens* v. *Virginia,* Marshall established the supremacy of the Supreme Court over all state courts by granting the right of appeal from the decision of a state court on a constitutional or federal matter to the Supreme Court. His reasoning here was that otherwise there would be conflicting interpretations, with each state offering its own.

During John Marshall's tenure in office (1801–1835), the Supreme Court decided forty-four cases involving interpretation of every part of the Constitution. These decisions transformed the Constitution into a living document and established in practice the powers of the various departments of the government. What Marshall actually created was a new concept of government, called judicial review or judicial supremacy. In very few countries does the judiciary have such authority. In England, for example, it is parliament that has the supreme authority. But Marshall did more than this. He created a country of law, where decisions are made according to due process of law.

During the thirty-four years of his service, the decisions of the Supreme Court represented the thinking, the reasoning, indeed the expression of John Marshall himself, a man who was admittedly a conservative, a believer in the sanctity of contract and private property, and one who sincerely believed in "one nation indivisible."

It is remarkable that this woodsman, with little formal legal education, was able to win and hold the respect of his more learned associates so that they accepted his leadership and views, even though some, such as Joseph Story, were members of the opposite party. In part this acceptance was due to his personal magnetism, eloquence, humility, and unselfish devotion to high ideals. He always had a warm sense of humor and the backwoodsman's directness of approach. There was something about him that won respect and good will.

Marshall never regarded himself as a statesman whose task it was to develop domestic and foreign policies. He based his decisions solely upon the provisions of the Constitution and, in justifying his decisions, limited himself to building his arguments upon the Constitution as written. Constitutional lawyers today, who are much more erudite, have found fault with his argumentation, but there are many who still quote him and seek to emulate his direct style of reasoning. In Marshall's judicial opinions, the grounds are carefully prepared, argument building upon argument. Then the premise is stated. All possible objections and alternate solutions are then set forth and examined. Finally a conclusion is drawn so that it seems completely logical. Undeniably it was his persuasive, reasonable logic that won acceptance of the interpretations of the Constitution, not only by Marshall's judicial associates but by the disagreeing factions that were parties to the dispute.

One of Marshall's most difficult tasks was presiding over the trial of Aaron Burr for treason. This was after Burr had killed Alexander Hamilton in a duel, and public sentiment and President Jefferson strongly favored conviction. Despite public pressure, Marshall ruled that the evidence was not sufficient, and Burr was acquitted. Some historians have declared that Marshall was unduly partisan in favoring Burr and seeking to embarrass Jefferson, with whom he was unfriendly, but the wisdom of Marshall's decision has stood the test of time.

There were times, too, when John Marshall's position on the Supreme Court was threatened because of the boldness of his decisions. When Jefferson was President, there is evidence that leaders of the Republican party were planning to impeach Marshall. The plan was so serious that Marshall wrote a letter to a friend in Congress suggesting that it might be better for Congress to have the power to reverse an unpopular decision of the Court than to remove the judges who made it. However, the plan came to naught when the attempt to impeach his associate Samuel Chase resulted in the latter's acquittal.

During his early years in office John Marshall also wrote a five-volume biography of George Washington, whom he admired greatly. Marshall's married life, which had begun as a romance between a backwoodsman and a society girl, had some unhappy outcomes. His wife became afflicted with an incurable nervous ailment that left her an invalid for most of their married life. However, in their relationship, Marshall showed the nobility of his character, for he was always patient, thoughtful, and devoted. Indeed when Mary Marshall, whom he always called his "dearest Polly," passed away, December 25, 1831, he was inconsolable and thereafter kept a lock of her hair in a precious locket always with him. They had ten children, four of whom died in infancy.

The election of Andrew Jackson brought to the presidency a strong-minded executive who was antagonistic to Marshall. Jackson appointed justices of his own party, and there were now many more occasions when Marshall was in the minority. In one case, *Worcester* v. *Georgia,* the Supreme Court ruled that the state of Georgia could not dispossess the Cherokee Indians. Jackson, who sided with Georgia against the Indians, refused to enforce the decision, saying: "Marshall has made his decision; let him enforce it."

The last years of Marshall's life, after the death of his wife, were unhappy. His oldest son died soon after his wife. His own health was poor and he suffered constant pain. He died on July 6, 1835, in Philadelphia where he had gone for medical treatment, and he was buried in Richmond, Virginia. The liberty bell in Philadelphia cracked while tolling his death and was never used again.

The influence and work of John Marshall were enduring. In the transformation of a weak confederacy of colonies to a united, strong government, a government of law, John Marshall played a principal role. His vision, his eloquence, his personality, and the logic of his thinking were the ingredients that were needed to give sinews to our constitutional government and to make it truly "*e pluribus unum*" (one from many).

FURTHER READING

Corwin, Edward S. *John Marshall and the Constitution.*
Dunham, Allison, and Kurland, P. B., eds. *Mr. Justice.*

──Alexander Hamilton──

[1755–1804]

THE MORNING OF JULY 11, 1804, was already uncomfortably warm when the small group of tight-lipped men assembled in a clearing at Weehawken, New Jersey. It was a most unlikely place for this ancient ritual to be performed, and the cast of characters was headed by two of the young country's most prominent citizens, Aaron Burr and Alexander Hamilton. The early sun, slanting through the trees, pointed up the murderous hatred on Burr's face as well as Hamilton's strangely serene, almost hypnotic state. Burr had come to kill —and Hamilton, it would appear, had every intention of being killed.

The distances were marked off by each man's seconds. A nervous official began the fatal "Ready, aim, fire!" Hamilton shocked his supporters by raising his pistol skyward. By the time his finger had fired the harmless shot, Burr's accurate bullet had slammed into Hamilton, toppling him to the ground. Hamilton's friends did what they could for the stricken man, but after terrible suffering he died the following day.

The date of Alexander Hamilton's birth is problematic. It was assumed that he had been born in 1757 in Charlestown, in the British West Indian colony of Nevis, one of the Leeward Islands. Recent research now places the date as 1755, however. Since every biographer has emphasized Hamilton's precociousness, it now appears that although he was a genuine prodigy, he was two years older than the historians once thought him to be.

Hamilton's mother had been separated from her first husband, and she could not obtain a divorce. Hence, her marriage to James Hamilton, a wellborn but unsuccessful merchant, was technically irregular, stamping Alexander as an illegiti-

mate child. His mother taught him to read and write when he
was quite young, and Alexander would amaze all by reciting
the Ten Commandments in Hebrew when most of his little
playmates were learning their first words.

Times were hard for the family, and James Hamilton became so frustrated with his failures that he deserted his family in St. Croix. When Alexander was eleven, his mother died,
and the orphan went to Christiansted, the capital of St. Croix,
where he managed to get a job as a lowly clerk in a large
countinghouse. Almost daily the slender red-haired Alexander
won promotions from his pleased employer. The boy had fire
and a head for business; he was resourceful and welcomed
responsibilities; he was a natural leader of men who were
twice his age. Within two years Alexander was practically
running a vast business which involved world trade, banking,
profit-and-loss statements, bills of lading, high finance, and the
intricacies of economics. All this was invaluable preparation
for the time when George Washington would call upon Hamilton to become the new nation's first Secretary of the Treasury.

It was an "act of God" which altered Hamilton's life. The
island of St. Croix was lashed by a vicious hurricane that
scattered death and debris in its wake. It was a frightening
experience for the survivors, especially for the impressionable
and articulate Hamilton, who was an eyewitness to the terrors
of the storm. He wrote a lurid account of the horror he had
lived through and circulated it among his friends. A Presbyterian minister, Hugh Knox, who had taught Hamilton, urged
the boy to submit it to a newspaper for publication.

When the "hurricane letter" appeared in print, it became
the talk of the islands. Knox used the letter to impress Hamilton's uncles and aunts with the need to continue his protégé's
schooling, and they advanced enough money to send the boy
to Knox's alma mater, Princeton.

Once again, a strange quirk of fate reshaped Hamilton's
future. His application to Princeton was rejected because he
had wished to enter in midyear. Rather than wait, Alexander
went to New York in 1773, and was accepted at King's College (now Columbia University), where he was plunged into
the mainstream of anti-British movements that were to alter
the entire course of our country's history.

Soon Hamilton became a familiar figure at mass meetings
in City Hall Park. The Boston Tea Party had just taken place,

and the fiery Hamilton gathered crowds around him while he assailed the repressive policies and practices of the mother country. When he was not studying natural law and Old Testament ethics at King's College (which had a faculty of three), Hamilton was busy writing pamphlets in support of the colonists. When an Anglican clergyman denounced the First Continental Congress, Hamilton struck back in 1774–1775 with two important pamphlets: *A Full Vindication of the Measures of the Congress from the Calumnies of their Enemies* and *The Farmer Refuted.* British informers had him marked as a rabblerouser, and his life was in danger.

Although Hamilton excelled as an orator and writer, he yearned for military action. Joining up with a patriotic band of volunteers, "The Corsicans," he drilled daily before classes. Soon after he became captain of an artillery company.

In the early days of the Revolutionary War, Hamilton participated in battles on Long Island, in White Plains, and in Princeton. The young officer's exploits were repeatedly brought to the attention of General Washington, who promoted Hamilton to lieutenant colonel and made him his personal aide-de-camp. As Washington's confidential secretary, fluent in French, he carried out many missions for the general, especially those involving allies such as Lafayette. Because desk work made Hamilton restless, he importuned Washington for front-line assignments, and finally distinguished himself in action at Monmouth and in the Yorktown campaign of 1781.

With the war over, Hamilton married Elizabeth Schuyler, the daughter of a wealthy New York politician, and eventually became the father of eight children. After deciding to become a lawyer, he studied diligently and in 1782 was admitted to the bar and opened law offices on Wall Street. As a rising young attorney, he helped to found the Bank of New York, and he was chosen as a delegate to the Continental Congress. It was within the next few years that Hamilton made his great contributions to our country as a thinker, planner, and statesman.

For several years, Hamilton had been giving thought to the form that a United States government should take. As early as 1778, in letters to New York representatives to the Continental Congress, Hamilton was outlining his suggestions. His ideas concerning the type of government which would work best featured the following highlights:

1. Congress would have many more powers than were delegated to it in the weak Articles of Confederation. It would be permitted to raise money by levying taxes (commerce, land, poll), to conduct all foreign affairs, to sign treaties, and to declare war.

2. Congress would seek foreign loans in support of the fledgling democracy. (France and Spain eventually lent the money which helped the Confederation to continue.)

3. A new branch of government—an executive division with departments of War, Marine, and Finance—was essential. (This was the origin of our present cabinet system. The chief executive, to be indirectly elected by the people, would serve for life and have an absolute veto.)

4. A national bank was required. Shares would be sold to the public, and subsequent profits would be divided between the government and individual shareholders.

5. The wealthy citizens must be wooed to lend their private funds to the government. If they could be shown that such support would be profitable for them, they would be cooperative. Such citizens would find it in their interest to back the paper money issued by the government since their prosperity would depend upon the soundness of the American dollar. In Hamilton's words, "The passions of avarice, ambition, and interest govern most individuals."

6. State authority would be limited to matters concerning the rights of property and life among individuals. The central government must be strong and supreme (Jefferson, on the other hand, believed in supremacy of the state governments).

Many of Hamilton's friends were highly critical. Such a government would not be democratic, they asserted; it would be in variance with the great traditions of democratic Athens. Hamilton replied: "The ancient democracies never possessed good government. When they assembled, the field of debate presented an ungovernable mob." If Hamilton's program were followed, his opponents continued, the control of the country would reside in the hands of affluent, powerful, corrupt people. Hamilton countered by saying, "Experience has by no means justified us in the supposition that there is more virtue in one class of men than in another."

By 1786 the former colonies had reached a disastrously low ebb. Inflation was strangling the country, and each state contributed to the madness by printing more worthless paper money. The army could not be paid, and the repayment of the loan to France was impossible. Hamilton and others had been calling for a convention of all the states which would draw up a revised and workable constitution. Now their voices were heard by desperate state legislatures which agreed to send representatives to Philadelphia in 1787 to a convention called by the delegates to the Annapolis meeting. (This Annapolis convention was marked by Hamilton's address which called for this Constitutional convention.) Hamilton, a New York delegate, was there with the "Federalists," those who wanted a federal constitution to replace the Articles of Confederation. Their opponents, the anti-Federalists, were also known as "Republicans."

At Philadelphia, Hamilton delivered an impressive five-hour speech in support of his theories of government. In addition to the proposals listed earlier, Hamilton advocated a congress of two houses, composed of an intelligent elite of property owners. He drew a graphic picture of the chaos which the country could avoid by giving maximum powers to a strong executive branch. In private discussions off the floor of the Convention he was eloquent in influencing the men who were to do the actual writing of the Constitution.

When the document had been completed, Hamilton's work began in earnest. He sparked the New York State Convention in Poughkeepsie in 1788, beating the drum successfully for adoption of the Constitution in the face of difficult odds. Now it became a matter of increasing the ground swell for ratification. Hamilton joined forces with John Jay and James Madison as authors of a series of persuasive letters to the New York press. (Hamilton wrote the first essay in the collection of eighty and about fifty of the others.) These letters, published in book form in 1788 as *The Federalist,* are masterful interpretations of the Constitution. In lucid prose, the letters analyze the principles of free government in so enduring a fashion that modern constitutional jurists consult them regularly for the clarity of their exposition.

Hamilton's foreign birth was an asset to him in his role as one of the founding fathers. He could campaign more vocally for a powerful federal government because he was not hampered by the parochial state loyalties which his colleagues possessed. The Pennsylvanians, Virginians, *et al.*, were loath to relinquish their personal powers, but Hamilton, whose New York roots did not go as deep, could foresee one united nation in place of a union of independent states.

One of the paradoxical aspects of Hamilton was his support of a constitution which went counter to many of his own beliefs in that it gave greater power to the masses. How could a man who had characterized the people as "turbulent and changing; they seldom judge or determine right" and as "a great beast" be in favor of a democratic government and popular suffrage? The answers to these questions must acknowledge Hamilton's freedom from personal bias when larger issues were at stake. It is to his credit that he would sacrifice some of his private prejudices in order to gain the other benefits which he saw in the Constitution. Despising anarchy, he feared that if the states rejected the Constitution then anarchy and a military dictatorship were inevitable.

As Washington's Secretary of the Treasury, Hamilton had the opportunity to implement his ideas on government finances. Under his leadership the National Bank opened for business in 1791. Thomas Jefferson and others believed that the Bank was unconstitutional, feeling that Hamilton had overstepped his authority. Hamilton's constitutional interpretation was exceedingly important in this case. He believed that Congress, in the best interests of the country, had the right to use any powers that were not specifically denied to it by the Constitution. This doctrine of "implied powers," later reinforced by Justice John Marshall in the *McCulloch* v. *Maryland* case (1819), has been a most significant feature in strengthening our national government.

Hamilton proceeded to move the country from bankruptcy to solvency. One of his plans was for the federal government to assume the debts of the individual states. James Madison was the leader of the opposition group, and in order to defeat Madison, Hamilton needed the voting strength of his bitter rival Thomas Jefferson. A deal was worked out between the two men. Jefferson would help Hamilton if Hamilton would agree to work for the future location of the nation's capital on the banks of the Potomac River.

That may have been the last time Jefferson and Hamilton ever exchanged a civil word. Jefferson, allowing his intense

326 of GREAT THINKERS

jealousy to influence his sounder judgment, accused the scrupu-
lously honest Hamilton of having mismanaged treasury funds.
Hamilton was cleared by an investigation but he decided to
resign from the cabinet in 1795. He was overworked, sickened
by the personal abuse which had been heaped upon him, and
in financial difficulties. "I am not worth more than $500," he
said at the time. "My slender fortune and the best years of
my life have been devoted to the service of my adopted
country."

The feud between Burr and Hamilton had been brewing
for a number of years. When a tie vote for the presidency
between Burr and Jefferson threw the election into the Fed-
eralist-controlled House of Representatives, Hamilton chose
to favor his old enemy rather than Burr. In 1804, when Burr
entered the New York gubernatorial campaign, Hamilton was
once again instrumental in seeing him defeated. Burr was
furious. He demanded that Hamilton retract certain charges.
When Hamilton ignored the request, Burr challenged him to
the duel which led to the disaster in Weehawken. Hamilton's
acceptance of the challenge is hard to explain because he
hated dueling (his own son Philip had been killed in a duel
three years earlier) and apparently he had no intention of
firing at Burr.

Charming and witty to some, arrogant and overbearing to
others, Hamilton inspired mixed emotions in his contemporaries. Subsequent generations have come to appreciate his outstanding contributions to his adopted land. Modern conservatives look up to him, but some liberals criticize him for his
lack of faith in the common man. To Woodrow Wilson he was
"a very great man, but not a great American." But to a leading
political scientist, Saul K. Padover, "Only George Washington
himself excelled him in the durability of his achievements as
the early builder of the Republic."

FURTHER READING

Taylor, G. R., ed. *Hamilton and the National Debt*.
Wise, William. *Alexander Hamilton*.

Johann Gottlieb Fichte

[1762-1814]

JUST AS Karl Marx and Friedrich Engels in 1848 sounded the opening bell of what was to be a long battle to transform capitalist society into communist society, so forty years earlier, Johann Gottlieb Fichte, in his *Addresses to the German Nation*, sounded a clear call to the spirit of nationalism of the Germans (Germany as a nation was then merely an idea, for it was composed of many different feudal states). His exhortation was to inspire his countrymen in many battles and to awaken similar nationalistic feelings among other peoples down to the present day. If nationalism is a central concept in the modern world, in Fichte's writings we can see that concept at its inception. In arousing this powerful force, Fichte believed it to be the means for the salvation of the Germans when their fortunes were at a low point. Speaking in Berlin in 1807, when that city and much of Germany was under the yoke of the conqueror Napoleon, he showed once again that the pen is mightier than the sword; indeed, one pen raised many swords.

Fichte's idea was not an inspiration of the moment. He had prepared long and hard for this occasion and his philosophical foundation was deep and strong. Born in Saxony, the son of a poor tradesman, he found his ability recognized early, and his education was subsidized by a wealthy patron. A good basic education was followed by some study of theology and philosophy. His fiery personality and short temper made it difficult for him to get along with teachers, patrons, and fellow students. When he turned to private tutoring to save himself from poverty, he found it difficult to hold a position for any length of time. His brilliance as a teacher was recognized, but his idealistic conception of human life which led him to judge his

327

fellow men by standards that were unusually high, together
with his dogmatic self-righteousness, made enemies of important people. He combined a rigorous moral code and radi-
calism, thereby alienating the romantics and the conservatives
alike.

Intellectually, he had been educated like Kant in the school
of continental rationalism and determinism. That man's reason was the means to understand the universe and human life,
and that the universe was a machine which turned out events
according to deterministic laws, he was quite sure. Then, as
Kant was influenced by Hume, so Fichte was "awakened from
his dogmatic slumbers" by Kant. He accepted Kant's "critical
philosophy" that showed the limitations of both reason and observation, and shifted the center of attention to the perceiv-
ing, thinking, and acting individual, man. As a result of his
liberation by Kant, he wrote a Kantian *Critique of Revelation*.
His name was omitted from the title page inadvertently, and
the work was ascribed to Kant. When Kant revealed him as the
true author, Fichte became famous. A university appointment
followed, but his refusal to compromise over what for him was
a matter of principle led to his dismissal. For a short time after
its founding he served as rector of the University of Berlin,
but his inability to work with others led to his resignation.
His death in 1814 resulted from a fever contracted while nursing his wife back to health.

Though his *Addresses to the German Nation* (1807) was
the book which most influenced the public, his *Vocation of
Man* (1800) is the most succinct statement of his world view,
and is the one that has been most studied by students of philosophy. In this book is stated, directly and without the philosophical jargon current at the time, his main position about
the nature of man and the foundations of philosophy. His aim
was to find a philosophy of life which would do justice to the
insights of the rationalistic school and to the criticisms of the
empiricists.

Taking his clue from Kant's notion of "practical reason"—
the insight which makes possible a moral life—he moved the
will to the center of his theory of man. Reason and sense perception were not rejected, but their employment was shown
to depend on an act of will. The *Vocation of Man* considers
in turn both reason and sense perception as possible bases of
a life for man.

Reason discloses the world as a deterministic order governed by universal and necessary laws. From this point of view man is a creature of the natural order, a cog in the world machine. Man does not act—rather nature acts through man. One can make no sense of human freedom on that basis. Sense perception, the empiricist basis of science and philosophy, is likewise inadequate. For the empiricist the world becomes a collection of ideas in the mind, and objective reality is lost. The will, which chooses the foundation and the method in the first place, is left to show the way. Thus in place of reason and its necessity, and perception and its subjectivism, is placed the will and its act.

On this approach, the world is understood as the arena of human action, and the acts of will constitute human freedom and self-realization. Related to and derivative from the will are, in addition to that on which the will acts (the world), an individual who wills and the ideal of perfection that guides him. The justification for man's action is his freedom, and that freedom is achieved simply by willing and acting in the light of self-imposed ideals.

What is here expressed in terms of the individual man (Fichte wrote his *Vocation of Man* in the first person singular) is applied to men in groups, since to conquer the objective world requires more power than one man alone can wield. Men must join in spirit and body to accomplish their goals. Thus Fichte accomplished the transition to the call to the nationalistic spirit which animated his *Addresses to the German Nation*.

Fichte, who stood halfway between Kant and Hegel, points toward two contemporary ways of thinking. His emphasis on the will and the act anticipated, as others had done in other ways, the twentieth-century pragmatism of James. His emphasis on self-affirmation suggests the way of thinking now called existentialism. More readable translations of his works and more adequate restatements of his views might well produce a revival of interest in him.

FURTHER READING

Mead, G. H. *Movements of Thought in the Nineteenth Century.*
Royce, J. *Lectures on Modern Idealism.*

──Thomas Robert Malthus──

[1766–1834]

IN ONE of his best-known works, *A Tale of Two Cities,*
Charles Dickens describes the end of the eighteenth century,
in which Malthus was growing up, in these words: "It was
the best of times, it was the worst of times, it was the age of
wisdom, it was the age of foolishness . . . it was the spring of
hope, it was the winter of despair. . . ." Thus did Dickens
describe living conditions in France and England, where a
few wealthy nobles lived in grandeur and looked hopefully
into the future, while the poor lived in grinding poverty and
squalor and had no future. As he grew to manhood, Malthus
could not easily forget the terrible living conditions of such a
large portion of the population. Later on, he was to have an
opportunity to make known the reasons for the misery of the
poor and to suggest ways to improve their lot.

Thomas Robert Malthus was born in 1766 in Rockery,
County Surrey, England, the youngest son of a very respect-
able family. His father, Daniel Malthus, was a learned, comfortable country gentleman among whose friends were most
of the well-known philosophers of the day, including David
Hume and Jean Jacques Rousseau. It was decided that young
Malthus would enter the church, so he was given a thorough
and excellent private education. He studied philosophy and
theology at Jesus College, Cambridge, graduating with honors
in 1788. He was ordained in 1797 and, for a short time, was
in charge of a small parish in his native county of Surrey.

It is interesting to note how as a young man Malthus became interested in the study of population growth. He and his
father were engaged in a long series of arguments over a number of ideas then being discussed in English intellectual circles
concerning the capacity of the human race to improve its

own conditions and to progress in the future. This was a period of tremendous social and economic upheaval and change in France involving the Revolution and its aftermath. The effects were not lost on Englishmen, and there was considerable discussion of the new social and political ideas relating to liberty, equality, and the better life.

In England itself, special problems related to the misery and general wretchedness of the working class and to the care of the poor and destitute were causing serious concern to the more enlightened thinkers of the day. The growth of the factory system was accompanied by the movement of thousands of people from farms and cottages, where they worked mostly outdoors, to overcrowded industrial towns, where they were compelled to work long hours in poorly lighted, poorly ventilated, and generally unsanitary buildings. The low wages paid by the profit-hungry factory owners forced all members of the family, including women and very young children, to work at these long and monotonous tasks to eke out a livelihood.

In 1793 William Godwin, whose plans for the amelioration of social injustice were impractical, although he had faith in human nature and was optimistic about the future, published a work entitled *Enquiry Concerning Political Justice and Its Influence on Morals and Happiness*. In this work he declared that "all government, even the best, is an evil." He further stated that human nature is susceptible to perpetual improvement so that man, in time, would become a perfect citizen behaving in such a way that maximum individual and collective benefits would result. Godwin concluded that, with the elimination of government and the application of man's innate reason to his living habits, productivity would so increase that people would be able to satisfy all their material needs and wants by working only one-half hour per day.

A similar study, written by M. Condorcet, appeared in France in 1794, suggesting that science and reason would assure all good things to man in the future.

Daniel Malthus, the comfortable country gentleman, accepted their views as a practical possibility of things to come and defended the ideas of these writers. Thomas Robert Malthus, his son, opposed them, partly for the sake of argument and partly because he felt the ideas to be but vaguely developed and unrealistic.

Finally, young Malthus, in an attempt to convince his father of the error of his views, wrote out his reasons for objecting to the thesis presented by Godwin and Condorcet. At his father's request, Malthus agreed to publish his views, but was reluctant to sign his name to the document. Thus it was that in 1798, at the age of thirty-two, Malthus anonymously issued his very famous work, *An Essay on the Principle of Population as It Affects the Future Improvement of Society, with Remarks on the Speculations of Mr. Godwin, M. Condorcet, and Other Writers.* The work created an immediate sensation and aroused a great deal of controversy. For example, William Cobbett had this to say about Malthus: "Parson! I have, during my life, detested many men; but never any one so much as you." Conversely, in 1800 the English Prime Minister William Pitt withdrew a proposed law for the relief of the poor because of his regard for Malthus, "whose opinions he was bound to respect."

Malthus' work is credited with initiating the science of population study, or demography, as it is called today. This essay was also a prime influence in bringing about the first regular census of the people in England, in 1801. Moreover, Charles Darwin credited Malthus with giving him the basic idea for the theory of evolution by natural selection. During his lifetime, Malthus revised, amended, and enlarged this work into many editions, the sixth and last during his lifetime appearing in 1826.

Simply stated, Malthus demonstrated that the optimism expressed by Godwin, Condorcet, and others concerning the future of the human race was in strict contradiction to the rather cruel and universal laws of nature. In other words, the basic and fundamental causes for the poverty and distress of the bulk of the population are not due to any man-made political institutions or laws, which could be corrected in time, but rather to a combination of nature's immutable biological and economic "laws." According to Malthus, the growth of population itself is an insurmountable obstacle to human progress and happiness because nature's laws indicate that population tends to increase at a much faster rate than does the food supply needed to sustain such a growing population. His famous formulation of this principle was illustrated by the use of the following series of whole numbers:

POPULATION	1	2	4	8	16	32	64	128	256
FOOD SUPPLY	1	2	3	4	5	6	7	8	9

The first series above indicates that the population tends to double itself, or increase in a *geometric progression*, every twenty-five years, while the second series indicates that the food supply, or the ability of the earth to produce food and other life-supporting goods, increases according to an *arithmetical progression*. A basic problem, as Malthus saw it, revolved around the passion that exists between the sexes. To Malthus this is a permanent and pervasive human trait resulting in excessive growth of population unless checked in some way. It is easy to see why Carlyle, after reading Malthus' thesis, which indicated that Nature plants in man instincts which forever condemn him to starvation, misery, penury, and death, called economics "the dismal science."

In later editions of his *Essay* Malthus wrote that while the ultimate check to overpopulation is the limited food supply (famine), there are other checks to population growth, both positive and preventive. Positive checks are brought about by war, epidemics, and plagues, which increase the death rate. Preventive checks, such as moral restraint and delayed marriages, tend to decrease the birthrate. As a practical policy, Malthus suggested that people, especially poor people, be discouraged from early marriage or from raising families without adequate financial resources. Furthermore, he was opposed to giving relief payments to the poor since he believed that such payments only tend to aggravate the situation by financing the birth of additional children.

The controversy stirred up by the appearance of the first edition caused Malthus to realize that he would need more time to restudy and defend his thesis. He arranged to take a three-year tour of the Continent where he visited Sweden, Norway, Finland, and Russia. He had to avoid France because of the political difficulties then existing between the English and French. Upon his return to England at the age of thirty-eight, he married, and in 1806 he accepted a post as professor of political economy and history in a college established by the East India Company in Haileybury, near London. He thus became the first person in the history of England to bear the title "Professor of Political Economy." He remained at this position until his death in 1834.

Malthus did not have an easy time maintaining and defending his basic thesis that the poor are themselves reponsible for their own misery because they marry too young and have too many children. In effect he was creating a good excuse for the wealthier and propertied classes to disassociate themselves from the inevitable fate of the working people. His opposition to greater equality, welfare, and relief assistance, because of his belief that such actions only bring forth more mouths to feed, made him very unpopular with the masses. Although he was criticized in his own day by being called "that black and terrible demon that is always ready to stifle the hopes of humanity," much of this criticism was unjustified, because Malthus was not deliberately trying to "stifle the hopes of humanity." He was simply trying to demonstrate and explain the existence of basic economic laws concerning a struggle between man and nature, a struggle in which, it seemed to him, nature is destined to be the winner. Malthus did not create this gigantic struggle, he merely called attention to its existence. Neither did he praise disease, war, pestilence, or misery. He only focused a spotlight on the effect they would have on man's eternal battle for survival. Malthus himself, in fact, was characteristically kind and "his sentiments were benevolent, his temper mild and easy, his nature loyal and affectionate; and he was cheerful." His life was spent in the placid existence of a scholar and teacher, and despite his poor speaking voice (caused by a cleft palate), he was admired and respected by his students, who often affectionately addressed him as "Pop."

Malthus was a contemporary and friend of David Ricardo, one of the most original economic theoreticians of all time. The two men met often and exchanged opinions in letters. Ricardo accepted the implications of Malthus' theory about population, but he went further to give a pessimistic view of a struggle for survival among three classes, the workers, the industrialists, and the landlords, which became the basis of the modern science of economics. Together Malthus and Ricardo demolished Adam Smith's optimistic view that everything will work out fine if the immutable laws of economics are merely allowed to function with a minimum of interference.

Today, the question of population growth has lost none of its importance, although some of its aspects have changed. Certainly in countries like China, India, and several in South

America, the struggle between population and food supply is still very much alive. However, modern technology and the development of scientific methods in agriculture, as well as the opening up of new areas of the world suitable for food production, have so greatly increased the supply of food that larger populations can be maintained, even at higher standards of living. Though the basic elements of his thesis are accepted as true, Malthus did not anticipate these scientific changes. For example, the England of Malthus' time had to feed a population of 10.5 million people. Today it provides a much better diet to 55 million people. In 1800 the population of the United States was only 5.5 million and today it is approaching 200 million. Not only do we generally have and enjoy more and better kinds of food, but at times we have had surpluses causing serious price problems to the farmers of the country. In addition, especially in modern Western societies, the birthrate has been kept within limits by parents desiring to have fewer children in order to give them more attention and financial support. For example, in such large countries as France and Italy, the birthrate has tended to remain stationary or to decline in the past half century. It also should be noted that in richer countries, the upper-income families tend to have fewer children. This, in effect, is one of the preventive checks that Malthus wrote about.

Malthus made two major contributions to the development of economic thought. One, dealing with his theory of population, has always been associated with his name. The other, however, dealing with the theory of economic crises, was largely overlooked until 1939, when John Maynard Lord Keynes credited him with the basic idea for Keynes's underconsumption theories.

In 1820, Malthus published another great book entitled *Principles of Political Economy, Considered with a View to Their Practical Application,* in which he indicated that population problems were not the only ones in store for mankind. Malthus was worried about the possibilities of recurring "gluts" or crises caused by general overproduction and underconsumption. This would happen, reasoned Malthus, because the capitalists continually did all the saving and investing they could, thereby constantly increasing the supply of capital. In turn, this capital would be used to produce huge amounts of consumer goods, but the parsimony of the middle class, and the general poverty of the working class forced to live on subsistence wages, would be reflected in insufficient demand. The result would be a general contraction of investment, a drop in prices, and a large number of unemployed workers, or, in other words, what we call today a depression. Malthus' suggestion to prevent depressions was to encourage increased spending for consumption and to discourage saving, in order that there be adequate demand for current production and output. For example, he suggested "that the employment of the poor in roads and public works, and a tendency among landlords and persons of property to build, to improve and beautify their grounds, and to employ workmen and menial servants" would help bring consumption and production into balance. In effect, this was one of the proposals made by Lord Keynes and followed by President Franklin Roosevelt during the Depression of the 1930's, in an attempt to stimulate the American economy.

Later on, Malthus was called a pessimist because he was constantly calling attention to the inevitable struggles of the various classes of society with one another, as well as with nature. Yet he did have good advice and practical suggestions intended to improve economic society. Indeed, his willingness to face the stark realities of conditions in his time, his astuteness in seeking basic causes of the conditions, and his independence and courage in announcing these causes and proposing practical remedies set a new pattern of economic thought.

FURTHER READING

Glass, Victor D. *Introduction to Malthus.*
McCleary, George F. *Malthusian Population Theory.*
Oser, Jacob. *Must Man Starve? The Malthusian Controversy.*

Georg Wilhelm
—Friedrich Hegel———

[1770–1831]

SOME CONSIDER Hegel the greatest, the most fruitful of all philosophers; others regret his influence. That his ideas entered powerfully into the mainstream of Western thought is undeniable. Much of his language and thought was used by Marx; but whereas Hegel originated his dialectic process of reasoning within an idealistic philosophy, Marx accepted the initial ideas of Hegel's view of history and fully applied the dialectic to a materialistic philosophy. If one studies Dewey, Whitehead, or Sartre, one will note how frequently a phrase, an argument, or a method seems to come from Hegel. Dewey acknowledges that "acquaintance with Hegel has left a permanent deposit in my thinking," and Hegel is often credited with being a precursor of modern existentialism.

Perhaps Hegel's greatest actual influence stems from his assertion that history must be understood in terms of the total interweaving of cultural patterns and human events, both horizontally in geography and vertically in time. He saw, before geological and biological evolution were accepted, that all reality is in process. All things, he believed, moved toward the eternal enrichment and self-realization of the Whole, "the Absolute Mind." On the way, men participate in the process through living their lives, suffering and enjoying, and creating new cultures. To the extent that they are alert to values and live meaningful lives, they temporarily share in the mind of the Absolute. There are reminiscences of Aristotle and Spinoza here. Hegel thought he was expressing the real truth of Christianity, but most Christian theologians disagree; they see the uniqueness of Christianity in its vision of a God who is personal as well as absolute and who bestows not merely a glimpse of eternity but personal immortality.

337

Hegel's external life was a quiet one spent mainly in learning, writing, and teaching, in over half a dozen widely distributed centers of German culture. He did some traveling in Europe, and immensely appreciated the different cultures he found, each with its own characteristics. Throughout his life he spent much of his time enjoying the arts. He took little outdoor exercise, was physically frail, and always looked worn. He was, until his last twenty years, quite poor. He married at age forty-one and was an affectionate, devoted husband and father. He was always interested in education, and a number of his writings show a sympathetic insight into the nature of the psychic changes from childhood to adolescence to manhood. He realized the importance of a youth's freeing himself from parental and local controls to achieve independence.

At the age of sixty-one, Hegel died, of cholera in Berlin, where he had held the university chair of philosophy for thirteen years. During those years he had become very famous. He was regarded as the "official philosopher" of Prussia, mainly because of his lavish praise of the government and especially of certain financial and legislative acts. Part of his motivation is found in his passionate desire for a centralized government that could bring well-being to Germany, after the devastation and poverty caused by the Napoleonic invasions. Hegel was never a warmonger. He hated war. But he thought wars inevitable in a world of greedy, violent, shortsighted men and nations. He praised the heroism of soldiers and civilians, and this is taken by some to mean he was praising war. He was not. He did think that all change takes place through antagonisms and struggle, but did not believe that violence is the desirable way. There can be rules of the game in business, in the arguments of politicians, and in interinstitutional struggle; that there often are not is a fact of life. It seemed to him that there would never be effective international rules because there would never be a superior governing power to enforce them.

Hegel was a nationalist but not a jingoistic one. He was too fond of other cultures for that. He considered the modern national state the most effective social unit possible for man and the necessary foundation for human advance. He thought direct government by the mass of people impossible, but he thought their voices should be represented.

Though Hegel was profoundly aware that all things change,

he was against change through revolution by the masses. He was deeply conservative—but it is entirely wrong to attribute totalitarian ideas to him. He objected strenuously to the state's interfering in family life, religion, art, science, or business. However, he felt that it should make some arrangements to help the extremely poor and the uprooted. He thought England's proposed land reforms in 1830 were far behind some in Europe. Laws must be made known to all and administered openly and fairly. Obedience to law is necessary to provide the conditions for human growth and enrichment in all the private spheres.

Hegel thought cultures around the world, past and present, most successful when the whole group had strong unifying ideas and emotions. Then the *Zeitgeist*—the pervading spirit of the times—entered into all activities and in turn was made plain through them. There would always appear one foremost nation, representing in itself the most advanced culture peculiar to the times. This one nation, often with an outstanding leader, would find itself burdened with world leadership. But a profound underswell of movement in another direction would already be at work; the very strengths of the leading culture would prove weaknesses against this new, strong antithesis; power and wealth would change hands, and a new era be on its way. The rights of the old and the new would clash, and one side would go down. Hegel saw the profound essence of tragedy in the fact that in all struggles there is right on both sides, honor and heroism on both sides, and eventual failure for all concerned. Yet everything is not lost. The best values of both sides are conserved, integrated, and transformed in the next form that the everlasting world process advances.

Hegel's own great cultural love was the Greek city-state, with its unity, its community, and its creativeness. "If it were permissible," he writes, "to yearn for being something which we are not, the longing for classical Greece would be permissible." Why is it not permissible? Because there is no going back! Reality is in eternal process, and a man attains dignity and freedom by participating in the culture into which he was born. For this reason Hegel thought that it was wasteful and foolish for philosophers of his day, when a university professorship was the normal career open to a philosopher, to be attached to no institution, "living their philosophy," like Socrates. Neither should the philosopher be a monk, as in the Middle

Ages. Hegel believed that the essence of life in his day lay in
social interconnectedness, with institutions playing a major
role. He maintained that the ordinary, unglamorous, punctual
life of a professor, so abhorrent to Kierkegaard, Schopenhauer,
and Nietzsche, could be a life filled with freedom and courage
of thought. "What really matters is to remain faithful to one's
aims."

Hegel thought philosophy must be professional, like law or
theology, and that its *practice* is in education, in the living
dialogue between teacher and student, both of whom should
keep abreast of historical and contemporary philosophical literature. Hegel often said philosophy should be a science. He
did not mean scientific in the modern sense of orientation to
reliable, tested knowledge about the natural world; rather that
philosophy should become professional and cooperative—a
mutual, logical endeavor among competent thinkers, not the
individual production of a lone thinker. As against logical intellectual endeavors, he calls "feeling," "intuition," and "belief"
nonscientific activities. The latter, however, produce the non-
logical, dynamic value content of philosophical reflection. The
"Truth," which in his terminology is a name for the "Whole,"
is a togetherness of rational and nonrational "moments" (dimensions, stages, or aspects). In this concept, Hegel synthe-
sizes Enlightenment values with Romantic values.

Hegel is devoted to freedom and skillfully interprets its
many forms. He holds all history to be man's progression in
the consciousness of freedom. The largest freedom is a life in
which mind and spirit reach high levels of activity in art, religion, and philosophy in harmony with the laws of Absolute
Mind. Like Kant, he asserts that morality requires full respect
for man as an end in himself, not as a mere thing or animal.
Moral action is truly moral only when moral law is freely followed by the conscious self; it is not action enforced by external law or the dictates of authority.

Hegel uses the term "morality" for the intentions and actions
of a person as a private individual, and the term "ethics" for
the realm of wider social and political duties. The state, for instance, has ethical duties in maintaining order and protecting
rights.

Hegel's basic philosophy is an intricate, all-inclusive system.
It explains reality as an Absolute Whole, which is both subjec-

tive and objective in nature, and works out its purposes in an endless process whose method of change is dialectical—that is, a movement from a given situation, the thesis, toward its opposite, the antithesis, and thence to a third position, the synthesis, which conserves and elevates the essential characteristics and values of the other two in a new form. Each synthesis has its own negation, and the process goes on as before, always producing richer and higher syntheses. The growth from childhood to adolescence to manhood is an example of this triadic movement.

One name for the Absolute is Spirit, and Hegel reminds us that "The Spirit bloweth where it listeth." It is free; it is bound by nothing but its own nature. The strictly ordered, in the sense of the logical or rational, is within the Spirit, not vice versa. In this concept, which places will deeper than reason in the godhead, Hegel is Augustinian and Lutheran rather than Thomistic. Hegel regards philosophy as the approach to the Spirit through human reason; and he regards religion, especially Christianity, as the approach through symbolic representations, metaphors, and intuitive images. But Absolute Mind, Spirit, God, and two other terms, the Notion and the *Idea*, all denote the same object, the living, spiritual, organic Whole.

Because Hegel saw the Whole as living and concrete, logical abstractions were to him unsatisfactory ways of explaining reality. A great difficulty in his style follows from this. He never was content with simple, unqualified statements, but was forever connecting each idea with others from different fields of discourse. Nothing can be explained by itself; it must always be connected with the total organism. He could not treat an object from merely the abstract view of physics, biology, or psychology, with no reference to the other truths about the object, especially the unmeasurable ones.

Nevertheless, he did try to clarify his meaning through different approaches. In his great *Science of Logic*, he analyzes and interprets the Absolute, here called the *Idea*, through the categories of thought. (*Idea* should be pronounced "ee-day-ah," Greek fashion, to distinguish it from the ordinary word "idea." The *Idea* means, as with Plato, the ultimate true reality, but for Hegel it includes not only disembodied pure essence, but essence united inextricably with dynamic, concrete existence—with being which is not an empty form, nor an inert mass-mechanism, but life.) The *Idea*, or any sample of it, can be discussed through the categories that thought uses: such categories as being, nonbeing, and becoming; or mechanism, chemism, and teleology; or theoretical mind, practical mind, and free mind. Hegel shows the organic relationship among all the categories, beginning with the emptiest, mere being, and ending with the richest and fullest, Absolute Spirit.

In one of his first books, and one of richest insight, *The Phenomenology of Spirit*, he treats the immense variety of human experience, paralleling that of the individual with that of the race, and seeing both as expressing the experience of the Spirit, the Absolute. His other books include *The Philosophy of History*, *The Philosophy of Right and Law*, and *Lectures on Aesthetics*.

Whether one agrees with Hegel or rejects his theories, there is common agreement that one must be acquainted with his philosophy.

FURTHER READING

Barrett, William. *What Is Existentialism?*
Easton, L. D. *Hegel's First American Followers.*
Kaufmann, Walter. *Hegel: Reinterpretation, Texts, and Commentary.*
Stace, W. T. *The Philosophy of Hegel.*

David Ricardo

[1772–1823]

ANY INDIVIDUAL astute enough to amass, through his own efforts, the sum of ten million dollars, is *ipso facto* considered to be a person of great ability. At the age of twenty-five, in 1797, David Ricardo had already acquired this enormous fortune. However, Ricardo's claim to recognition by posterity does not rest on his ability to make a lot of money in a short time. Instead, he is generally considered as the most important representative of the "classical" school of economics, the name given to those who, at this time, systematically unfolded the basic principles underlying the operation of the capitalist system, along with a historical explanation of its growth and development. Ricardo's works have left an indelible impression in such areas as labor and wage theories, rent, profits, and international trade.

David Ricardo was born in London in 1772, where his father, a member of the London Stock Exchange, had settled after leaving Holland. Earlier, a branch of the family, which included such noted individuals as the philosopher Spinoza and the writer Isaac Pinto, had lived in Portugal. His education was mostly in commercial subjects and, at the age of fourteen, his father took him into his business at the Stock Exchange. Young Ricardo, who had innate good judgment, a cool head, and a great capacity for hard work, was able to master the intricacies of the stock market in a relatively short time. However, when he was twenty-one years old, Ricardo was disowned by his father for leaving the religion of his family to become a Unitarian and to marry a beautiful Quaker girl. With the help of a few exchange members who admired his ability, he was able to obtain a seat on the London Stock Exchange in his own right. Within four years he had amassed enough money to last him the rest of his life, and he decided to devote much of his time to study and research. At first he was interested in the sciences, such as mathematics, chemistry, and geology; but after reading Adam Smith's *Wealth of Nations,* he decided to spend his time exclusively in the study of political economy. In this field he became quite famous in his own lifetime, and in 1819 was elected to a seat in Parliament, where he quickly became England's leading expert on economic policies. Ricardo did not forget others less fortunate than himself, for he supported from his own funds two schools and a home for destitute people.

Ricardo's first literary effort brought him immediate recognition and fame. It was in 1809, at the age of thirty-seven, that he published his views and ideas on a serious banking problem of the day. The pamphlet was called *The High*

Price of Bullion: A Proof of the Depreciation of Bank Notes,
in which Ricardo explained that the Bank of England notes of
that period were depreciating in value, and that the amount of
their depreciation was related and equal to the premium being
offered for bullion or gold. In this same essay, Ricardo became
the first economist to use the word "laws" to describe the
forces that tend to regulate economic behavior and activity.
Thereafter, in quick succession he published several additional
works, such as *Essay on the Influence of a Low Price of Corn
on the Profits of Stock* (1815), *Proposals for an Economical
and Secure Currency, with Observations on the Profits of the
Bank of England* (1816), and his major work, *Principles of
Political Economy and Taxation,* which appeared in 1817. In
1820 his essay on the funding system, in which he advocated
a pay-as-you-go policy for governmental expenditures, was
published in the sixth edition of the *Encyclopædia Britannica.*
The following year he founded the Political Economy Club,
the first of many societies for the study of economic problems
which subsequently were established in many other countries.
He continued to write and publish up to the time of his death
in 1823. In fact, he was so prolific a writer in his later years
that several of his manuscripts were published after his death
and, as recently as 1955, Cambridge University Press required
ten volumes to reissue his works and correspondence, including previously unpublished materials and notes.

Ricardo was loved and respected during his lifetime for his
"kindliness of manner" and for his efforts to reform Parliament,
to provide greater freedom for the press, and to emancipate
Roman Catholics. He was a profound and original thinker and,
in the words of one of his earliest biographers, "in point of
deep, clear and comprehensive intellect, he had no superiors,
and very few, if any, equals either in Parliament or in the
country."

It was this intellect that led Ricardo to observe the many
changes with their attendant problems that were taking place
in the eighteenth and early nineteenth centuries. Especially
troublesome for the English were the readjustment problems
resulting from the war against Napoleon. As is generally true
in any country after a major war, the public debt had sky-
rocketed, taxes were quite heavy, the cost of living was rising
faster than wages, the landowners, hoping to maintain high

prices, were opposing foreign grain importation, and the growing shipping industry was seeking concessions from the government. Furthermore, the growth and establishment of the factory system during the early years of the industrial revolution created additional areas of conflict between the workers and the new capitalist class. These were hard times for the people, and a particularly pressing problem of the period was the high price of "corn," which in England meant any edible grain (wheat, oats, barley, rye, etc.). As food prices continued to rise, it became necessary to use poorer agricultural lands, leading to higher rents for the better situated or more fertile land. The problem of rent had been discussed by many writers in France and England during the eighteenth century, and even in the United States it occupied a central position in the works of Henry George as late as the end of the nineteenth century. The problem of rent was a source of conflict between the aristocratic landlords, the hereditary owners of the land, and the rising class of industrialists or capitalists who had little liking for the landlords. Ricardo, in fact, was one of the rising industrialists and often their spokesman. Ricardo's explanation of the basis for land rent is probably his most famous theory and the one that is always associated with his name throughout the world.

Ricardo started off by defining rent as "that portion of the produce of the earth which is paid to the landlord for the use of the original and indestructible powers of the soil." Rent arises because a differential exists between soils of different fertility. For example, when a country is originally settled there is an abundance of all types of land. Since there is no scarcity of fertile soil no one will pay for the use of any land as long as unappropriated amounts of land remain. However, as the population increases and more and more land is put under cultivation, a point is reached where land and soil of a poorer quality or location must be utilized. As soon as this takes place, land of superior quality begins to command a differential called rent, and the amount of the rent is measured by the difference in the qualities between the inferior and superior lands. This continues to hold true as each parcel of poorer land is brought under cultivation. The diagram illustrates this principle:

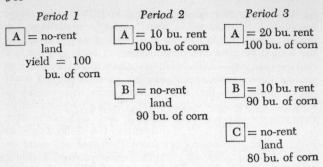

Period 1

$\boxed{A}$ = no-rent
land
yield = 100
bu. of corn

Period 2

$\boxed{A}$ = 10 bu. rent
100 bu. of corn

$\boxed{B}$ = no-rent
land
90 bu. of corn

Period 3

$\boxed{A}$ = 20 bu. rent
100 bu. of corn

$\boxed{B}$ = 10 bu. rent
90 bu. of corn

$\boxed{C}$ = no-rent
land
80 bu. of corn

In period 1, when the original, abundant, well-located, highly fertile land A is the only land under cultivation no rent arises even though the yield is 100 bushels of corn. In period 2, when inferior land B is used and produces 90 bushels of corn, then land A requires 10 bushels of corn as rent, and land B becomes the "no-rent" land. In period 3, when even less desirable land C is farmed and produces only 80 bushels of corn, then it becomes the no-rent land and land B must receive 10 bushels of corn as rent. Land A now requires 20 bushels of corn as rent. In each case it is the difference in yield between two parcels of land that determines the amount of rent. Ricardo was careful to point out, however, that a shift to poorer quality or less accessible land does not always occur. Instead, more intensive cultivation of the superior land may result in more output so that, if an additional investment of capital and labor on land A were to increase the return by 85 bushels of corn, whereas the same investment in land C would result in an increase of only 80 bushels of corn, then of course land C would not be used.

This theory of rent is based on the principle of diminishing returns, which states that when successive units of labor and capital are applied to a given quantity of land, a point will be reached beyond which further addition of labor and capital will yield less than proportional increments of output; in other words, the ratio of output to input will be diminishing. Ricardo's ideas were similar to those expressed by his contemporary and very good friend Thomas Robert Malthus in his *An Inquiry into the Nature and Progress of Rent, and the Principles by Which It Is Regulated,* published in 1815. In this essay, however, Malthus listed a third principle underlying the theory of rent. While Ricardo was satisfied with stating that the limited quantity and varied quality of land, plus the fact that the most fertile soil is relatively scarce, were the basic reasons for the existence of rent, Malthus insisted that rent could not be paid unless the land produced more than enough to keep and sustain those cultivating it. Therefore, reasoned Malthus, it is not essential for new land to come under cultivation before rent arises; instead, if the price of the produce rises, or if the cost of production goes down, then rent will occur on any land under cultivation. Furthermore, reasoned Malthus, high rents are a sure sign that a country's land is fertile, its agricultural products abundant, and the nation wealthy.

Ricardo disagreed with this analysis. Instead, he saw high rents as a cause for high food prices, which in turn would lead to a demand for higher wages, thus reducing the profits of employers. He concluded, therefore, that the interests of the landowners are in direct opposition to those of the workers and capitalists, and so he vigorously opposed the Corn Laws, which were designed to regulate the importing and exporting of grain and other cereal products in order to keep those prices and, in turn, land rents high. Thus, Ricardo was as firm a believer in free trade as was Adam Smith but for somewhat different reasons.

In this connection it is interesting to note the paradox that the wealthy Ricardo was arguing against the landowners, while Malthus, a humble college professor, was defending the landowners.

Ricardo also developed an important theory concerning wages and the distribution of the shares of wealth in a society. He declared that "profits depend on high or low wages, wages on the price of necessaries, and the price of necessaries chiefly on the price of food." One of his more important conclusions was that the price of labor, that is wages, would tend to remain at a level sufficient only to permit workers, "one with another, to subsist and perpetuate their race, without either increase or diminution." In case wages should ever rise above this subsistence level, the population would be stimulated to increase and the resulting competition of workers for jobs would in time force the wage rate to fall. In effect Ricardo was agreeing with Malthus in concluding that the poverty of the masses really is of their own making. This so-called "iron law of wages," as well as Ricardo's theory that the true value of commodities is determined solely by the amount of labor expended in their production, was later used by Karl Marx as the basis for his theories of the exploitation of the working class by capitalists and landowners.

Historically, writers on the history of economic thought, while recognizing the great contributions made by Ricardo, have tended to classify him, as well as his friend Malthus, as pessimists. However, they did not consider themselves to be pessimistic in outlook. Rather, they both believed that they had discovered "economic laws" more important than Adam Smith's "natural laws," which stated that society is guided by an "invisible hand" leading to the general welfare of all. Instead, Ricardo saw a world full of antagonism and conflict among the various classes concerned with the economic process, and governed by the law of diminishing returns which puts a limit on the amount of food production, and in which wages can never long remain above the subsistence level. These dire predictions, especially the ones concerning wages and food supplies, fortunately have not come true, because of such unanticipated factors as labor unions, productivity, and government regulation. Workers are able generally to command incomes which permit them a standard of living far above the level of subsistence, and historically, since Ricardo's death, agriculture has suffered more from "overproduction" than from "underproduction."

It has been said that Ricardo's contribution to the evolution of economic thought "makes him seem like a giant among pygmies." He succeeded better than any of his predecessors in isolating the chief categories of the economic system. His concern with the distribution of income in an economy focused attention on class conflicts and the importance of social and historical factors in economic analysis. He was a man of great perseverance, possessing strong powers of abstraction and synthesis, which enabled him to construct a sweeping theoretical system. The methods he used to develop models for economic analysis dominated economic thinking for almost a century. He can truly be called a "founder of modern economic science."

FURTHER READING

Blaug, Mark. *Ricardian Economics.*
Franklin, Burt, and Legman, G. *David Ricardo and Ricardian Theory.*

——John C. Calhoun——
[1782–1850]

ON MARCH 4, 1850, a tall, gaunt, and haggard figure, barely able to drag himself along, tottered into the chamber of the United States Senate and sank wearily into his seat. Torn as he was by the wracking cough of the consumption that was devouring him, his face was drawn and wan; his dark luminous eyes, cavernously deep-set in an angular, square-jawed face, stared forth in a pale image of their ancient fire. Too weak to do so himself, he begged permission of the chair to allow his friend, James M. Mason, Senator from Virginia, to read the speech he had prepared.

John C. Calhoun was dying. Indeed he was not to live out the month. But he was come to take his last stand before a crowded Senate chamber on the critical issues that were threatening to tear the country apart. When it had become known that the ailing Senator from South Carolina would address the Senate on March 4, probably for the last time, all Washington turned out to hear him. There was scarcely room to breathe in the galleries. Sitting immobile throughout the reading of his carefully written address, silent and inscrutable, seated just in front of Mason, he seemed to be speaking from beyond the grave through the voice of his colleague on the floor. He fittingly symbolized the dying cause that he upheld.

It was, of course, in this very chamber that only a few days earlier Henry Clay had risen, at the age of seventy-three, to make his plea for the last "great compromise" designed to prevent the foundering of the Republic on the rock of slavery. The issue of the expansion of slave territory, which had more than once before threatened the unity of the nation, had been precipitated anew by the series of events following upon the recent war with Mexico. In the summer of 1849, California, just acquired as a territory and burgeoning forth in a population explosion brought on by the discovery of gold near Sutter's Fort, had drawn up a constitution excluding slavery and was applying for admission to the Union. If she were to be admitted, the balance of free and slave states, at fifteen each, would be broken. Two more senators from a free state were more than southern radicals were willing to accept. The crisis was aggravated by several other questions agitating the country: there was the conflict over the status of slavery in the newly acquired territories of the Mexican Cession other than California; Texas and New Mexico were engaged in a boundary dispute; abolitionists were clamoring for the abolition of slavery in the District of Columbia, and southerners for a strengthened fugitive slave law. To put these issues to rest Clay had set forth a series of proposals in an "omnibus" bill that, by granting the wishes of the North on the admission of California as a free state and those of the South on a more stringent fugitive slave law, and by compromising the other issues, offered some hope of reconciling the interests of the two sections in a peaceful resolution of the conflict.

Joining Clay in his plea for reason and moderation, Daniel Webster, who with Calhoun and Clay made up the great triumvirate of the congressional leaders of their time, was to take the Senate floor three days after Calhoun's dramatic appearance and speak out in support of the compromise measures. For this famed 7th of March speech, the last great oration of his career, Webster was to bring down upon his leonine head the condemnation of the antislavery people of the North. Because he endorsed a compromise that included the return of fugitive slaves, New England humanitarians never forgave him for this speech. They rejected, as an apostasy and betrayal of his own lifelong antislavery sentiments, his plea for conciliation and accommodation.

Of the three giants dominating these fateful debates of February and March 1850, it was Calhoun alone who turned his back upon compromise and accommodation. If his message of March 4 spoke of compromise, it was on a note of futility and despair. If it spoke of accommodation, the only accommodation it would countenance was one that meant surrender of the North to the South. In taking this line, Calhoun, as spokesman for the South, was defining the extreme slaveholder's position. Clay had called for sacrifice, compromise, and understanding. Calhoun spoke of rights, justice, and the Constitution. "The great and primary cause" of the present crisis, Calhoun declared, "is that the equilibrium between the two sections has been destroyed." The South had been excluded from the new territories, penalized by a protective tariff, discriminated against by a despotic government. One by one the ties holding the Union together were snapping apart:

> The Union cannot . . . be saved by eulogies on the Union, however splendid or numerous. The cry of "Union, Union, the glorious Union!" can no more prevent disunion than the cry of "Health, health, glorious health!" on the part of the physician can save a patient lying dangerously ill. . . .

> How can the Union be saved? There is but one way . . . and that is by a full and final settlement, on the principle of justice, of all the questions at issue between the two sections. . . .

> But can this be done? Yes, easily; not by the weaker party, for it can of itself do nothing—not even protect itself—but by the stronger. The North has only to will it to accomplish it—to do justice by conceding to the South an equal right to the acquired territory, and to do her duty by causing the stipulations relative to fugitive slaves to be faithfully fulfilled—to cease the agitation of the slave question, and to provide for the insertion of a provision in the Constitution, by an amendment, which will restore to the South, in substance, the power she possessed of protecting herself before the equilibrium between the two sections was destroyed by the action of this government. . . .

> If you, who represent the stronger portion, cannot agree to settle them on the broad principle of justice and

duty, say so; and let the states we both represent agree to separate and part in peace. If you are unwilling we should part in peace, tell us so; and we shall know what to do, when you reduce the question to submission or resistance.

In concluding with a scarcely veiled threat of secession, Calhoun had reached the end of a long road, a road that he had embarked upon some twenty-odd years before. This was a marked departure from his career up to 1828, for his early life as a public figure had been characterized by devotion to nationalism.

John Caldwell Calhoun had been born, of Scotch-Irish descent, in the Abbeville district of South Carolina on March 18, 1782. His father, Patrick, born in North Ireland, had left when still a child and had migrated to the colonies, settling ultimately in the back country of South Carolina after brief sojourns in Pennsylvania and western Virginia. He acquired over thirty slaves in an area where slaves were uncommon, attained some prominence in his community, serving in the colonial and afterwards in the state legislatures. In 1770 he married Martha Caldwell, the daughter of another Scotch-Irish settler. Her brother, John Caldwell, after whom young John Calhoun was named, was murdered by Tories during the Revolution.

When John was fourteen, his father died. The opportunities for gaining a liberal education in the Carolina hinterland at that time were slim. What young Calhoun could absorb—and it stayed with him until he came to Congress in 1811—was a strong antinational bias that permeated the area in which he grew up. His county had opposed ratification of the Constitution fiercely; and in his boyhood days, from father, neighbors, and schoolteachers, the sensitive ears of Calhoun heard nothing but imprecations on the central government. Apart from that he received little education; in fact, his reading and writing were so rudimentary that he developed habits of bad spelling that remained for life. Fortunately for his career, in his late teens he had the advantage of being tutored for a time by his brother-in-law, the Reverend Moses Waddell, a Presbyterian minister who afterward became one of the South's outstanding educators and the president of the University of Georgia. In 1802, Calhoun was admitted to the junior class at Yale College and was graduated with distinction in 1804. He then studied at

Tapping Reeve's famous law school in Litchfield, Connecticut, and in 1807 was admitted to the Carolina bar. In 1808 and 1809 he was a member of the South Carolina legislature, and in 1810 was elected to the national House of Representatives.

Here Calhoun joined Henry Clay as a leader of the young "War Hawks." When the war he wanted with England materialized, he became, and remained for fifteen years thereafter, a foremost advocate of nationalist measures, including support of a program of armed strength, encouragement of manufactures through high protective tariffs, construction of national roads, and the chartering of the Second Bank of the United States.

It is part of the irony of events that had Calhoun's public career ended before 1828, he would have gone down in the pages of history as a great nationalist, and not as the most tragic expounder of sectionalism in this country. The unique place he has won for himself in the American political tradition is due entirely to the second half of his public life, when he confronted the dilemma in which he found himself as a representative of the slaveholding South. Here he stands in the mainstream of the development of the American "conservative" mind. As its exponent he was "a brilliant if narrow dialectician," in the judgment of one historian, "probably the last American statesman to do any primary political thinking." It has been said of Calhoun that he "possessed neither Webster's brilliant rhetoric nor his easy versatility, but he surpassed him in the ordered method and the logical sequence of his mind. He never equalled Clay in the latter's magnetism of impulse and inspiration of affection, but he far surpassed him in clearness and directness and in tenacity of will."

If any man's career may be said to have reflected the change in relationship between the North and the South, it was John C. Calhoun's. In confronting the great issues of the day he faced the hopeless task of fighting, as the phrase had it, "against the census returns." Although the South was growing throughout the period preceding the Civil War, the North was growing even faster. In 1790, the populations of North and South were about equal. By 1850, the North counted 13,500,000; the South only 9,600,000. The North had grown commercially and industrially and had concentrated in it the mobile wealth of the nation; the South remained agricultural.

A correspondingly growing disparity in political strength between the two sections seemed inevitable. The central problem for Calhoun, then, was how, in a democracy, to protect the interests of a conscious minority against the will of the majority. In devising his solution, the theory of "concurrent majorities," he made his contribution to the conservative political tradition of the nation. At heart he always remained a Unionist as well as a Southerner: he wanted to contrive a way in which the South could remain in the Union and protect its position within that Union. By this theory of the "concurrent majority," which would give any interest group, such as the South, a veto over any act passed by a Congress controlled by a majority, such as the North, Calhoun was doing nothing less than providing a rationalization for minority veto of a majority act.

How could this be effected within the constitutional framework of the United States? Calhoun had two answers. For his first remedy, far from being original, he went back to the doctrine of "nullification" or state "interposition," as set forth in Madison's and Jefferson's Virginia and Kentucky Resolutions of 1798. In his *The South Carolina Exposition and Protest,* published anonymously in 1828, and directed against the high protective tariff, which he regarded as not only discriminatory against the agrarian South in favor of the industrial North but also as unconstitutional, Calhoun invoked the "compact" theory of the Union which held that the "sovereign" states were to judge the constitutionality of acts of Congress. If Congress exceeded its delegated powers by enacting a protective tariff, any one of the states could "interpose" its authority to block enforcement of the law, declaring it null and void. Congress might then choose between acquiescing in nullification or proposing a constitutional amendment specifically granting to it the desired power. Since ratification of such an amendment would require approval by three-fourths of the states, Calhoun thought that this was a sufficient safeguard for the interests of the minority South.

Because nullification failed for lack of united support within the South, Calhoun was subsequently driven to a more extreme, if more sophisticated, instrument for implementing his doctrine of the "concurrent majority." This was the constitutional amendment that he referred to in his March 4 speech.

It was his idea that there should be two presidents, one for the North and one for the South, each having veto power over acts of Congress. He had expressed this as early as 1833, shortly after becoming a senator (he had resigned the office of Vice-President under Andrew Jackson to become a senator), and last formulated it in the posthumously published *Disquisition on Government.* Since, he held, government by numerical majorities was inherently unstable, it should be replaced by one that organically represented the whole community, both majority and minority. Society should not be governed by counting heads but by considering the great economic and geographic interests. In order to protect the minority against the predatory majority, it must be given "a concurrent voice in making and executing the laws or a veto on their execution." Short of that, the South would have to seek security in secession. Loving the Union as he did, his conviction that existing constitutional safeguards could not protect a minority from being taxed to death ultimately forced him to the logical extreme of secession.

Had Calhoun done no more than develop his doctrine of the "concurrent majority," he would have left his mark upon American political theory with this ingenious, if easily transparent, attempt to provide a rationale for the special interests of his class and section. As such it stands as a monument to the capacity of the human mind to rationalize and justify self-interest. But there were other facets to his thinking which distinguish him as a keen dialectician and as a truly seminal thinker and which have earned for him the description of being the "Marx of the master class."

Calhoun was a frank apologist for the slave system. As early as 1837, he said in Congress, "Slavery is, instead of an evil, a good—a positive good." And he propounded a theory of history that justified the slave system:

> It would be well for those interested to reflect whether there now exists, or ever has existed, a wealthy and civilized community in which one portion did not live on the labor of another; and whether the form in which slavery exists in the South is not but one modification of this universal condition.

As a labor system, slavery was no more ruthless or exploitative than the system of capitalistic wage labor, he maintained. In fact, it was more humane in that the slaveowner had an interest and a responsibility toward the health and maintenance of his property in sickness and in old age, in good times and bad.

Calhoun never showed his brilliance of mind and his skill as a dialectician to greater advantage than in the way he rang all the changes upon the dialectical elements present in a very complex situation. His first thought was to save the South by cementing an alliance with the equally agrarian West against the industrial North. Failing that, he thought to appeal to the self-interest of northern capitalists by calling for a "planter-capitalist collaboration against the class enemy," the enemy of all property. In 1847, he reminded northern conservatives that "the interests of the *gentlemen* of the North and the South are identical." The South, he held, was the more stable society and had much to offer as a conservative force. He argued further that it was to the interest of capitalist elements in the North to suppress abolitionist agitation because the overthrow of slavery in the South would prepare the ground for social revolution in the North. In this he was prescient in his analysis of power relationships because the alliance he sought in the pre-Civil War era has actually come to pass in the twentieth-century alliance between northern conservatives and southern reactionaries. But Calhoun never did find among the northern capitalists the response for which he had hoped; and, failing this, he was not above reversing his field and turning to the "wage slaves" of the North for support of the slaveholding aristocracy. It was one of his own followers who pointed out in the House of Representatives in 1837 that the southern planters stood in relation to northern capital "precisely in the same situation as the laborer of the North" and that the slaveowners were "the only class of capitalists . . . which, as a class, are identified with the laborers of the country." Hope as he might to turn to his advantage the tensions and contradictions within the northern capitalist structure, Calhoun was doomed to frustration. He and the South lost the race with time because the conflict between capital and the southern planter came to a climax before the conflict between labor and capital.

The close identification of Calhoun's thinking with the interests of an outmoded social structure and his putting it to the service of a small class devoted to the perpetuation of an exploitative economic system have inevitably and forever linked it with the conservative tradition in America. This is unfortunate in an important sense, because Calhoun, in his speculations, touched upon a vital problem in political theory: how to protect the individual and minority groups against the tyranny of the majority in a democracy. This is precisely the kind of threat against which the Bill of Rights is designed to protect political and intellectual minorities. But Calhoun was not the least bit concerned with protecting the rights of dissenters to express unpopular opinions in politics, or with the protection of religious heterodoxy, or with the civil rights of ethnic minorities. The only rights he was interested in vindicating were those of a *propertied* minority with vested interests and considerable power at that time.

By addressing himself to the problem of minority rights from the narrow viewpoint of a social-sectional class, and a reactionary one at that, Calhoun missed the opportunity to make a contribution to that liberal tradition under whose banners intellectuals have generally traveled in our times. But to have done this, he would have had to transcend the limits of his own class and social environment.

FURTHER READING

Coit, Margaret L. *John C. Calhoun.*
Current, Richard N. *John C. Calhoun.*

———Arthur Schopenhauer———

[1788–1860]

ARTHUR SCHOPENHAUER, called the German philosopher of pessimism, wrote the following comments concerning
the happiness of man:

> So long as we are given up to the throng of desires
> with the constant hopes and fears, so long as we are the
> subjects of *willing*, we can never have lasting happiness
> and peace.

> Happiness, accordingly, always lies in the future or
> else in the past, and the present may be compared to
> a small dark cloud which the wind drives over the sunny
> plain; before and behind it all is bright, only it itself
> always casts a shadow.

Although Schopenhauer's personal background and the
world situation of the early nineteenth century account for his
personal pessimism and although his doctrine of the "will"
gives a philosophical basis to pessimism, there is more in his
philosophy than emotional despair.

In 1793, Schopenhauer's father, a wealthy merchant who
desired freedom, left the free city of Danzig with his family to
go to Hamburg, when it seemed that Danzig might be annexed
by Prussia. Later, the father was adamant that the son should
enter the business field. Against his inclinations, Arthur pursued the father's wishes because of his love and respect for
him, but when, in 1805, his father, who had exhibited signs
of mental illness, committed suicide, the son plunged into
depression: "The truth which life showed to me clearly . . .
was that this world was not the work of an all-merciful god,
but that of the devil who called creatures into being in order
to delight in their torment."

358

After his father's death, Arthur studied at the University of Göttingen where he became a student of Plato and Kant, and where he developed his musical talent. Subsequently, he studied medicine, psychology, and psychopathology at the University of Berlin.

Arthur's mother, a popular novelist of the day, moved, after her husband's death, to Weimar where she preferred a life that was free of responsibility in association with some of the intellectuals of the day. On one occasion Goethe commented that her son would achieve fame. This comment was one of the sources of bitter rivalry between mother and son. The mother, likewise, disliked Arthur's interest in philosophy. In fact, when he completed his philosophical doctorate dissertation, *On the Four-Fold Root of the Principle of Sufficient Reason,* in 1813, she pinched her nose because she detected the pharmaceutical odor of "root" in the title.

In a bitter argument one day, the mother pushed her son down some stairs. This action ended any affection between the two, and the son never saw the mother again, although she lived on for twenty-four years. His relationship with his mother may explain his hatred of women. Once Schopenhauer said of them that they are "not even a necessary evil." Again, he said that they ". . . should never be allowed altogether to manage their own concerns, but should always stand under actual male supervision, be it of father, of husband, of son, or of the state. . . ." Some commentators have pointed out that the unhappiness of his family life also explains the personal pessimism that underlies his philosophy.

In 1818, he completed the document that expressed the core of his philosophy, *The World as Will and Idea.* The tremendous ego of Schopenhauer, which some modern psychologists would explain as a cover for insecurity, impelled him, on sending his manuscript to the publisher, to write that it was "clearly intelligible, vigorous, and not without beauty," and that it "would hereafter be the source and occasion of a hundred other books." Sixteen years later the greater part of this edition, which had almost no buyers, was sold for waste paper!

In 1820, Schopenhauer started lecturing at the University of Berlin. Having a disdain for the philosophy of the German philosopher Hegel, and being egotistic about his own appeal, he scheduled his lectures at the university at the same hour that Hegel was lecturing there. Schopenhauer, not drawing students from Hegel's lectures, canceled his own lectures. Disappointed and disillusioned, he gave up his teaching career.

Both Hegel and Schopenhauer, as well as Fichte, were greatly influenced by Kant. Indeed Schopenhauer's animosity toward Hegel stems not only from Schopenhauer's personality clashes with Hegel but also from Schopenhauer's disagreement with some of Hegel's interpretation of Kantian concepts of metaphysics. Kant professed an idealistic hypothesis—reality exists in the mind of man. Hegel, Fichte, and Schopenhauer accepted the hypothesis but with varying extensions of it.

Kant stated that two worlds exist: one outside the mind of man, a world consisting of objects, or "things-in-themselves"; and one inside the mind of man consisting of a collection of sense data concerning the physical manifestations of the "things-in-themselves." Kant concluded that a "thing-in-itself" cannot be known. However, Schopenhauer said that it can be known and that it is blind will. Schopenhauer's basis of reality is will. On the other hand, Hegel, a champion and proponent of reason, claimed that reason is the ultimate of reality. Hegel confirmed the rational character of reality; Schopenhauer maintained the irrational character of will and debunked the notion of pure reason so popular with Hegel. Fichte wanted to dispense with the "thing-in-itself" and to declare the "ego," or "the thinking subject," as the ultimate of reality.

Schopenhauer spent the greater part of his remaining years attempting to seek fame and brooding about not achieving it though he did achieve fame late in life. Being financially independent, he had time to contemplate and encourage his concepts of existence. In contrast to his actual existence, he wrote: "To have all his [man's] wants satisfied is something intolerable—the feeling of stagnation which comes from pleasures that last too long. To overcome difficulties is to experience the full delight of existence."

The stage of Europe in Schopenhauer's days was being set for his philosophy. The ravages of the Napoleonic wars caused an air of pessimism to pervade Europe. The exuberance of the French Revolution was over; Napoleon was in exile at St. Helena. Prices were high; people were impoverished; food was lacking; morality was at a low ebb after the war. Disillusionment prevailed in young and old alike. Gone were the high hopes for freedom of the spirit and the emancipation of man that were fostered in the French Revolution when the feudal aristocracy was unseated. Reaction was in the saddle and the absolute rulers were back in authority with antidemocratic repression.

A reviewer said *The World as Will and Idea,* the basic work of Schopenhauer's philosophy, treats four areas: "The first part deals with the world as it appears, the second as it 'really' is, the third with temporary 'salvation' through aesthetic contemplation, and the fourth with enduring salvation through the denial of the will." It is a book that is distinctive in its straightforward, practical presentation of ideas, quite different from the involved metaphysical treatment of philosophy in other books of his time.

"The world is my idea," the famous opening statement in his book, gives some insight into the nature of the will. To Schopenhauer, man "knows not the sun and the earth, but always only the eye, which sees the sun, the hand that feels the earth." The world about man is only about him as an idea. Up to this point he was merely reiterating what Kant and Fichte had said about reality, that it was merely the figment of man's mind. However, Schopenhauer went beyond this to introduce a new and more basic dimension, the will. He asserted, "The objective world, the world as idea, is not the only side of the world, but merely its outward side; and it has an entirely different side—the side of its inmost nature, its kernel, the thing-in-itself." The "thing-in-itself" is what Schopenhauer calls the will—"the inner essence of man's nature." The will applies not only to man himself but also to all things in nature. What the scientist called the underlying force or life force in nature and man, he called the will.

Schopenhauer's will has broad characteristics; notable are the desire to live and the inclination to reproduce. He illustrates will's desire to live when "we see a dry seed preserve the slumbering force of life through three thousand years, and, when at last the favorable circumstances occur, grow up as a plant." He explains the will's inclination to reproduce when he states that "the reproductive organs are properly the focus of the will, and form the opposite pole to the brain, which is the representative of knowledge. . . . The former are the life-sustaining principle—they ensure endless life. . . ."

Schopenhauer hypothesized that if the world is will then life is evil. The desires of life are infinite; they are "like the alms thrown to a beggar, that keeps him alive today in order that his misery may be prolonged tomorrow." Pain is the stimulus in life. Man appreciates happiness only in presence of suffering. When man is plagued with wants and privations, he recognizes the loss of happiness. So, "as soon as want and suffering permit rest to a man, *ennui* [boredom] is at once so near that he necessarily requires diversion." Thus "life swings like a pendulum backward and forward between pain and *ennui.*"

Since the will has unquenchable desires, and since these cause pain to man, he lives in dire straits. How can man achieve any happiness in life? Schopenhauer's answer to this is the control of the will by the intellect. "Of ten things that annoy us, nine would not be able to do so if we understood them thoroughly in their causes, and therefore knew their necessity and true nature. . . . For what bridle and bit are to an unmanageable horse, the intellect is for the will in man." When man can overcome the will with the intellect, he begins to achieve happiness. "Unselfish intellect rises like a perfume above the faults of follies of the world of will."

The highest form of this "will-less" knowledge is seen in the genius. "Genius is the power of leaving one's own interests, wishes, and aims entirely out of sight, of entirely renouncing one's own personality for a time, so as to remain pure knowing subject, clear vision of the world. . . ." Schopenhauer used his idea of the genius to help to explain some of the genius's foibles and "oddities." The genius, being "will-less," becomes impervious to his surroundings; thus he seems "unusual" to one not in the same state.

What aids man in achieving this will-less state? Art and compassion! In the contemplation of an object of art—a tree, building, or mountain—man loses himself in the object, "forgets even his individuality, his will, and only continues to exist as the pure subject, the clear mirror of the object, so that it is as if the object alone were there, without any one to perceive. . . ." A man in such a state "is *pure*, will-less, painless, timeless *subject of knowledge.*" During the time that one contemplates an object of art, he is temporarily transcending

the pain and evil of life, and he experiences exalted happiness.
John Keats presented a similar philosophy about happiness in
these lines from "Ode on a Grecian Urn":

> "Beauty is truth, truth beauty,"—that is all
> Ye know on earth, and all ye need to know.

Schopenhauer maintained that music was *the* art that would
raise man above the conflicts of the will. "Music is by no
means like the other arts, the copy of the Ideas"; music is
"the copy of the will itself." The German composer Richard
Wagner agreed with Schopenhauer's theory of music and even
sent him an autographed copy of *The Ring of the Nibelung*.

By means of compassion, man can achieve a will-less state
or salvation. Compassion, according to Schopenhauer, is the
temporary extinguishing of the will, with all its cravings and
desires, and the temporary identification with the suffering
will of another. Schopenhauer found compassion expressed in
Hindu literature. He maintained that compassion could release
man from the bondage of the individual's will and thereby
alleviate the suffering within himself. This release cannot be
totally achieved in life because life is the embodiment of the
will. However, the saints did acquire a high degree of compassion.

By means of his doctrine of the will, Schopenhauer interpreted religion and death. Religion, said Schopenhauer, is
contrary to all that man has ever experienced. Man, possessed
with the "will to live," sees death all about him. Man dies in
countless ways each day, despite his desires and inclinations to
live. In fact, Schopenhauer notes that in life man exerts his
greatest energies in the reproduction and raising of his species.
Despite these energies, man knows he will die. To counter this
inevitability, man devises gods who have the power to save
man from death. Schopenhauer agreed that Christianity saw
suffering and evil in the world. In fact, the original teachings
of Christianity were pessimistic. However, he concluded that
man saw himself as a source of evil and that the teachings of
religion were pervaded with optimism. Consequently, if man
could achieve immortality, religion would fade away.

Death of man, according to Schopenhauer, is the initiation
of man's perpetual "nonexistence." After death man does not
suffer, for suffering demands life. However, the will of man,
the basis of reality, is indestructible. When the body of man

decays, his will is untouched by death because the will exists
outside the domain of space and time. The body of man is a
physical or phenomenal thing. In birth, the will takes on the
structure of an animal body. The will, being eternal, existed
before acquiring a body, and exists after shedding a body.
Thus man's identity, according to Schopenhauer, does not
exist except as an idea in man's own thinking. The will has
identity but only becomes recognizable when it takes on a
physical character.

In later years, Schopenhauer's philosophy was widely accepted. Because the ideals and democratic efforts of 1848 were
frustrated, because science questioned theology, and because
biology stressed the struggle for existence, Schopenhauer's
works were being read, and they expressed or explained the
despair of the day. Schopenhauer the pessimist ironically became the optimist, for he lived to see his fame, collecting all
the articles which were written about himself. On his
seventieth birthday in 1858, he received acclamations from
throughout Europe. However, on September 21, 1860, he
sat down to breakfast alone and died of a heart attack. Never
marrying, Schopenhauer had one faithful companion throughout life—a poodle named Atma (world-soul). The boys of his
day called the dog "Young Schopenhauer."

Schopenhauer had an influence upon the thinking of the
German philosopher Friedrich Nietzsche, upon the naturalistic
writers Henri Bergson and William James, and upon other
philosophers. He sought for an answer to the eternal questions
with which philosophers have grappled: What is reality?
What is truth? What is the path to happiness? The kernel of
Schopenhauer's contribution was to develop and analyze a new
conception as a dimension of human behavior, the conception
of the will. He pointed philosophy away from abstract idealism
and concern with pure reason, and directed it toward realism
and search for new conceptions.

FURTHER READING

Aiken, Henry D., ed. *Age of Ideology.*
Gardiner, Patrick. *Schopenhauer.*

John Henry
——Cardinal Newman——
[1801–1890]

"THAT only is true enlargement of the mind which is the power of viewing many things at once as one whole, of referring them severally to their true place in the universal system, of understanding their respective values and determining their mutual dependence."

Thus, John Henry Newman, renowned scholar, educator, fellow at Oxford's Oriel, religious thinker, and leader of the Oxford movement, described the effect of basic liberal arts education in his widely recognized volume *The Idea of a University* (1858). This was a man whose scholarship led him to gather his facts, to test them with Aristotelian logic, to synthesize, and to write. When beset with a problem, he drew up a thesis, investigated, researched, and interpreted his findings as his brilliant and thoroughly trained mind was able to do.

Born on February 21, 1801, the eldest of six children of banker John Newman and Jemima Fourdrinier, John Henry began his studies at a private school in Ealing, London. At the age of sixteen he was admitted as a commoner to Trinity College, Oxford.

Newman's independence of mind was evident at Oxford from the first. He made no attempt to disguise his disgust for the loose morals and excessive drinking which prevailed, and his companions found futile their attempts to embarrass him into conformity. Shy, retiring, and earnest in manner, John Henry's early days at the university were lonely. Perhaps this loneliness was rendered more acute by the fact that the Newman household which he had left was such a happy one. Members with a variety of interests enjoyed each other's company, played, and worked together. John Bowden, three years his senior, was his first friend at the university. Newman said that they became inseparable: reading, walking, and boating together. Bowden's name for Newman was "the great man" or "Joannes Immortalis."

John Henry's Oxford career was endangered by the failure of his father's bank, a shock from which the elder Newman never fully recovered. However, the son was able to continue his scholarly efforts.

At an unusually early age, Newman achieved the singular honor of election to an Oriel Fellowship on April 12, 1822. Ordained to the Anglican ministry shortly before his father's death in 1824, he was able to support, in part, an Oxford education for his brother Francis, as well as to render financial aid to his mother and other members of his family.

If one were to characterize Newman's long life, the theme of suffering and inner conflict would appear to run as a constant thread throughout. There is loneliness, uncertainty, and inner search for truth, coupled with misunderstanding and persecution, both before and after his embracing the Roman Catholic faith. Pain was inflicted at times by friends, at other times by strangers, and even by members of his own family. Through all, John Henry Newman displayed patient endurance which never faltered in the face of opposition from within or from without.

He speaks of three conversions. The first occurred when at fifteen he was converted from skepticism to God. In his *Apologia* he says that God touched his heart and describes his great change of thought.

In 1827 his illness, followed closely by the sudden death of his sister Mary, resulted in what Newman refers to as his second conversion. His work on the Fathers of the Church had laid the foundations. At this period his sermons were characterized by the call "to holiness rather than peace," to purification of religious belief as disciplined faith in emulation of the Fathers of the Church. After his friend Keble's sermon in 1833 on "National Apostasy" (with which Newman held that the Oxford movement began), Newman addressed his clergy with *Tracts for the Times*. In fact, after this he wrote several "incendiary pamphlets" under the caption "Choose Your Side." In opposing the "liberals," Newman makes clear that he referred to the spiritual liberals who were making reason the sole judge of religious truth, thus weakening faith.

He maintained that politics had no place in his discussion.

His third conversion took place during the summer of 1839, while engaged in a profound study of the Church in antiquity. He came upon the history of the heretical Monophysites of the mid-fifth century. The parallel between the Monophysites and Eutychians of the fifth century and the Anglicans and Protestants from the sixteenth to the nineteenth struck with unprecedented force. Newman says, "It was difficult to make out how the Eutychians and Monophysites were heretics, unless the Protestants and Anglicans were heretics also; . . . difficult to condemn the Popes of the sixteenth century without condemning the Popes of the fifth." This marked the beginning of a long struggle that ended with his leaving the Anglican Church and asking for admission to the Roman Catholic Church on October 8, 1845.

Thus his major conversions evolved from youthful skepticism to evangelicalism, then through the Tractarian movement (the *Via Media* "middle road"—the Anglican's position between Roman and Protestant with an emphasis on spiritual reform expressed in the *Tracts*) to his final acceptance in the Church of Rome.

Close friends played an important role in this development, and no study of John Henry Newman would be complete without a look at some of these great minds.

In 1816 it was Walter Mayers, a young clergyman teaching at Ealing, who lent Newman books, all from the school of Calvinism, from which Newman learned a direction which he "almost never lost." Dr. Whately, a gentle, encouraging instructor, attracted Newman to the cause of the evangelicals, a cause in which he persisted for several years, gradually being drawn from it by contact with Oxford scholars. Newman says Dr. Whately not only taught him to think but to think for himself. He inculcated some of the most prominent features of the Tractarian movement into his young student. Dr. Pusey was the scholarly professor of Hebrew, authority on the Scriptures, without whose influence the Oxford movement could never have succeeded. Pusey revived Newman's interest in the Church Fathers. He aided in securing a collection of the works of the Fathers which Newman kept to his dying day.

Then there was the empiricist Froude. His interest was not the early Fathers but the Medieval Church. The story of Thomas à Becket, revealing the conflicting forces between church and state, was his favorite topic. Newman called him an "Englishman to the backbone." It was Froude who worked to bring Newman and the gentle Keble together. The relationship, however, was confirmed for Newman by his interest in Keble's theories on faith and reason, although Newman was not entirely satisfied with the latter's unphilosophical approach.

The ailing Froude's invitation for a trip to Italy in 1832 was an awakening for young Newman, who had never before observed anyone or any place outside a small area of England. His own determination to visit Sicily unaccompanied, his illness during this excursion, and his enforced wait at Palermo for transportation stimulated a tremendous desire to return to England: "We have work to do there."

His trip to the Mediterranean was the occasion of some of his most beautiful poetry. The famous "Lead Kindly Light" was composed while the sailing vessel was becalmed off Sardinia on the return voyage. In the poem he recorded the ordeal he had endured in his conversions, together with the premonition of things to come. In a personal note to Anne Mozley, he referred to his need for direction from without.

Many other individuals exerted considerable influence on the sensitive soul of this man as he struggled in search of truth, eager to repair abuses in society and in the church of his day. One of his greatest hardships when he finally did break with the Anglicans was leaving some of these friends, while one of the brightest moments of his later life was renewal of communication with them.

John Henry Newman's kind heart, his genuine interest in fellow human beings, and his awareness of the social evils resulting from materialism in England, formed him as one of the nineteenth century's outstanding intellectual and religious leaders.

The period 1833–1841 was considered a turning point of history by the participants of the Oxford movement. Disturbed by the political involvements and social pressures which seemed to be stifling the intellectual and spiritual life of the Church of England, Newman and his followers began a search for truth. These men were fervent Anglicans, thoroughly distressed by the fact that their church leadership was, to a considerable degree, in the hands of "smug parsons" and "privileged aristocrats." Accordingly, they issued a series of ninety pamphlets called *Tracts for the Times,* which identified, as a result of intensive study and search for the truth, early Catholic doctrines and practices. Newman's sincere efforts to revive the spirit of ancient Christendom relied to a great extent on the Bible.

As inheritors of the Age of Enlightenment, the people of the nineteenth century were often thought to be promoters of "arrogant independence" and "lawless freedom." In contrast, Newman and his fellow Tractarians followed their convictions as loyal Anglican clergymen in such matters as their opposition to the fight for emancipation from the established church of the Irish Catholics. The cause, championed by Peel and O'Connell, appeared to Newman and his associates to be a kind of treason.

In the *Apologia pro vita sua,* written in 1864 in answer to the accusations of untruth by Dr. Kingsley, Newman describes in a simple, forthright style, documented by letters and other memorials, his slow and painful struggle with religious convictions to the time of his conversion from Anglicanism to Roman Catholicism. The struggle was intensified by the fact that he had had a deeply grained, lifelong conviction that the Church of Rome was wrong. Since he had been so committed to the Anglican cause, the struggle to reverse the position and espouse the Church of Rome was extremely difficult, and the fear of discovering himself wrong again was intense. This pain of separation was amplified by the fact that his closest friends were not able to go along with him. Who could describe the effort it must have cost a scholar who was to give up Oxford, his beloved St. Mary's, and finally Littlemore, his last Anglican parish?

In addition to the heartrending process of slow separation there was the slander, misrepresentation, and misunderstanding of which he was the victim. In his *Apologia* this man of sixty-three describes the efforts he made to avoid unsettling others and his attempts to keep them from hasty action. This must have been a revelation to those who so violently accused him during the years of decision.

Once the step was taken and Newman had embraced the Catholic faith, his troubles were not over. The chain of misunderstanding and disappointment continued. This extraordinary scholar was unable to convince others of the depth of his sincerity.

Partly because of a language barrier, partly because of a lack of understanding of the culture and scholarship he represented, and partly through lack of discretion on the part of his friends, his efforts to cooperate with Rome were slighted. Hope and enthusiasm were aroused by projects such as the establishment of a Catholic university in Dublin, the proposed translation of the Bible, and the project for a branch house for Catholic students at Oxford. In each case, jealousy, greed, or misunderstanding entered and the project had to be abandoned.

Out of one of the most disheartening of these projects, the Catholic University of Dublin, grew *The Idea of a University*, which expressed his views of the purposes of a university education and which is used to this day as a classic in educational philosophy.

Newman's profound analysis of basic education was written at a time when there were Newtonian overtones advocating specialization in education, when Darwin's theories were upsetting the scriptural accounts of creation, when science was assuming an increasingly important role, when materialism was a growing force. To those who advocated education for a particular profession, Newman said, "Society itself requires some other contribution from each individual besides the particular duties of his profession," and again, "the perfection of intellect, which is the result of education and its beau ideal, to be imparted to individuals in their respective measures, in the clear, calm, accurate vision and comprehension of all things, so far as the finite mind can embrace them, each in its place and with its own characteristics upon it." The discussion of the role of theology in education; of literature, of physical science, and elementary studies contains challenges no educator can afford to ignore.

One of Newman's last works, *Grammar of Assent*, was published in 1870. Here Newman presents clear definitions, with explanations and illustrations, of terms necessary for understanding the principal truths and mysteries of the Catholic faith as they were worked through his mind, trained originally in Anglican schools of theology. The easy reference to the ancient classics, to the philosophy of all ages, is somewhat indicative of the scholarship and clear reasoning of this great thinker, who had almost reached the age of seventy.

The second part contains the first sketch of what philosophers would today call "phenomenology" of conviction and belief. It is considered by some an "epoch-making contribution to Christian thought."

Despite the long struggle and the painful lack of acceptance, a happy ending did come. Restrictions on registration of Catholics at Oxford were lifted as a result of the Act of Parliament in 1871. Later, restrictions on the part of the Catholic hierarchy on Catholics attending secular schools were also lifted. It was, indeed, too late for the organization of a school for Catholics in Oxford, but it was not too late for Oxford to recognize one of its glorious alumni.

Trinity College, for the first time in its history, awarded to John Henry Newman an honorary fellowship. Shortly after this, on May 12, 1879, Pope Leo XIII bestowed on him the red hat of Cardinal, thus rendering John Henry Cardinal Newman a prince of the Catholic Church.

During a century when England was changing from a rural to an industrial society, when Ireland had severe religious and economic problems, when traditions were being uprooted, when liberals, radicals, and conservatives were competing for power, when materialistic philosophies were spreading, and science was challenging the very rules of life, John Henry Newman stood as a beacon of scholarship, advocating steadfast faith, a disciplined mind, and high ideals of human behavior.

Were he alive a century after the appearance of his *Apologia,* the growth of the spirit of ecumenism, the vast development of education together with the emphasis on the participation of the laity in the life of the Catholic Church, which he advocated, would convince Newman that he had not pioneered in vain.°

FURTHER READING

Bouyer, Louis. *Newman: His Life and Spirituality.*
Trevor, Meriol. *Newman: The Pillar of the Cloud.*
————. *Newman: Light in Winter.*

° Clubs for Catholics at nonsectarian institutions of learning are called "Newman Clubs" in memory of John Henry Newman, founder of the Oxford movement.

——Benito Pablo Juárez——

[1806—1872]

BENITO JUÁREZ had come a long way since his childhood as an Indian boy when, barefoot and in tattered cotton
trousers, he had known hunger and abject poverty. Now he
was governor of his state of Oaxaca. It would be so easy to
settle into the usual pattern of governmental inertia, to make
no enemies, to forget the injustices he had known as a youth.
But he could not forget. He thought of Hidalgo and the
priest, Morelos, who had led uprisings of his people for freedom from Spain in the early nineteenth century and had paid
for their ideals with their lives. Juárez, the short, stocky, full-
blooded Zapotec Indian, with black hair, craggy face, and
piercing black eyes, sat in a black frock coat in his governor's
chair and determined that, no matter what the cost, he would
bring about reforms.

Benito had been born in the tiny village of San Pablo de
Guelatao, Oaxaca, Mexico, the first day of spring, 1806. At
this time Mexico was still ruled by Spain, and the government
was controlled by grandees who had been born in Spain and
who had huge landholdings. The clergy also exercised a powerful influence, both politically and socially, possessing large
tracts of land, that had been granted to them centuries before,
and controlling education. Below the grandees on the social
scale were the Creoles, those of pure Spanish ancestry who
had been born in Mexico. Next were the mestizos, who were
the offspring of intermarriages between Spaniards and Indians; and finally, there were the full-blooded Indians, who
had almost no rights and lived in poverty, exploited by those
in power.

Benito was orphaned at an early age but was fortunate
enough to be adopted by an uncle for whom he worked as a

sheepherder and who arranged for his initial schooling. These
boyhood years had a great influence upon his life. His outdoor
living as a herdsman developed his fortitude, stamina, and
powers of concentration. Loneliness and privation held no
fears for him. His meager schooling by the harsh methods of
rote learning imposed by the local priests gave him an abiding
determination to find a better way of education.

When he was twelve, he ran away to the city of Oaxaca
where he was taken in by Don Antonio Salanueva, who became his godfather and patron and made it possible for him
to attend law school.

Juárez was fifteen in 1821 when Mexico won its independence from Spain after bloody revolutions. However, the forces
that had united in revolt were now torn apart by their conflicting interests. On one side were the Liberals and on the
other were the wealthy landowners and many Church officials
who feared the consequences of reforms that would emancipate the masses. The young law student Juárez aligned himself heart and soul with the Liberals and, despite personal
dangers, fought for reforms.

In 1831 he became a lawyer and in 1834 was admitted as
an advocate. In his memoirs of this time, he revealed his belief in government by elected representatives and the necessity of education to produce an intelligent electorate. For the
rest of his life he never wavered from this belief in democracy. At this time, too, he married Doña Margarita, beginning
a relationship of devotion and love that helped to sustain him
through unbelievable hardships and reverses.

In 1847, Juárez was elected governor of the province of
Oaxaca. In taking office he said that he had always worked
for "fulfillment of the law that has always been my sword
and shield." He was to maintain this faith in a government of
laws throughout his life, though many of those around him
would seek dictatorial powers for themselves and even for
him. Juárez' administration as governor began in an atmosphere of debt and suspicion on the part of those who feared
his liberalism. However, he succeeded in placing the state's
finances in a strong position, in expanding education by building more than three hundred schools and eight normal schools
for training teachers, and in making some legal reforms that
established greater justice for the poor. Although he did not

approve of the civil power of the Church, he did not at this
time move to disturb it.

During the Mexican war with the United States, the Conservatives returned to power under the virtual dictatorship of
Santa Ana. The difference between the two men becomes
evident when one considers the following statement made by
Santa Ana about Juárez: "It is amazing that an Indian of such
low degree should have become the figure that we all know."
Juárez was not only ousted from the government in 1852, but
he was imprisoned and almost murdered before he escaped
into exile in New Orleans.

In 1855 the Reformers under Alvarez returned to power in
Mexico, and Juárez returned as national Minister of Justice.
In this office, Juárez instituted reforms despite the bitter opposition of the Church authorities and the Conservatives. He
secured adoption of the *Ley Juárez* ("the laws of Juárez,")
which removed the special privileges of the upper classes,
gave the civil government control of Church property, set up
a Bill of Rights allowing appeal to the Supreme Court on civil
rights, and made the President of the Supreme Court an
elected official. Juárez was elected President of the Supreme
Court and was next in succession to the presidency.

In 1857, the liberal Mexican government, now under President Comonfort, adopted the Constitution of 1857 which included the *Ley Juárez* as well as measures to strip the Church
of its civil authority. In retaliation, governmental officials were
excommunicated by the Church, and an armed revolution led
by General Zuloaga and the Conservatives forced President
Comonfort to resign and flee the country.

Juárez thus became the legitimate constitutional head of
government, but he had few followers, no army, and almost
no resources. Foreign governments, including the United
States, recognized Zuloaga because they feared Juárez, the
reformer. Again Juárez narrowly escaped assassination as he
fled north to Veracruz, but his determination to establish justice, freedom, and democracy in his country never flagged. In
a letter seeking aid, he said: "They have invoked the sacred
name of our religion . . . to destroy at one blow the liberty
that Mexicans have won at the cost of sacrifices of every
kind."

While in Veracruz he decided to make the issue of his

struggle clear and issued his Manifesto of July 7, 1859, separating Church and state, nationalizing Church lands, requiring civil control of marriages, births, burials, and guaranteeing freedom from injustice. Juárez's enemies vilified him as anti-religious in a country whose people were devout Roman Catholics, but Juárez maintained that he could be religious and at the same time seek reforms for the good of the people.

In 1861, Juárez finally achieved victory and returned to Mexico City as the lawful head of the government. However, his trials were far from over.

The nation, impoverished by civil wars and the corruption of the prior administration, was unable to pay its foreign debts, and France, Spain, and Great Britain threatened occupation. Juárez' statesmanship and his commitment to honor the debts of his country averted this incident.

Internally, there was bloodshed, violence, and treachery. Many of his supporters sought their own aggrandizement. Few had his patriotic idealism. Yet, he had patience, stamina, shrewd common sense, integrity, and vision which enabled him to hold the support of men of different temperaments.

In 1864, the French Emperor Napoleon III placed Maximilian upon the Mexican throne, and again Juárez became a hunted outlaw with a price upon his head, though he was the elected President of Mexico. Juárez would not surrender but continued guerilla attacks and propaganda for freedom from foreign imperialism. Finally Napoleon was compelled to withdraw his forces, and Maximilian was captured and executed in 1867.

Once again Juárez returned to the presidency and again he sought to institute reform and solvency. Recognizing the importance of education in a democracy, Juárez, in 1871, reorganized and expanded the educational system under civilian control. He also made changes in the structure of the government, modeling it more after the United States. Throughout his life, Juárez had remained steadfast to his purpose of improving the lot of the Mexican people by establishing a democratic government of laws with justice and freedom of civil and religious beliefs. If his struggle seemed herculean, perhaps it was because his thinking was far in advance of his time in Mexico. Even the great Latin American liberator San Martín had thought that the best form of government for Latin America was a monarchy, not a democracy.

When Juárez (he died in 1872) was followed by Porfirio
Díaz, a dictator, it seemed that all the gains in reform would
be eradicated, but the seeds of liberalism had been sown better than Juárez himself had realized, and Mexico moved in-
exorably toward democracy. Benito Juárez, the little Zapotec
Indian who became Mexico's greatest president, was me-
morialized on a hillside of Oaxaca in a bronze statue, holding
a book in his hand. On the book is carved a single word: "Reform." The great French author, Victor Hugo, said of him that
America had produced two great men, Lincoln and Juárez.

FURTHER READING

Baker, Nina B. *Juárez, Hero of Mexico.*
Smart, Charles A. *Viva Juárez!*

———Sören Kierkegaard———

[1813–1855]

HE WAS CERTAINLY A PECULIAR FIGURE walking
through the streets of Copenhagen, his high silk hat suppress-
ing a mass of unruly fair hair, his umbrella tucked under his
arm. Worse, the curvature of his spine made him lean until it
seemed that he must fall over backwards, and his spindly legs
moved in a crablike, mechanical gait, a fashion that suited
the purposes of the street urchins who followed at a not-so-
respectful distance, chanting tauntingly, "Either or, either or!"

Fortunately, Sören Kierkegaard was able to accept his physical appearance with a wry humor that instinctively grasped
the irony of the situation. Although his brilliant mind found
no reflection in his physical appearance, it was scarcely dimin-
ished by it. Long ago the Danish philosopher had learned to
accept the disparity between his physical and mental powers,

and had renounced the former for the latter. Kierkegaard
lived in the world of the intellect, and yet his own intellect
paradoxically realized the insufficiency of a world ruled entirely by reason. Thus he wrote: "It was intelligence and
nothing else which had to be opposed. Presumably that was
why I who had the job was armed with immense intelligence."

The task to which Kierkegaard was alluding was to lead to
a dual revolution: against the rational philosophy of Hegel
(Hegel believed that "the real is the rational and the rational
is the real") and against the practitioners of Christianity of
Europe, who seemed to him to be hypocritical—a revolution
that ultimately cast Kierkegaard in the role of a nineteenth-
century Luther.

In 1813 Sören Kierkegaard was born, the seventh and last
child of Michael Pedersen Kierkegaard of Copenhagen, then
the intellectual center of Scandinavia. From the outset his life
was dominated by the figure of his father, and later he quite
frankly admitted that it was love of his father that enabled
him to understand love of God. At an early age he was a par-
ticipant in his father's religious discussions, but he had no
friends his own age. As he says in his journals, he never really
had a "childhood" in the real sense, but his relationship with
his father was rich enough to bridge this deficiency.

The years of his boyhood and youth were outwardly uneventful, but despite the outward appearance of calm, there
was much turmoil, both within the Kierkegaard household
and within young Sören himself. It seemed as if a curse had
fallen on the elder Kierkegaard and his son. Within the space
of a few years Kierkegaard's mother and five of his six brothers died. These events served to unmask the silent despair of
his father, a despair that undermined the faith of both father
and son and plunged both into a melancholy that was to become the dominant note in Kierkegaard's life. This despair
stemmed from the father's belief that these deaths were the
direct result of his having blasphemed God when he was a
boy and of the irregularities that preceded his marriage to his
second wife, who had also been his servant girl. Sören came
to share this belief and later described the crumbling of his
father's faith as "the great earthquake" that shattered his
world and left him stranded "inwardly torn asunder." However, despite great internal suffering and struggle, Kierkegaard
continued to wear the mask of the literary rake and wit, a

mask that quite concealed his melancholy. And he continued in this aimless fashion until the death of his father ushered in the second stage of his life.

It was during this stage that the most momentous event of his outwardly uneventful life occurred. In 1840 he became engaged to Regine Olsen, and then a year later he mysteriously and unexpectedly broke off the engagement without any justification or provocation. This sudden action was the turning point of his life and the vital influence on his thought. Afterward he wrote, "Had I had faith I would have remained with Regine." But the fact is that he did not remain with her; he felt that it was not his destiny to marry, but rather to make another choice. Thus, although he earnestly desired the comforts of domestic life, he renounced them. Like Abraham who was called upon by God to sacrifice his only son, Isaac, Kierkegaard felt that he had been called upon to sacrifice Regine and his one happiness in order to achieve a spiritual life. The inner agony of this painful decision was intensified by the caddish behavior he adopted to discredit himself and lessen Regine's suffering. Thus he lived in the years 1840–1845.

There was no dichotomy between Kierkegaard's life and his thought; they were merged into one. And thus it is quite natural that the writings of this period should focus on the dynamics of choice. *Either/Or* deals with choice, and *Fear and Trembling* focuses on the Abraham-Isaac story, which is after all only a thinly disguised analysis of his decision to break with Regine.

Kierkegaard was an existentialist thinker; that is, he believed in the *existence* of man as a free-willed, important personality, not subject to mechanical rules of nature but able to determine his future, and hence his "essence," by making decisions. To Kierkegaard existence is not some abstract thing residing placidly in the realm of pure thought, as Hegel declared, but rather it is something that touches man to the core of his being and daily must be reaffirmed through "either/or" choices. Sören Kierkegaard felt the fear and trembling of the "either/or" choice because he had made it, and it was of this that he wrote. It is in making such choices and leaping into the unknown that one begins to become a "self."

Either/Or, written before he was thirty, set forth Kierkegaard's basic belief. The choice for mankind is between the apparent reality of pleasure and sensations and the verity of ethics, moral law, and personal identification with God. This is no minor choice, but one between "everything" and "nothing."

For Kierkegaard there could be only one choice: God. He chose not what he regarded as the pseudo Christianity practiced by some but a spiritual "leap to God," brought about by faith, not intellect, by individual suffering rather than by any systematized institution, by a process of individual elevation through the overcoming of anxiety, temptation, and fear. He rejected the complacency of accepted dogma and the ecclesiastical comfort of a "being" person in favor of the dynamic striving of the "becoming" person.

Now Kierkegaard determined to launch an attack upon ecclesiastic abuses in Denmark, on false religionists, and on all institutions constricting freedom. In *Attack upon Christendom,* written in an ironical tone, he criticizes false clergy who have sought the placidity and influence of a church haven and have debased the high ideals of Christianity.

In *Concluding Unscientific Postscript,* he attacks the scientific rationality of Hegel as representing an erroneous and smug definition of a static world, as if any human being could ever solve the riddle of existence. Kierkegaard argued, rather, that the world is an ever-changing, "becoming" universe under a transcendent God, with choices open to individuals and with courage required to make the choice.

Behind the acid wit of his pamphlets are two major ideas. The first is that men "must reach the category of the individual"—that is, stop being herd animals and experience the agonizing dilemmas of choice in "fear and trembling." It is an attack on the herd mentality, and a cry for individuality and freedom. The second idea is that the illusion that Europe was still following the ideals of Christianity had to be destroyed. This was a direct result of his first idea, for without free individuals to experience the religious element, according to Kierkegaard, religion could only exist as ritual and ostentation, which is what he said Danish religion was.

During the last few months of his life, Kierkegaard played the role of a nineteenth-century Luther trying to reform the Church, elevating the personal above the institutional. He also believed himself to be a latter-day Socrates, for his approach was Socratic: irony and wit were the main weapons of this gadfly who caustically stung the inflated pride of those he considered hypocritical Christians. And just as Socrates did, he, too, caused public resentment. Kierkegaard became the target of counterattacks that went far beyond his own criticism in vituperation and vilification. His learning, his sincerity, and even his unattractive physical features were sneered at, ridiculed, and lampooned from the lecture platform and in periodicals.

As the furor increased, Kierkegaard's strength waned. He had literally expended all his energy on these polemics. In October 1855, as the last of his pamphlets went to the printers, he collapsed in the streets. Taken to Frederick's Hospital, he refused to retract his works or to receive communion. And it was in this way that Sören Kierkegaard, deeply religious and yet regarded by many in his own day as inimical to Christianity, died, at the age of forty-two.

Kierkegaard has had a greater influence on the twentieth century than on his own; his influence was not exerted until after the First World War. He forecast the dread result of enslavement of the mind that eventuated in Nazi Germany. Because of his attack on the herd or mob, he has great importance in an age when individuality is slowly being submerged, and when terms like "organization man" and "the lonely crowd" are in use. But, above all, he was one of the first existentialists, one of the first to attack the abstract rationality of the German idealists such as Hegel. Thus all the existentialist philosophers of this century owe a debt to Kierkegaard, a debt that is readily acknowledged. Finally, as a religious thinker, Kierkegaard has had great influence on modern theology. His fundamental approach has been developed by such Protestant theologians as Karl Barth and Reinhold Niebuhr. It is in this way, through his tremendous importance in the twentieth century, that the strange, melancholy man who lived for but forty-two years in the nineteenth century came to have a lasting influence after his death.

FURTHER READING

Aiken, Henry D., ed. *Age of Ideology.*
Brown, James. *Kierkegaard, Heidegger, Buber, and Barth.*
Friedman, Maurice, ed. *Worlds of Existentialism.*

Lowrie, Walter. *Kierkegaard: A Life.*
————. *Short Life of Kierkegaard.*
Wolf, Herbert C. *Kierkegaard and Bultmann.*

————John Stuart Mill————

[1806–1873]

IN 1867 in the British House of Commons, a man sixty-one years of age stood up and made the first speech ever made before that august body in defense of woman suffrage. Though he was far from convincing to his colleagues and though woman suffrage did not come to Great Britain for another half century, that speech was the culmination of a plan that had started many years before, in fact, even before he was born. The man was John Stuart Mill, recently elected member from Westminster, an important district in London. He had run as an independent and was elected on the basis of his reputation as a thinker of integrity.

The plan referred to was formulated by his father James Mill, and by his father's friend Jeremy Bentham, the intellectual leader of a reform group known as "philosophical radicals." In the year 1806, when the first son, John Stuart, was born to James Mill and his wife, Mill conceived of the idea of educating him to become the leader of the reform movement in England. John was not to be sent to school, since the schools of the time merely indoctrinated their pupils into acceptance of the status quo. He was to be given a private education by his father so that he would not waste time learning things which would have to be unlearned later. John was taught Greek at the age of three and Latin at the age of eight. By the time he was twelve, he had read almost all the major classical authors in the original. He studied literature, history, mathematics, and science. When he was about twelve or fourteen, he was turned to economics and philosophy, the combination of which, in the eyes of the reformers, was the key to the reformation of society.

John spent about a year in France when he was fourteen, learning French and dancing and attending some university lectures. When he was old enough to attend a university in England, his father and Bentham consulted on this question and decided against sending him, since the universities had little to teach him that they wanted him to learn and both major universities (Oxford and Cambridge) were under ecclesiastical control. He therefore continued his studies under his father's tutelage. He gave us a rather graphic description of his relation to his father in his *Autobiography* (1873).

When he was eighteen, he was given the task of editing Bentham's work on judicial evidence. The result was published in five volumes as Bentham's *Rationale of Judicial Evidence*. Shortly after this, and perhaps partly as a result of this exhausting work, Mill had what he called "a crisis in my mental life," what we might call a nervous breakdown. He seems to have plumbed the depths of despair; he asked himself whether, if all the ends which he hoped to achieve were realized, he would then be happy and he could only answer, no. He came out of this crisis (on his own) with the help of the inspiration provided by the emotional content of the poetry of Wordsworth and Coleridge, and the influence of Harriet Taylor whom he subsequently married.

With his father's assistance he secured a position as an examiner of correspondence for the East India Company, a quasi-civil-service position. After a career in this company he retired to a life of writing and travel, which he interrupted in 1865 when some citizens of Westminster asked him to stand for Parliament. He served one term (to 1868) and was defeated when he came up for reelection, largely because his reform ideas were in advance of his time.

In addition to his career as an official in a quasi-governmental organization, Mill had a more important and influential career as a reformer and writer who was, in effect, the conscience of the age. Writing in his spare time and on vacations, he turned out hundreds of newspaper and magazine articles, and an amazing variety of very important books on many subjects. His books became classics in his own lifetime. Indeed, John Stuart Mill was regarded as the greatest economist of his age. He was assisted in his writing by his wife, Harriet Taylor, to whom he dedicated several of his works.

The focus of his interest was what he called "the moral sciences," which comprised history, the social sciences, then in their infancy, and philosophy. His earliest work, which was in economics, culminated in his *Principles of Political Economy* (1848). This book brought up to date the theories of taxation, rents, wages, wealth, and production in the tradition of the classical political economy of Adam Smith and David Ricardo.

But his main contribution was to show that the laws of distribution are not immutable, as the classicists had declared, but subject to change and control. He conceded that agricultural production was beyond the control of society because it was dependent upon nature: e.g., diminishing fertility of soil, blights, weather, and human incapacities. Malthus and the classicists had taught that the immutable laws of production and distribution forever doomed workingmen to minimum subsistence (Ricardo's "iron law of wages"). For this reason economics had come to be known as the "dismal science." Now Mill was saying that the production of goods could not be controlled, but the distribution could be. By taxes, by laws, and by expropriation society can take from one individual and give to others. Simple as this thought was, Mill was the first to give wide expression to it and to see its consequences.

The theoretical basis was set down for raising the standard of living of the workers by deliberate policies of government. This was an entering wedge for socialism and while Mill was not a socialist in the present-day meaning of the term, he did call himself one, and his economics was the basis of English Fabian socialism.

Prior to the publication of his *Political Economy* he had completed his *System of Logic* (1843), the first comprehensive study of logic based explicitly on empiricist (experiential) principles.

Mill's greatest interest and most noteworthy contributions to both the thinking and the practice of his generation and later ones lay in the fields of ethics and politics. This clear-thinking, sober, and dedicated reformer lived close to the great political events of the period from 1820 to 1870. During the French Revolution of 1830, Mill and a friend rushed over to Paris to see the progress reform was making on the Continent. His reflections on these events were reported to newspaper readers in Britain. He did the same during the French Revolution of 1848.

The earlier French Revolution of 1789 had aroused in Great Britain a sharp reaction against change. The groups in power in Great Britain prevented the reforms necessary to enable the country to digest the many changes brought about by the industrial revolution. The factory system, which led to the rise of industrial towns, spawned many abuses and much suffering. Mill saw the solution not in any revolutionary upheaval but in a rational reform of Parliament.

The year 1832 saw the fulfillment of the hopes of the reformers in the passage of the Great Reform Bill of 1832, which eliminated the "rotten boroughs" and extended suffrage. Mill shared the hopes of the reformers at that time, but by 1840 he was reevaluating the situation and coming to realize that reform was a more complicated problem than could be solved by extending suffrage as some earlier reformers had supposed.

Later in his life he pulled together his thoughts on the problem of democratic government and produced one of his most important books, *Considerations on Representative Government* (1861). This book is the work of a reformer grown to maturity. The point of departure is the doctrine of Bentham as presented in James Mill's brief *Government* (1820). Originally an article for the *Encyclopædia Britannica*, this is a didactic summary of the Benthamite position that representative government is the cure for the political ills of mankind. Tyranny is government that is not truly representative of the interests of the ruled. The cure for tyranny is an adequate system of representation—the outlines of which James Mill proceeded to draw.

Mill placed the problem of reform in its historical setting. Influenced by the conception of progress that had been developed in France in the eighteenth century, e.g., by Condorcet, he saw mankind moving through stages in its historical development, each stage related to the state of knowledge at that time, each stage preparing the next. The culmination of the development was the achievement of representative government. Thus, representative government is not the solution for all people at all times, but only for those people who are prepared to undertake its obligations.

Mill developed a system of representative government in which men of knowledge have special weight in governmental councils. In the first place, additional education is rewarded with additional votes in the election of representatives. In the second place, the administration of affairs is in the hands of experts. Finally, the drafting of legislation is turned over to trained legal specialists. The people elect a representative body to check on the activities of the governors and as a forum to discuss public issues for the enlightenment of all. The aim of this government is to provide for the well-being and liberty of all.

Mill devoted a separate study to the problem of liberty. His *On Liberty* (1859) is still the classic work in that field. With great foresight, Mill saw that liberty in the modern world is threatened not so much by government as by the society in which custom may suppress individuality. He set down a principle which should regulate the relation of the individual to society: There is a sphere of action in which society has only an indirect interest, and in that sphere the individual should be free to do as he chooses. It consists of the inward domain of consciousness, the choice of a way of life, and associations with other mature individuals. These require freedom of thought and discussion, freedom of tastes and pursuits, and freedom of association. The main body of Mill's essay is devoted to the extended argument for freedom of thought and discussion, an analysis of the conception of the individual presupposed by his theory, a study of the relation of the individual to society, and the discussion of some troublesome examples. His justification of liberty is in terms of its results, not in terms of a doctrine of God-given or natural rights. Liberty is best because it is most likely in the long run to produce the greatest happiness of the greatest number. It thus becomes clear that the defense of liberty requires a theory of the good life for man, a moral theory.

His lengthy essay *Utilitarianism* (1863) is an account of the doctrine that was the cornerstone of the way of thinking of the philosophical radicals. The underlying question is "What is the good?" This is a central question of philosophy, and one of the oldest. The utilitarians (as the philosophical radicals came to be called) said that the good is that which promotes the greatest happiness of the greatest number, happiness being defined in terms of a preponderance of pleasure and the absence of pain. This view, which philosophers call "hedonism," had been stated by Bentham with great force. Mill accepted it with qualifications, qualifications made necessary by criticisms which had been showered on Bentham. The central qualification concerns Mill's recognition of qualitative differences among pleasures. Spiritual or mental pleasures, he said, are qualitatively superior to bodily pleasures, to the point where they cannot be compared quantitatively.

Mill also struggled to do justice to Kant's view that it is the motive that determines the morality of an action. Although he did not accept that doctrine, Mill did admit that the motive determines the moral quality of the actor, but he insisted to the end that the moral quality of the act is determined by its results.

The legacy of John Stuart Mill is the legacy of the open-minded, rational inquirer who searches for a reasonable solution to all disputed questions and does not make up his mind until he has considered all the evidence. Raised as a doctrinaire believer in one solution to all problems, he had to work his way to openmindedness. His friends and opponents alike recognized his honesty, his understanding, and his fairmindedness. Gladstone called him "the saint of rationalism."

FURTHER READING

Packe, Michael. *The Life of John Stuart Mill.*
Stephen, Leslie. *The English Utilitarians.*

——Henry David Thoreau——

[1817–1862]

THE FOLLOWING ITEMIZED LIST for the building of a house, among the most famous in all American history, belongs to the noble experiment undertaken from 1845 to 1847 by Henry David Thoreau of Concord, Massachusetts:

Boards	$8.03½,	mostly shanty boards
Refuse shingles for		
roof and sides	4.00	
Laths	1.25	
Two second-hand		
windows with glass	2.43	
One thousand old		
bricks	4.00	
Two casks of lime ..	2.40	That was high
Hair	0.31	More than I needed
Mantle-tree iron	0.15	
Nails	3.90	
Hinges and screws ..	0.14	
Latch	0.10	
Chalk	0.01	
Transportation	1.40	I carried a good part on my back
In all $28.12½		

All his life, Thoreau was a critic of the herd spirit and a non-conformist; it was in consonance with that attitude that he decided to build a modest house in the woods near Walden Pond and take Nature as his bride. "I went to the woods," Thoreau explained, "because I wished to live deliberately, to front only the essential facts of life, and see if I could not learn what it had to teach, and not, when I came to die, discover that I had not lived."

The story of Thoreau's life in the woods is told in his American classic, *Walden*. A more influential product of those two years of semi-isolation and meditation is the essay "Civil Disobedience." That lucid statement of Thoreau's principles, like a rock thrown into a pond, has created rings of ripples, which have subsequently encircled our globe and have profoundly influenced such men as Mahatma Gandhi and Martin Luther King, Jr. Thoreau's rebellion was against the materialism of his prospering country, against the idea that happiness consists of counting money or material possessions. Thoreau's nineteenth-century protest in this respect has implications for our times.

Henry Thoreau, who spent almost all his years in a small New England town, would be astonished to see how far his ideas have traveled. Except for a few brief intervals, he lived a parochial existence in the Concord area, where he had been born in 1817. His father's family were English-speaking French, and his mother's people were Scottish. Although his father was taciturn, his mother more than made up for it; she was known as "the greatest talker in Concord." Young Henry acquired his mother's Scottish burr, and it flavored his speech for the rest of his life.

Concord was a splendid place for a youngster who loved the out-of-doors, and Henry was such a boy. His senses, being keener than most, allowed him to see the beauties of nature in sharp focus. As Ralph Waldo Emerson, Thoreau's great friend, said: "He saw as with microscope, heard as with ear trumpet, his memory a photographic register of all he heard."

Thoreau's formative years, in short, were happy ones. Loved by his parents, his sisters and brother, nourished by good books and conversation, and insulated from worldly pressures, Henry had a childhood that he characterized as "ecstasy." After his graduation from public school he went on to Harvard, where his marks were good but not outstanding. In later life, Henry was critical of Harvard, feeling that it had not taught him much of value. When Emerson mentioned that Harvard taught all branches of learning, Thoreau added, "All the branches and none of the roots."

Many doors were open to Thoreau as a Harvard graduate. His classmates went on to become clergymen, doctors, jurists, and industrialists, and Henry chose to become a teacher. His first job at Concord's elementary school did not last long. The school-board members lifted their eyebrows at Henry's new educational theories, and they were shocked by his refusal to flog pupils. Henry resigned and, together with his brother John, opened an elementary school that was startlingly progressive. Thoreau's pupils would learn "by doing": they would experience things firsthand rather than merely read about them. Furthermore, misbehaving pupils would not be flogged but would be subjected to a talk on morals instead.

The school was successful, but Henry lost his interest in it when his brother died two years later. It was at that point that Thoreau began his lifelong friendship with Emerson. While at Harvard, Thoreau had read Emerson's important transcendentalist essay, "Nature," and it had stimulated him to keep a personal journal. A mutual friend showed Thoreau's notebooks to Emerson, who was so impressed with the young Concord schoolteacher that he invited Henry to live with his family and "to receive bed and board in exchange for what he chooses to do."

At Emerson's home, Thoreau met celebrities such as Nathaniel Hawthorne, Margaret Fuller, and Bronson Alcott. He imbibed the idealism of those romantic New Englanders who despised hypocrisy and sought after the truth of the heart. The conversation, often brilliant, was not lost upon Thoreau.

The opportunities for someone who wanted to earn a living as a writer were limited in Concord, however, and when Thoreau had a chance to get closer to New York's editors and publishers he took it. Emerson had managed to get Henry a job as a tutor to his nephew who lived in Staten Island. This was the kind of work which was ideal for Thoreau and close enough to the big city for him to get the writing assignments which would bring him a living. But a tour of the publishers' offices revealed that the only one willing to pay its contributors was the *Ladies' Home Companion*. As Thoreau "could not write anything companionable," he turned his back on New York after six months, moving back to his parents' home in Concord. There he helped his father by inventing a new process for making graphite, which brought substantial prosperity to their lead-pencil business.

The year was now 1845. Thoreau was twenty-eight, half-way through his life and with little to show for it, he felt. He had written some poetry (called "worsification" by James Russell Lowell), published a few magazine articles, lectured, taught school, done surveying and other odd jobs. Now it was time to stand back, take a hard look at his situation, and make some significant decisions as to the future. He had no interest in the material things of this world, scorning ostentatious wealth, creature comforts, and conspicuous consumption. The ideal life, as he pictured it, would be one of leisure, contemplation, and reading, all in a natural setting. Since any type of primitive habitation required some money, he reasoned that he could plan for an existence which required the barest minimum: "In proportion as a man simplifies his life, the laws of the universe will appear less complex and solitude will not be solitude, nor poverty poverty."

Retirement to Walden was the answer. Emerson had acquired several acres on the shores of Walden Pond, and he offered them to Thoreau as a retreat. Thoreau would pay his own way completely, build a house from scratch, eat whatever food he could grow or catch, and eliminate all nonessentials. In drawing up such a blueprint for living, he would be conforming to the principles set forth in one of his beloved documents, the Hindu Bhagavad-Gita: "He who is content with wisdom and clear-seeing, who is victorious over the senses, to whom a piece of dirt, a piece of stone, a piece of gold are all equal is established in the Rule. Let the man of the Rule hold himself always under the Rule, remaining in seclusion, utterly subdued in mind, without cravings and without possessions."

The list of expenses at the start of this biography appears in *Walden; or Life in the Woods*, Thoreau's account of his two-year experiment. Other statistics are equally interesting: the cost of his food came to twenty-seven cents a week; he earned $23.44 from the sale of farm produce; it cost him a grand total of $25.21 to live there for the first year!

He moved into his tiny dwelling on Independence Day, 1845. Characteristically, he put no lock on his door, stating that his domicile "belonged to nature as much as to man." In these spartan surroundings Thoreau found his Shangri-La. He explored the woods, fished, raised beans and potatoes, read widely, and contemplated. Occasionally some Concord citizens would drop in ("going to see Henry" became a town ritual) and occasionally Henry would leave the woods to do surveying and to pick up supplies.

At Walden, Henry had the time to write. He completed his first full-length book, *A Week on the Concord and Merrimack Rivers,* an account of a trip he and his brother had made six years earlier. Henry had to print it at his own expense because no publisher would accept the book. After one year, the company returned 706 unsold volumes out of the thousand it had printed. "I have now a library of nearly nine hundred volumes," Thoreau quipped, "over seven hundred of which I wrote myself."

Thoreau once noted: "By my intimacy with nature, I find myself withdrawn from man. My interest in the sun and the moon, in the morning and evening, compels me to solitude." It is ironic, therefore, that a man so withdrawn from mundane affairs should come to play as important a role as Thoreau did. His personal philosophy and his convictions, as reflected in "Civil Disobedience," have affected the lives of millions of people in the twentieth century.

Disapproving of the United States government's feeble protest against slavery, Thoreau had refused to pay his poll tax. This action led to his being jailed for a day when he strolled from Walden into Concord. An apocryphal story tells of Emerson's visit to the jail and his question: "Henry, what are you doing in there?" to which Thoreau replied, "Waldo, what are you doing out there?" After his release from prison, Thoreau returned to Walden and committed his protest to paper. Some of his major ideas appear in the quotations below:

Under a government which imprisons any man unjustly, the true place for a just man is also a prison.

It is not desirable to cultivate a respect for the law, so much as for the right.

That government is best which governs least.

The only obligation which I have a right to assume is to do at any time what I think right.

I cannot for an instant recognize that political organization as my government which is the slave's government also.

Any man more right than his neighbors constitutes a majority of one.

Those who, while they disapprove of the character and measures of a government, yield to it their allegiance and support are undoubtedly its most conscientious supporters, and so frequently the most serious obstacles to reform.

Unjust laws exist: shall we be content to obey them, or shall we transgress them at once? ... If unjust laws exist, civil disobedience is an effective way to oppose and change them.

It matters not how small the beginnings may seem to be: what is once well done is done forever.

If the injustice ... is of such a nature that it requires you to be the agent of injustice to another, then, I say, break the law. [When the Nazi officials on trial in Nürnberg after the Second World War said that they were merely carrying out the law in murdering enemies of the state, the Allied prosecutors quoted Thoreau to them.]

Absolutely speaking, the more money, the less virtue; for money comes between a man and his objects, and obtains them for him. ... The best thing a man can do for his culture when he is rich is to carry out those schemes which he entertained when he was poor.

There will never be a really free and enlightened State until the State comes to recognize the individual as a higher and independent power, from which all its own power and authority are derived, and treats him accordingly.

When Mahatma Gandhi urged the people of India to practice civil disobedience in their struggle for independence from Great Britain, he referred to the philosophy of Thoreau as his guiding star. Recently, in the American Negro's campaign for equality, the Nobel Peace Prize winner Martin Luther King, Jr., said: "The teachings of Thoreau are alive today, indeed they are more alive today than ever before. A sit-in at lunch counters, a freedom ride ... a peaceful

protest . . . all are outgrowths of Thoreau's insistence that evil
must be resisted and no moral man can patiently adjust to
injustice."

As abruptly as he had gone to Walden in 1845, Thoreau
left the woods in 1847. As he explained, "I left the woods for
as good a reason as I went there. Perhaps it seemed to me
that I had several lives to live, and could not spare any more
time for that one." He headed for Concord, living for a time
with the Emersons and then at his own home. His daily
routine remained basically as it always had been: each
morning he read, all afternoon he tramped through the
countryside, and in the evening he copied into his journals
all that he had seen and reflected upon.

Emerson described Henry as he saw him setting out for
his midday ramble. "Under his arm he carried an old music-
book to press plants; in his pocket his diary and pencil, a spy
glass for birds, microscope, jack-knife and twine. He wore a
straw hat, stout shoes, strong gray trousers . . . to climb a
tree for a hawk's or squirrel's nest."

Sadly enough, one of those excursions led to Thoreau's un-
timely death. In December 1861, he caught a severe cold from
lying upon the damp ground too long, counting the rings on a
fallen tree. Bronchitis and tuberculosis followed. Within a few
months it was apparent to all that Henry was dying. When a
religious acquaintance asked him whether he had made his
peace with God, Henry answered, "I have never quarreled
with him." When near the end and asked whether he saw the
land he was approaching, Thoreau barely had the breath to
reply, "One world at a time."

At Thoreau's funeral in May 1862, the eulogy delivered by
Emerson concluded with this statement: "Wherever there is
knowledge, wherever there is virtue, wherever there is beauty,
he will find a home." Henry David Thoreau, the man who all
his life marched to the music of his own drummer, could fall
into step with the other great thinkers of world history.

FURTHER READING

Canby, Henry S., ed. *Thoreau.*
Derleth, August. *Concord Rebel.*
Hoff, Rhoda. *Why They Wrote.*
Van Doren, Mark. *Henry David Thoreau.*

———Karl Marx———
[1818–1883]

"LET THE RULING CLASSES TREMBLE at a Communist revolution. The proletarians have nothing to lose but their chains. They have a world to win. Working men of all countries, unite!"

These words first appeared in 1848 in a small German-language pamphlet, the *Communist Manifesto*. Since then, the pamphlet has been reprinted innumerable times in all languages, and has undoubtedly become the most widely read single piece of socialist literature in existence. The *Communist Manifesto* was the joint product of two young and relatively unknown socialist writers, Karl Heinrich Marx and his lifelong friend and collaborator, Friedrich Engels. At the request of the League of Communists, an organization of workers, they wrote the *Manifesto* to set forth its platform and program. At the time, the term "socialism" generally was used to describe the collectivist theories of men like Robert Owen, François Fourier, and the Comte de Saint-Simon, all of whom Marx later classified as "utopian socialists" because they failed, according to Marx, to recognize the futility of trying to reform existing political, social, and economic institutions. By contrast "communism" was the term used to describe the working-class movement dedicated in the class struggle to the forcible overthrow of capitalism.

Strangely enough, Marx and Engels, who through their writings set in motion the international Communist movement, were themselves products of "bourgeois capitalism" and had received a substantial middle-class upbringing. Neither of them ever was a "worker" in their sense of the word. In fact, Engels, the son of a wealthy German textile manufacturer, for almost forty years used his income and later his inheritance to work with and support Marx and his family.

Karl Marx was born in Trier, Germany, on May 5, 1818, the third of nine children and the only son to live to maturity. His father, a prosperous lawyer, had converted from Judaism to Christianity. All members of the family, including Karl when he was about six years old, were baptized in the Protestant faith.

When Karl entered the University of Bonn at the age of seventeen, he intended to study law in accordance with his father's wishes. However, after one year he transferred to the University of Berlin, where he studied philosophy, history, and literature. He devoted all of his tremendous energy to his studies, partly because of their intellectual appeal and partly because he never engaged in any of the social activities of the typical German undergraduate. He had a seriousness of purpose and a maturity beyond his years. In fact, just before coming to the university he had persuaded his parents to permit him to become engaged to a beautiful and aristocratic girl, Jenny von Westphalen, whom he married seven years later.

As an example of his capacity for work, he told, in a long letter to his father, how he wrote three volumes of poems to his Jenny, "read Heineccius, Thibaut, and the sources," translated large parts of Tacitus and Ovid and two books of the *Pandects*, prepared a work of three hundred pages on the philosophy of law—and composed a play. In addition, he read many books on all subjects and "while out of sorts, got to know Hegel from beginning to end." This letter was written when he was nineteen years old.

In 1841, Marx received a Doctor of Philosophy degree from the University of Jena, where he had hoped to pursue an academic career. When his identification as a radical Hegelian and as a nonconformist prevented a university appointment, Marx became a free-lance journalist. He soon became editor of the *Rheinische Zeitung*, in which he wrote editorials denouncing the authorities for their harsh treatment of the poor. After five months the newspaper was suppressed, and Marx and his wife moved to Paris, where Marx felt he could become better acquainted with prevailing French socialist thinking. It was in Paris, in 1844, that Marx began his lifelong friendship with Engels.

After a series of expulsions from France, Belgium, and Germany (he was charged with treason in Germany), Marx finally settled with his family in London, where he spent the last thirty years of his life working in the library of the British Museum and producing huge masses of manuscripts, including his major, three-volume work, *Das Kapital (Capital)*.

The years in London were filled with grinding poverty, sickness, and personal tragedy for Marx and his deeply devoted wife. At this time Marx was rather stocky in appearance, with a broad forehead, prematurely furrowed by cares. His hair was full, black, and always disarrayed, and his face usually had an intense, serious expression. The family was constantly hounded by bill collectors, pawnbrokers, and landlords. Once, when a child died in infancy, Mrs. Marx had to borrow the money for the coffin from a stranger in the neighborhood. From time to time Marx worked as a journalist and, for a while, was the English correspondent of the *New York Tribune*, but most of his meager income came from his friend Engels. It is all the more astonishing to note the monumental works Marx turned out in the midst of these tribulations. All the while, this dedicated theorist, whose ideas dictated social upheaval, has been described as "lovable in his dealings with children; those of the neighborhood called him 'Daddy Marx,' and looked to him for sweets, not in vain."

The work of Karl Marx has had a great influence in world history. There are those who criticize his contributions to economics, sociology, history, and philosophy, but they cannot ignore what he wrote in these areas. Principally, Marx is regarded as a great thinker in economics who was also a practical revolutionary and who used his studies of economics and history to forge ideological weapons to be used in a worldwide political struggle for the liberation of the proletariat. In fact, in the *Manifesto* and in *Das Kapital*, Marx was trying to analyze the trend of his times and to show that world society was in a process of change that would inevitably transform the capitalist system into a socialist one.

As he and Engels looked about in Europe in the 1840's, they saw men, women, and children working long hours under inhuman conditions and for pitifully low wages so that the mill and factory owners could realize maximum profits. With revolution or the threat of revolution challenging the old order in

Europe, Marx believed that the program he had set down in the *Manifesto* was capable of being achieved in the near future.

Despite the lip service paid to the ideals of liberty, equality, and fraternity, there was very little freedom of speech or of assembly, and the notion of the divine right of kings was still enforced by the ruling despots. Abortive revolutions occurred in France, Belgium, Germany, Austria, and Hungary in 1848; but lacking leadership and direction, the revolts failed. Before long the old reaction had returned in full force. It was almost seventy years after the publication of the *Manifesto* that the first successful "proletarian revolution" finally took place in 1917, in Russia, the least industrialized of all the major countries of Europe and therefore the one containing the smallest working class.

The fundamental basis of Marx's works begins with the philosophy of Hegel. Hegel had been the head of the philosophy department at the University of Berlin and had died only five years before Marx became a student there. Partly because of the failure of the French Revolution and partly because the German national pride had been hurt by the invasion of Napoleon, the German philosophers rejected the writings of such French rationalists as Voltaire and Rousseau and adopted Hegel as their guiding spirit.

Hegel viewed the historical process as a conflict between old and new forces. The old thesis is in effect locked in a struggle with its antithesis, a struggle that results in a synthesis, which produces, in turn, the new age or time period and a new thesis. To this process Hegel gave the name "dialectic," by which he meant the dialogue between a previous age and its successor, resulting in a periodic transformation of society. Furthermore, Hegel argued, the dialectical process is inevitable, and any attempts by man to change his society by force and violence away from this natural development of the old giving way to the new are doomed to failure.

The Hegelian system of thought became very popular among European intellectuals who were sadly disillusioned by the failure of the French Revolution to permanently establish liberty, equality, and fraternity for all. Now they saw that it was not their inability to overcome the forces of evil that had caused the Revolution to fail. Instead, Hegel's dialectical process explained the failure: the appropriate historical factors for this social upheaval were not present.

In Berlin, Marx had joined a radical new group called the Young Hegelians, who were opposed to the docile acceptance of the status quo advocated by the original Hegelians. The old Hegelians held that any state or institution in existence was rational and good because it was the synthesis of previous cultural conflicts. The Young Hegelians disagreed; they argued that intellectuals had a duty to use their reasoning powers to criticize the existing irrational and evil institutions and thereby assist man to move in the direction of a better society.

Marx readily accepted this duty and began to attack the institutions and governments of his time. By placing the Hegelian process of history in a materialistic framework, Marx developed his famous theory of "dialectical materialism," which holds that all social evolution is determined by material and economic forces. In his book *Introduction to the Critique of Political Economy*, Marx put it this way: "The mode of production in material life determines the general character of the social, political, and spiritual problems of life." Marx emphasized the idea that neither religion, literature, art, moral behavior, nor even governments, but rather the economic forces and environment, are the determining factors in civilization. In fact he believed that economic considerations are responsible for the form and development of religion, literature, art, morals, and government. In addition, it was clear to Marx that "the history of all hitherto existing society is the history of the class struggle." History, to Marx, was a long record of conflict between the rich and the poor, the exploiters and the exploited. In the distant past it was the masters against the slaves, in the Middle Ages it was the knights and lords opposing the serfs and vassals, and in modern times under capitalism, the bourgeoisie was exploiting and oppressing the working proletariat.

To Marx there was a visible pattern in all of these class struggles; namely, that, according to the dialectical process in history, each lower class would free itself from, and in time replace, the upper classes. He wrote, "From the serfs of the Middle Ages, sprang the burgesses of the first towns; and from these burgesses, sprang the first elements of the *bourgeoisie*." It was inevitable that just as the capitalist had replaced the feudal lord, so would the proletarian replace the capitalist. With the victory of the proletariat, Marx saw a radical change taking place in the class-struggle process. A proletarian victory would result in the withering away of the state, since the state is only an instrument by which one class dominates another. Once the working class were victorious, a one-class society consisting only of proletarians would emerge. The advantages to be had were obvious: all benefits would accrue to all people. Despite his complete belief and confidence in the ultimate, predestined victory of the proletariat, Marx held that communism should be achieved by political action and even by armed revolution. To this task he devoted the rest of his life.

After developing his materialistic interpretation of history with its many psychological and sociological overtones, Marx analyzed, in *Das Kapital*, the existing economic system and developed his theory of surplus value.

All wealth, according to Marx, is produced by the worker, since land is a passive agent and capital is simply labor in another form. The value of a commodity, then, is measured and determined by the relative amount of socially necessary labor contained in it. Labor itself, like any other commodity, also has a value determined by the amount of labor necessary to produce it. In other words, labor sells in the market place at a price equal to its cost of production. This will be seen as a restatement of Ricardo's "iron law of wages," which stated that workers will receive only enough wages to subsist and to reproduce themselves. The worker is at the mercy of the capitalist, who owns the means of production because of the existence of the institution of private property. The worker can earn enough in six hours to obtain his daily necessary minimum subsistence level. However, the capitalist does not let him stop at that point. Instead, the worker is forced to work twelve hours, since the capitalists set that number of hours as the length of the working day. During the hours when he works for nothing the worker produces surplus products, which the capitalist sells. The profit is then shared with the landlord for the use of his land, and with the banker for the use of his money. To Marx this was a subtle way of stealing from the workers, no different from the forcible appropriation of lands and goods which took place in earlier societies.

From this exploitation of the working class, Marx believed he foresaw two important developing consequences. The first consequence he thought would be the ever-increasing concentration of industry into larger business units. This prediction, made around 1848, has proved to be accurate in all the industrial countries of the world. The widespread development of public stock issues, however, has limited this concentration to *control* as opposed to *ownership*; but for Marx, the effect is nevertheless the same.

The second consequence Marx thought he foresaw was the ever-increasing number and misery of the working class. The size of the working class has certainly increased, but in most industrial countries their misery has not. In fact, money wages and real wages (the goods and services that can be purchased by money wages) have increased both absolutely and relatively for workers—because of the growth and development of labor unions, protective labor legislation, cooperatives, and enlightened employers.

Much of what Marx wrote failed to stand up against the test of time. Some of his economic theories have been modified or refuted by later economists; his philosophy has been called one-sided; and his prophecies have not come to pass, although others have adapted them to the changing circumstances of history. Yet no review of the history of economic thought or of the development of contemporary social and political institutions can fail to give considerable space to Marx and his works. When he first became associated with socialism, it was a disorganized and ineffective movement. His contribution was to give the movement a purpose and a rational philosophy grounded in painstaking research and detail. He provided those who believed as he did with the spirit necessary to turn their movement into a powerful force for reform. He created "scientific socialism," and was the first to integrate the fields of history, economics, and sociology. From his day on, it would not be possible to discuss any facet of life without due reference to its economic aspects.

Although Marx died at the age of sixty-five, it is conceded that most of his theories had been formed before he was twenty-seven years old. At his funeral, which only eight people attended, his friend Engels said that Marx was "the most hated and the most calumniated man of his time," but in spite of that "he died beloved, revered, and mourned by millions of revolutionary fellow workers from the mines of Siberia to the coasts of California." The seeds of his ideas, sown in apparent futility in the nineteenth century, were to influence such renowned authors as George Bernard Shaw and Émile Zola and were to take root in the minds of such political leaders of the twentieth century as Lenin in Russia and Mao Tsetung in China. Through revolutions that were brought about by these leaders and others, millions of people in many countries live under governments that pledge allegiance to the theories of Karl Marx, even though there are varied interpretations of those theories and visible differences among existing Communist governments.

FURTHER READING

Berlin, Isaiah. *Karl Marx: His Life and Environment.*
Bober, M. M. *Karl Marx's Interpretation of History.*
Mehring, Franz. *Karl Marx: The Story of His Life.*
Schlesinger, Rudolf. *Marx: His Time and Ours.*
Sprigge, Sylvia. *Karl Marx.*
Wolfe, Bertram D. *Marxism: One Hundred Years in the Life of a Doctrine.*

——Herbert Spencer——

[1820–1903]

In 1858, Herbert Spencer was considering the publication in book form of some essays he had written on economics, philosophy, sociology, and psychology, when he realized that there seemed to be an underlying factor in each of these fields, the factor of evolution. He had first expressed this idea in *The Development Hypothesis* in 1852, seven years be-

fore Darwin's *Origin of Species*. The magnitude of his theory
staggered him as he started to think of its application in all
areas of human endeavor: history, sociology, chemistry, astronomy, morality, etc. Almost forty years old and in poor health,
could he hope to develop his theory in all these diverse fields?
He determined to make the effort, to devote his life to this
grandiose project in scholarship.

Spencer had received little formal education. The son of a
teacher, he was taught chiefly by his father and an uncle who
was a clergyman. He had almost no knowledge of Greek and
Latin, which were an expected part of a good education in
his day, and little formal training in his native language (he
once boasted that he was almost totally ignorant of English
grammar). He was nonetheless intelligent and intellectually
curious.

Despite the limited formal education he had received, Spencer, with a keen, logical mind and a gift for organizing and
clarifying, was able to become an assistant schoolmaster in his
home town of Derby at the age of seventeen. Shortly afterward he found use for his abilities as a mathematician in a
civil engineer's position with the London and Birmingham
Railway. When this position ended, he commented cryptical-
ly, "Got the sack—very glad." He now had free time, which
he used in developing hobbies, such as collecting fossils,
phrenology, and planning a variety of unsuccessful inventions.

Spencer then turned to journalism. He found a position as
a subeditor of the *Economist*. In this position he formed friendships with such intellectual leaders of his day as George Henry
Lewes, Thomas Huxley, and Marian Evans (later to become
the famous writer George Eliot).

Spencer could not live in such circles on his limited salary,
so he seriously considered migrating to New Zealand for what
he called "better luck under fairer skies." With his scien-
tifically methodical mind he set down in opposite columns all
advantages and disadvantages of such a venture. Each such
item was given a specific numerical value. When he added all
points the total was almost three to one in favor of New Zealand. The total score was so heavily weighted because of the
high number of points he gave to a "more profitable living
wage" and "prospective excitement in marriage" in New Zealand.

However, all this planning and computation failed to move

him to action. He was assailed by doubts as to his ability to find a wife in any land. Many years later he wrote, "It seems likely that this abnormal tendency to be critical has been a great factor in the continuance of my celibate life."

When his uncle died, leaving an inheritance that permitted him to give up his editorial position on the *Economist* and to devote his entire time to writing, the venture to New Zealand was promptly abandoned. Spencer already had written a number of papers on scientific subjects. He was slowly formulating his theories of living which he felt applied to all fields of human knowledge, and he was anxious to publish his theories in order to reach a wider audience.

The great age of Kant, Fichte, and Hegel was ripe for change. Kant had demolished reason and had shown the primacy of feeling and sensation. Philosophic thought concentrated on abstract metaphysics. At the same time industrialization and science were gathering momentum and focusing on practical problems of living and on obtaining practical answers to them. The French positivist, Auguste Comte (1798–1857), was saying that it was time to abandon the puerility of metaphysics and to look for some positive answers to real problems. For these answers, he looked to science, the world of Boyle, Faraday, Franklin, Joule, and Linnaeus. Comte was saying that the function of philosophy was to unify the sciences in order to improve human life. This was an idea that Spencer accepted and developed.

The first seven years of Spencer's new career in philosophical writing were spent in formulating the basic principles of what he called his "synthetic philosophy," or "new scientific philosophy," which he felt would revolutionize the world.

In 1860 he completed his *First Principles*, in which he presented the basic foundations of his philosophy. Later volumes would apply these principles to biology, sociology, psychology, ethics, and government. For Spencer, philosophy was the "universal science" from which the basic generalizations of all other sciences are derived. The exposition of basic principles applied to all scientific fields and eventually grew into a work of eighteen volumes. No other person of the nineteenth century had the energy or tenacity to undertake or complete such an immense project. Although he had little formal background in these subjects, Spencer had a voracious mind that could absorb and organize ideas that he heard about or read in articles. These ideas he assimilated, analyzed, and developed.

Spencer based his system on two theories: the theory of evolution and the theory of dissolution. The famous slogan "survival of the fittest" was not Charles Darwin's but Herbert Spencer's. In his writing he extended the principles of evolution from the earth to the heavens. All of nature, according to Spencer, is progressively and regressively rhythmical. All of life is an integration of matter and then a dissipation of forces. In other words, everything in the universe changes from chaos to creation to chaos. The formation of planets, nations, men, cultures, morals, art, science, religion—all things pass from embryonic stages, birth, youth, prime, old age, to death and decay.

In Spencer's *Synthetic Philosophy* we have what he considered "the universe in miniature." He dealt with the birth of the stars and planets, the evolution of the earth on which man lives, the life of man, the growth of man's intellect, and the progress of his spirit. All civilization is a part of this rhythmical cycle. Society develops from the family, families become clans, clans grow into states and nations, nations grow into empires and, hopefully, may develop into a world federation. In the end, however, all will dissolve into the nothingness from which it came.

Spencer's predecessors, Hegel and Comte, had also held elaborate theories of historical development, but their interest was primarily in human ideas and institutions. They made no attempt to formulate universal laws that would apply to life as a whole or even to the physical universe. On the other hand, Darwin was careful to disavow any supposed ethical implications of his theories.

It remained for Spencer to speculate freely about the cosmos and to formulate a total world view in terms of a concept of gradual evolutionary growth and development. The concept and the task were a monument to the ability, energy, and egotism of the man.

Spencer became recognized as the leader of the controversy on evolution which raged in the Europe of his day. Without systematically studying the writings of other psychologists, he wrote one of the most important texts on psychology of the nineteenth century. His writings on biological subjects made him one of the most talked-of men in England. He also was one of the most dogmatic intellects of his century. His mind was utterly closed to any idea that was not his own. He became so obsessed with the formation of synthetic formulas for life that in the words of one of his friends, "He stopped living." Another contemporary considered him "all brain and no heart."

Spencer's attitudes may have been affected in part by the condition of his health. During the early years of his writing career, he drove himself without letup. At thirty-five he began to have peculiar sensations in the head and to experience severe insomnia. These reactions preceded a general nervous breakdown, from which he never recovered completely. A year later his physician advised him to give up living alone and to live with some family where he could be properly cared for. In the midst of this developing illness, he continued preparing the first draft of his *Synthetic Philosophy*.

Whatever the cause, Spencer's boastfulness of his own utter lack of emotion indicated one of his greatest weaknesses. He had no understanding of that part of life which "mind cannot regulate but the heart must feel." In youth he was very friendly with Marian Evans (George Eliot), and their mutual friends expected an engagement. However, his only written comment about her in later years was as follows: "Usually heads have, here and there, either flat places or slight hollows, but her head was everywhere convex." His hobby of phrenology apparently outstripped his emotions. Later, on a majestic ocean voyage to America his only entry in his journal referring to the journey was "Terrific disturbance from fog whistle—getting bored." He commented not a word about the beauty of Niagara Falls—only about its height, tonnage of water, and approximations of water pressure.

But because of, or in spite of, personality quirks, the work went doggedly on.

As soon as the first draft was completed, his friends secured advance subscriptions to finance the remaining steps of publication. Six hundred people agreed to underwrite costs, and Spencer seemed certain of enough income to continue his work without financial worry. He planned to issue his works in quarterly installments. When first copies appeared with his strong antireligious viewpoints expressed, many of the six hundred advance subscribers withdrew support entirely and he was compelled to use funds from his inheritance. He came near complete financial ruin, but his friends somehow were able to get together enough funds to keep his work going. Spencer was determined that his philosophical writing be completed so that it might revolutionize the thinking and scientific concepts of mankind.

After he finished *Basic Principles,* he turned to the sociological and political fields in which the principles of evolution and dissolution also applied. Spencer felt that justice in men's hearts grows out of the trends in society. The social structure of the human race is the highest expression of all life, and the law of social progress is inflexible. Through the ages there has been an evolution from "the belief that man exists for the benefit of the state to the belief that the state exists for the benefit of individuals." In education he urged that more time be given to science and less to literature and the so-called cultural subjects.

Spencer was suspicious of a powerful state control. He insisted it should be "limited to preventing breaches of equal freedom of its members." He completely distrusted the military Prussian state in Europe in his day. "The growth of state power," he said, "means militarism and imperialism." The philosopher Spencer had such little faith in governmental institutions that he carried his manuscripts to the printer himself instead of trusting them to the post office.

As he grew older, his health deteriorated. He used earplugs to shut out noise and confusion. His mind harassed by financial worries, his temper short, and his body weakened, he was able to dictate only a few hours at a time.

His friends offered him financial donations so that he could continue his work, but he refused to accept their charity. His printers suffered a financial collapse, and Spencer issued a statement that, owing to unavoidable circumstances, he could not complete his manuscript.

Upon this circumstance, several scientists and philosophers —one of them being John Stuart Mill, his greatest professional rival—anonymously and very generously gave $7,000 for the continuation of his work. His friends had to pretend that more subscriptions had been received.

As the years wore on and volume after volume of his works came from the press, Spencer's friends began to compare his efforts to combine all sciences in an encyclopedic compendium to the attempt of Thomas Aquinas (1225–1274) to unite knowledge in a theological context. In each case scientific progress and advances in philosophical thinking have outmoded some of the work of the author. Spencer still remains important in the field of ethics and in political theory. The very opposite of Marx, who was his contemporary, Spencer is remembered as a champion of individualism and a rigorous opponent of every form of socialism.

In his late years (he lived until eighty-three in spite of his illnesses), Spencer wrote his autobiography. He pointed with some pride to his Quaker parentage. "I have never shown the unfailing diligence that was common to them," he said, "yet there has not been shown by me as great an amount of altruistic feeling." In this autobiography he speaks of other personal faults. He records his "early divorce from religion" and "youthful indifference to a sense of duty," in a sense almost apologetic for having been the "scientific skeptic" of his age. He does speak with pride of his "early freedom from moral fear." This was a matter of great pride to the aged Spencer, the philosopher who was the spokesman of the age of agnosticism.

Worse for Spencer than the decline of his health was the decline of his fame and reputation. The basic formulation of his philosophy had been quite early in his life; his renown came comparatively early in his career. The remainder of a long life was spent in defending those views against hostile attack from many sides.

Scientists exploded one error after another in his voluminous scientific writings; religious leaders attacked his attitudes against religion. The British imperialists attacked his viewpoints against war; socialists took strong opposition to his strong stand for the rights of the individual and for limiting the power of the state.

As his early life was lonely, so his old age was spent in pathetic desolation. Yet his influence was profound upon philosophy and all branches of learning which he sought to attune to an emerging age of science.

FURTHER READING

George, Henry. *Perplexed Philosopher.*
Rumney, Jay. *Herbert Spencer's Sociology.*

——Mary Baker Eddy——

[1821–1910]

RELIGIOUS BELIEFS are most unique and personal in that their acceptance and growth can neither be predicted nor explained by logic or scientific proof. Although most of the world's major religions originated hundreds, if not thousands, of years ago and their rise was usually quite slow, there have been some exceptions, such as the Church of Christ, Scientist, founded by Mrs. Mary Baker Eddy in 1879. In less than fifty years more than two thousand branch churches and societies adhering to the tenets of Christian Science were formed throughout the world. In spite of this movement's obvious variance with prevailing orthodox beliefs, its numbers and influence are still increasing.

Today, Christian Science and Mary Baker Eddy are virtually synonymous. Although folktales and written history tell of individuals with seemingly chronic or incurable ailments who occasionally have been cured by so-called "faith healers," it is extremely unlikely that anyone would have had the temerity to predict the birth of a religion based on this type of phenomenon. Even more remote was the possibility that the founder and organizer of such a movement would be a woman, at a time in American history when women were not permitted to vote and were limited to activities centering about the home. Yet if all of these nigh-impossible obstacles were to be overcome, one would accord little chance of doing it to a woman who had very little formal education, who could not get along with friends or family, and who was a virtual pauper and incurable invalid suffering from a progressive form of spinal paralysis at the age of forty-one. Not only did this "miracle" come about, but in this process Mary Eddy became a millionairess long before she died.

Mrs. Eddy is as controversial a figure as one could possibly find among world-famous personalities. Until the 1930's there were but two main sources of information about this most remarkable woman: two biographies that flatly contradicted each other. The first was written by Sibyl Wilbur as an official biography, approved by the leaders of Christian Science and recommended by Mrs. Eddy in her own handwriting. Thus, one might expect that this biography would be completely reliable. Yet Stefan Zweig, in his book entitled *Mental Healers,* calls it a most ornate example of literary embroidery, written for the edification of the "believer," so as to "exhibit the discoverer of Christian Science in a rose-colored light and wearing a halo."

Zweig refers to the other biography, written by Georgine Milmine, as the "black" biography, because it portrays Mrs. Eddy as an ill-tempered hysteric who was a hypocritical, deceitful, and grasping individual. A more recent "unofficial" biography by Edwin Dakin indicates that the plates for the "black" version were purchased by a friend of Christian Science and destroyed. The true irony of this situation is that the "black" biography did not succeed in making Mrs. Eddy appear to be ridiculous, but, as Zweig said, "makes her interesting; whereas the 'rose-colored' biography, with its idolization, makes an unquestionably interesting woman seem incurably ridiculous."

Mary was the youngest of six children born to Mark and Abigail Ambrose Baker on July 16, 1821, at Bow, near Concord, New Hampshire. Her parents were hard working New England farm people. Mark Baker also was a man of local prominence who served as a justice of the peace and as deacon of the local Congregational church. Mary seems to have inherited her father's iron will, but not his strong body and balanced temperament. Due to her frail health, she was unable to attend school regularly. As she also was relieved of most of her farm and household chores, Mary was left to her own devices. She used this leisure time most profitably, in reading a wide variety of books and in writing bits of prose and poetry.

In 1843 Mary Baker married Washington Glover, a hale, young New Englander who had started a small contracting business in Charleston, South Carolina. Unfortunately her happiness was cut short only six months later when her husband contracted yellow fever and died while on a business trip. Mary was left penniless, and only the aid of Glover's Freemason lodge members enabled her to return to the Baker homestead in New Hampshire. Three months later her one and only child was born and christened George Washington Glover. It is noteworthy that during Mary's brief interlude of happy married life her letters tell of her good health and happiness.

In 1853 Mary Baker married a traveling dentist named Daniel Patterson, who had all the vigor and health that she seemed to lack. However, this marriage also proved to be disastrous. After ten years of alternate care and neglect he enlisted in the army, and was captured and imprisoned for the duration of the Civil War. Soon after his release Patterson deserted his wife. In 1873 she obtained a formal divorce from him. Mary's last matrimonial venture was also tragic and relatively brief. In 1877 she married Asa Gilbert Eddy, the first of her followers to practice Christian Science publicly. He died in 1882 after a brief illness, during which both the best of Christian Science and conventional medicine were to no avail.

There still is a great deal of controversy concerning "when, how, and where" Christian Science was born. One version claims that it was born when an ex-clockmaker named Phineas Quimby cured Mary Baker of a form of paralysis in 1862 after the conventional doctors had classified her as incurable. Until then Quimby had been very successful in convincing receptive patients that, after stroking their heads with his moistened fingers and listening to their symptoms, he could deny the reality of their illnesses and effect "mental cures" by modifying their feelings.

Mary Baker wrote in *Retrospection and Introspection,* which was published in 1891, that she discovered the "science of divine metaphysical healing" in February 1866, when she "gained the scientific certainty" that all causations and effects were mental phenomena. She claims that this discovery occurred after she had been severely injured by a fall on an icy street in Lynn, Massachusetts. She lay critically ill for three days, and was declared to be a hopeless case by her attending doctor. After receiving no relief, she took up her Bible, opened it so that she could read an account of Christian healing (Matthew 9:2), and experienced an immediate recovery.

This incident was followed by an intensive study of her textbook, the Bible.

During the next four years Mary Baker existed through the generosity of others. During the day she would spend her time by telling all who cared to listen of the marvelous cures that the mind and faith were capable of performing, while most of her nights were spent in writing a book that would eventually be published as her principal work, *The Christian Science Textbook*, first entitled *Science and Health* when issued in 1875.

The year 1870 was a great turning point in Mary's life as she was able to put her theories into practice. Her vehicle was twenty-one-year-old Richard Kennedy, a worker in a box factory. Mary was convinced that she had finally found the long-sought impassioned disciple, and entered into a formal contract with Kennedy. This agreement provided for Mary to teach her discoveries to him in return for his pledge to provide for her living expenses and to share equally the proceeds from his yet nonexistent practice. Two months after Kennedy hung up his shingle in Lynn, Massachusetts, his office was overcrowded with patients who came to receive the benefits of the "new mental cure."

Mary Baker was so delighted to find that her method was practical that she decided to spread further her principles of "Moral Science" (the name "Christian Science" had not yet been devised) by teaching trustworthy practitioners her "mental" system. She inaugurated three-week courses consisting of twelve lectures each. The original fee of $100 was soon raised to $300, with an added stipulation that every member of the class must pay Mrs. Eddy 10 percent of the income received from practicing or teaching the science.

In 1876, Mary Baker and a few of her pupils formed the Christian Science Association. Three years later she and a selected number of her followers organized the Church of Christ, into which the earlier association was merged. In 1892 Mary Eddy and some of her followers founded the Christian Science mother church in Boston, called the First Church of Christ, Scientist. Today the mother church, together with the branch churches or local congregations spread throughout the world, constitute the organization of this movement.

Christian Science is a religious system based on the words

and works of Jesus Christ. It is "the scientific system of divine healing"; it is the "law of God, the law of good, interpreting and demonstrating the divine Principle and rule of universal harmony." Christian Science's uniqueness is indicated by its distinction between what is real and what is apparent or seeming but unreal. Thus the only reality of sin, illness, or death is the fact that they seem real to ordinary human belief until God removes their disguises. The adherents of this faith are taught to overcome all forms of error or evil on the basis of its unreality, through spiritual understanding.

Mrs. Eddy was very active in every important activity of her Church. Thus, in 1892, she founded the Christian Science Publishing Society as an agency of the Church of Christ, Scientist. A few years earlier she had founded and edited a monthly magazine, the *Christian Science Journal*. Fifteen years later she founded a weekly, the *Christian Science Sentinel*. She did not establish her best-known publication, a daily newspaper called the *Christian Science Monitor*, until she was eighty-seven years of age. This newspaper is widely respected as one of the best papers today, as it reports the news of importance without resorting to sensationalism and scandal.

Unfortunately for Mrs. Eddy, her later years (she lived to eighty-nine) were marred by controversies, lawsuits, personal attacks on her integrity, even by the author Mark Twain, and the necessity of disproving rumors of her death by granting an interview at age eighty-five to hostile reporters. Yet it is even more remarkable that those with whom she quarreled could not help adoring her. One of her earliest pupils, Daniel H. Spoffard, while involved in a lawsuit with Mrs. Eddy, remarked that she had "brought into my life its most illuminating truth." Mrs. Augusta Stetson, after excommunication from the Christian Science Church, said, "I gladly accept this crucifixion at the hands of my superiors. It is but another step in my climb to our leader's own Christlike level."

Mary Baker Eddy was a great thinker in the sense that she synthesized many of the teachings of Jesus Christ, which she believed to have remained virtually dormant for close to two thousand years, by reviving his healing ministry. However, Mrs. Eddy conclusively showed her followers that the true practice of Christian Science is not limited to the healing of the sick, but is applicable to every type of human need.

Further Reading

Dakin, Edwin F. *Mrs. Eddy.*
Wilbur, Sibyl. *The Life of Mary Baker Eddy.*
Zweig, Stefan. *Mental Healers.*

—————Léon Walras—————
[1834–1910]

"So far as pure theory is concerned, Walras is, in my opinion, the greatest of all economists." This is the way another great thinker and economist of modern times, Joseph A. Schumpeter, characterized the work of Marie-Esprit Léon Walras, a French economist who was born at Evreux, France, in 1834. Schumpeter made this statement because he believed that of all original work developed by economists since very early times, only Walras' "will stand comparison with the achievements of theoretical physics." In view of the fact that Walras twice failed the competitive examination to enter the Polytechnical Institute, this praise adds an ironical twist to his distinguished career.

As a young boy Léon moved around a great deal, living in Paris, Lille, Caen, and Douai, because his father Antoine Auguste Walras was at different times a teacher of philosophy and rhetoric, an educational administrator, and finally an economist. At the age of eighteen, Léon graduated from the lycée at Douai with a bachelor-of-letters degree. In order to prepare himself better for the examinations of the Polytechnical Institute, he spent another year at the lycée and obtained a bachelor-of-science degree. After his two failures to enter the institute, he enrolled in the School of Mines, but remained only a short time because his temperament was not suited to an engineering career. He now turned to the study of literature, journalism, and philosophy. When his published works failed to satisfy the public or the critics, his father persuaded him to "dedicate his life to the development of economics as a science."

There followed some twelve years in which Walras tried in several different ways to achieve the goal his father had set for him. He began by obtaining positions on two magazines, the *Journal of Economists* and *The Press*, neither of which lasted very long. He tried to establish a journal dealing with economic topics, but this also failed. Subsequently, he developed a strong interest in the cooperative movement, an interest that remained with him throughout his lifetime. To assist the movement, he and his associates founded a bank for producers' cooperatives in 1865, with Walras as the managing director. Within three years the bank also failed, and Walras was forced to accept rather menial employment to support himself.

Thus far, it was amply clear that his career was wholly unsuccessful both commercially and academically. His articles had been refused by the publishers, he was unable to obtain a teaching position in France, and the bank failure ended any hopes for a business career.

Although Léon had had no formal training or preparation in economics, he apparently obtained an insight into theoretical economics from his father, who had established a reputation as a first-class economist with the publication, in 1831, of a well-received book entitled *On the Nature of Wealth and the Origin of Value*. It was this lack of any recognized formal training in economics that prevented Léon from obtaining any kind of academic position in France. It was only through a stroke of good luck that he was able eventually to settle down in academic surroundings and produce his great works.

In 1860 an International Tax Congress was held in Lausanne, Switzerland. The Council of State of the canton of Vaud offered a prize for the best paper on the fiscal problems of the canton. Walras' paper advocating the nationalization of the canton's land was considered "well and closely reasoned" but won only fourth place. Nevertheless, he apparently made a very strong impression on some of the judges because ten years later, when the canton of Vaud reorganized the faculty of law of the Academy of Lausanne, Walras was invited to become the first occupant of the newly established chair in economics, in spite of the fact that he had never had any prior experience as a teacher. Thus it was not until 1870, at the age of thirty-six, that Walras obtained his first formal position in the field to which he had decided to devote his life. He remained in this position, teaching, writing, and elaborating his theories, until 1892, when he resigned for reasons of health. After his retirement he remained near the university and continued his research and writing until he died in 1910. Despite the fact that he lived the last forty years of his life in Switzerland and was extremely grateful to that country for the opportunities it had granted him, he remained a French citizen to the end.

Walras was a prolific writer, and despite his many disappointments and difficulties, he managed to produce more than one hundred books and articles. Among the best-known and more important of his works are *Elements of Pure Economics*, published in two parts: *Theory of Exchange* (1874) and *Theory of Production* (1877). This entire work went through several editions—the last definitive one being published in 1926. Other important books by Walras are *Mathematical Theory of Social Wealth* (1883) and *Studies in Social Economics* (1893). In this latter book, Walras concerned himself with the economic effects of communism, private property, nationalization of land, and public finance. In a later book, *Studies in Applied Economics* (1898), Walras indicated a serious interest in the practical problems of monopoly versus free competition, the money, banking, and credit situation, the effects of stock-market speculation, and other areas of economics.

In his later years, Walras was deeply concerned with the social and moral implications of economic theory, and devoted much effort to developing plans to improve the welfare of the people. He was a candidate for the Nobel Peace Prize in 1906, for which he submitted an essay on the subject of land nationalization. The eventual winner that year was Theodore Roosevelt, for his efforts in helping to end the Russo-Japanese War.

Walras' fame as a great thinker rests on several important innovations he contributed to the development of economic science. He is recognized as the codiscoverer of the marginal-utility theory of value, the founder of the "Lausanne" or "mathematical" school of economics, and the originator of "general equilibrium economics."

In describing what economists today call "marginal utility," Walras used and refined the term *"rareté,"* which had originally been introduced by his father. To Léon Walras it meant "the intensity of the last want satisfied by consuming one unit of goods." In other words, the effective usefulness of a particular good must be measured in relation to the quantity of that good in the individual's possession.

The concept of marginal utility was fundamental to the development of the Walrasian system of general equilibrium analysis, which tried to cover the entire field of value and price relationships by using comprehensive mathematical formulas. Walras believed that the determination of the conditions by which equilibrium is established in the market place is the one and only important task of pure economics.

Basically, Walras envisioned two separate markets: the market for goods and the market for the uses and services of the factors of production, that is, land, labor, capital, and the entrepreneur. In bringing these two markets together, Walras was not thinking of only a single commodity or good, but instead visualized the entire economy as a series of interdependent markets which included all commodities and all productive factors. In each market, however, the prices for products and the prices for services are determined by the following same set of laws: (1) In any one market there can be only one price for the same class of goods. (2) The price of any commodity is such that the amounts offered and the amounts bought are equal. (3) The price results in maximum satisfaction for the maximum number of buyers and sellers.

Thus an individual goes to the market with a given stock of goods and a certain "disposition to trade," and proposes a particular set of prices. If, at the proposed prices, supply and demand are equal, equilibrium is established at once. However, if supply and demand are not equal, prices will continue to change until a point of equilibrium is reached. Value then becomes a clear matter of preference between the relative usefulness of goods to an individual. This preference helps to establish the pricing process, which, in effect, is a ratio between one commodity and another. Prices, therefore, are mutually determined because goods constitute reciprocal demands for each other. This last concept led Walras to develop another very important idea in economics, that of "opportunity cost." This idea holds that in the time needed to create one type of commodity, the factors of production must forgo the opportunity to create another type of commodity. This also holds true for the consumer. If he buys one product with his limited income, he must give up the opportunity to obtain another.

To develop these ideas fully, Walras designed a system of equations to show the interrelationships of all of the functional parts of the economy. In this way he tried to make economics a pure science, similar to the natural sciences. In addition—unlike Jevons and Gossen who had also developed marginal-utility concepts, which they tried to apply to particular or specific parts of the market—Walras produced his theory of general equilibrium encompassing the fields of exchange, production, capital, and money in a unified system for the entire economy. In this concept, he was building on the ideas implicit in the work of another Frenchman, François Quesnay, who had developed the *Tableau Economique* more than one hundred years earlier. In fact, Walras was convinced, at the end of his career, that all types of social phenomena, including political, economic, religious, and intellectual aspects of life, are tied up with each other in a very intimate fashion. In this sense, Walras was reacting to the things he had seen in France during his developmental years.

In 1848, the pain and distress of the working class were quite apparent. Wages were depressed, and housing and working conditions were unbelievably poor. The conditions for future revolutionary explosion were plain. The use of force to effectuate change was abhorrent to Walras, even though he objected to society permitting some men to exploit others. He favored change, but he wanted it to be slow and scientific. It was this desire that produced his determination to discover the scientific basis for economic behavior. Walras thought he had achieved his goal with the discovery of *rareté*, since he believed that it would lead to the optimum satisfaction of want, and that it would, with his system of equations, give maximum satisfaction both to buyers and to sellers.

During Walras' lifetime his work was not readily accepted by his professional contemporaries, and he did not gather any disciples around him. This was especially true of his native France, which withheld recognition of his work and refused to

consider the validity of mathematical economics until about
1915. Some recognition did come, however, during his lifetime, but from a distant shore. In 1892, the American
Economic Association elected Walras an honorary member as
a reward for his "eminent services to the science of Political
Economy." Later writers, realizing the tremendous value of
Walras' work, could say that there are very few economists
who have contributed so much to the permanent body of
established truth as Walras did. In 1954, Schumpeter concluded his study of Walras' work by saying, "It is the outstanding landmark on the road that economics travels toward the
status of a vigorous or exact science and . . . still stands at the
back of much of the best theoretical work of our time."

FURTHER READING

Hicks, J. R. "Léon Walras," *Econometrica*.
Schumpeter, J. A. *History of Economic Analysis*.

——William Stanley Jevons——

[1835–1882]

IN HIS RELATIVELY SHORT LIFE, William Stanley
Jevons became known not only as an economist of the first
rank but as an innovator in the disciplines of logic, mathematics, and statistics. Even those economic ideas of his which
are no longer considered valid today are still discussed in
textbooks as an illustration of the work of a penetrating mind
seeking solutions to difficult problems.

Seeking an explanation for the periodic rise and fall in
business activity, Jevons thought the answer was to be found
in noneconomic factors. He carefully calculated the average

duration of these business cycles in the period from 1721 to 1878 and found that they lasted 10.46 years, which closely corresponds to periodic appearances of spots on the sun. To Jevons, then, these sunspots were responsible for the business cycle because the spots changed the energy distribution of the sun and affected the amount of rainfall, which affected the growing of crops, which, in turn, impinged upon all business activity. Although discarded today as unrealistic, his theory did call attention to the need for research on factors causing business cycles.

Jevons was also a strong adherent of *laissez faire.* He believed that government should interfere with private business only (1) where there are many scattered activities which require general supervision and coordination, (2) where the activities are routine in nature, (3) where a reasonable amount of capital is required, and (4) where all work is performed in the open, under public control. Although *laissez faire* has been abandoned by almost all governments, Jevons' principles serve as a reminder of the intense individualism of the political leaders of his time as well as of ours.

William Stanley Jevons was born in Liverpool in 1835 to a Welsh family. In Liverpool he attended the Mechanics' Institute High School where he studied mathematics and science. His father, a Unitarian, published articles on economic and legal subjects and was said to have built the first iron boat used on the seas. Of the eleven children born into the family, only three lived to adulthood. Jevons' mother, a poetess, died when he was ten years old, and an older sister took care of him thereafter.

The family suffered a serious financial setback when the father's iron business failed. Despite this difficulty, he managed to send fifteen-year-old Jevons to a London school. After one year in the preparatory school, he was accepted into University College where he studied botany and chemistry. As an example of his fertile imagination and good mind, we have this entry from his diary written in 1852: "I have also had a talk about the origin of the species . . . I . . . firmly believe that all animals have been transformed out of one primitive form by the continued influence, for thousands and perhaps millions of years, of climate, geography, etc." Charles Darwin's *Origin of Species* did not appear until seven years later.

William was such a good student in the sciences that when
the newly opened mint in Australia asked the university to
recommend an assayer he was chosen for the job. He was only
eighteen years old and did not want to leave the University,
but conditions at home required him to contribute to the
support of two younger children. Furthermore, the job in
Australia paid a much higher salary than any he could command in England at that time.

Jevons remained in Australia for five years, during which he
saved his money in the hope that when he returned to England
he would have sufficient funds to continue his education. His
interest in meteorology there resulted in his first published
paper, "The Climate of Australia and New Zealand." In 1859,
as he had planned, Jevons returned to England after first
visiting Peru, Panama, the West Indies, and the United States.

Jevons now re-entered University College in London and
began to study mathematics and political economy. Within
a year he was able to write to his brother, then living in the
United States, "I have worked a good deal at political
economy; in the last few months I have fortunately struck
out what I have no doubt is *the true Theory of Economy.*"

He had already worked out in his mind the fundamentals
of the marginal-utility concept, which he stated thus: "As the
quantity of any commodity . . . which a man has to consume,
increases, so the utility or benefit derived from the last portion
used decreases in degree." Jevons was quite anxious to share
his discovery with the world, so he prepared a report which
he sent to the British Association for the Advancement of
Science in 1862. He was chagrined when the Association
took no notice of the work. A second paper, "On the Study of
Periodic Commercial Fluctuations, with Five Diagrams,"
fared much better, and he was allowed to read it to the
members of the association. This short paper was "the beginning of a new stage in economic science."

Jevons had developed a statistical technique to measure
what today are called "seasonal variations" and "secular
trends," using a series of index numbers which he devised
himself. It was the first time anyone had attempted to measure
statistically the actual results within the economy of changes
in the value of money. The uses he made of charts and diagrams as aids in business forecasting were also considered
unique. Furthermore, he was one of the first economists to

apply mathematical theories of probability in an attempt to solve economic problems. Of this early effort of Jevons', John Maynard Keynes, an outstanding economist of the present century, said: "For unceasing fertility and originality of mind, applied with a sure touch . . . to a mass of statistics . . . this pamphlet stands unparalleled in the history of our subject."

After completing his work at the university, Jevons tried writing for magazines and even operated a ghostwriting service, but the returns were poor. In 1863, he went to Owens College in Manchester as a tutor and soon advanced to a professorship. With the income from this position, he felt secure enough to marry and in 1867, at the age of thirty-two, he wed Harriet Ann Taylor, daughter of the owner of the *Manchester Guardian*, a famous English newspaper.

Jevons worked assiduously preparing material for his courses and at the same time wrote extensively. The combined work load soon overtaxed him and damaged his health permanently. In 1865 he published a book on *The Coal Question*, in which he presented a systematic review of the probable economic future of England in relation to its need of coal. The book obtained for the author an invitation to visit with Prime Minister Gladstone.

His reputation was further enhanced with the publication of a book on *Pure Logic* (1864), on which he had spent several years. This was followed by *Elementary Lessons in Logic* (1870) and the highly successful *Principles of Science* (1874), which was also printed in six foreign languages. For almost fifty years afterward, students in England read and studied Jevonsian logic.

Additional honors came his way. He was made a fellow of the Royal Society in 1872, the first economist since Sir William Petty was so honored in 1646. In 1876, Jevons accepted a professorship in political economy at his alma mater, University College in London. In 1880 he resigned to spend all his time completing his projected *Principles of Economics*. However, fate willed otherwise, for he unfortunately was drowned in August 1882, at the age of forty-seven.

Jevons' chief contributions in the field of economics are contained in the *Theory of Political Economy* (1871). From this book it can readily be seen how much Jevons's approach to the study of economics differed from that of his classical predecessors, including Adam Smith, David Ricardo, Thomas

Malthus, and John Stuart Mill. All of them were deeply interested in the political affairs of their day and looked to economics as an instrument to be used to improve the welfare of mankind. Jevons, on the other hand, avoided politics, and only sought to improve economics as a pure science. He was interested in developing the fundamental principles of political economy and thought that others, better suited than he, should try to put the findings to practical use.

The classical writers of the period maintained that the value of a commodity was determined by its cost of production; the prevailing economic ideas, as set forth in John Mill's *Principles of Political Economy* (1848), also strongly emphasized the supply side in the analysis of value. However, Jevons asserted that exchange value is determined primarily by demand, which in turn is influenced by subjective psychological factors. He pointed out that once labor is expended in the creation of an article, it has no influence on the future value of that article, except in a very roundabout way; it was Jevons who said that "in commerce bygones are forever bygones." Therefore, past labor cannot cause or create value, although it can be a determining factor. Jevons put it in the following tabular form:

Cost of production determines supply;
Supply determines final degree of utility;
Final degree of utility determines value.

In his use of the concept of the "final degree of utility" Jevons meant the same thing that was called "marginal utility" by Carl Menger and Von Wieser in Austria, "specific productivity" by John Bates Clark in the United States, "*rareté*" by Léon Walras, and "ophélimité" by Vilfredo Pareto in Lausanne, Switzerland. All these writers, working independently, arrived at this new concept by different methods at about the same time (1871), an extraordinary example of simultaneous discoveries.

Jevons' unique contribution was his development of the demand theory based on an analysis of human behavior. Jeremy Bentham had already pointed out that man is essentially hedonistic and that in all his actions he seeks out those things that give him pleasure, and avoids those things that cause him pain. Bentham even thought he could develop a "felicific calculus" which could be used to measure the dimensions of pleasure and pain to permit individuals to achieve the greatest happiness.

Jevons was interested only in trying to explain why people are willing to exchange goods in certain ratios. He did not try to develop any kind of measure of pleasure or pain as Bentham did, because he was convinced that it was impossible to consider pleasure and pain as units whose intensity could be measured or weighed. However, Jevons did believe that a theory of value and price could be based on an individual's ability to tell which of two pleasures or two pains is greater, and whether a given pleasure is stronger or weaker than the pain one must undergo to obtain it. In other words, according to Jevons' theory, an individual should be able to tell whether additional amounts of goods that he obtained by exchange or work give him pleasure equal to, greater than, or less than the sacrifice or pain he must endure to obtain those additional goods. Pleasure is defined as "any motive which attracts us to a certain course of conduct"; and pain, as "that which deters us from that course of conduct."

To this general framework, Jevons added his idea of the "final degree of utility," upon which the entire theory of exchange value, based on demand, rests. This is essentially a static and short-run theory in which supply is fixed. In the long run, adequate allowance must be made for changes in population growth, tastes of individuals, and political and economic institutions, all of which tend to affect supply and, therefore, ultimately, value. Jevons purposely chose to ignore "dynamic" or long-run situations in his analysis because he felt that the mathematical nature of his approach would be better understood in a static context, in which no changes of any kind were taking place.

"Utility," according to Jevons, is the pleasure derived from the use of a good, and this pleasure tends to decrease as the amount of the good used increases. Jevons was careful to make a distinction between "total utility," the pleasure obtained from the use of the entire amount of a good, and the "final degree of utility," the pleasure contained in the last or least amount of a good. For example, where there is a great supply of water, the final degree of utility of the last unit is zero, yet the total utility of water is beyond measure. Diamonds, on the other hand, are limited in supply and, therefore, the final degree of utility of the last one is very high. It is this last unit, according to Jevons, that determines the value or price of all units of the good.

Jevons supported his theoretical findings with diagrams and algebraic notations, developing an illustration for the principle of diminishing utility which was used by writers of introductory textbooks in economics for more than seventy-five years. He also was the first English-speaking writer to indicate that the supply curve of labor may be backward-bending, that is, that the utility of the wages the workers earn tends to decline. At the point at which the disutility or pain of the extra hour or unit of work equals the utility or pleasure of the extra wage, the worker will stop his work.

Jevons' knowledge of human behavior is further illustrated by his recognition that pleasure and pain will vary in duration and intensity, that there is uncertainty involved in exchanges to take place in the future, and that, therefore, the individual will discount or make allowances for these contingencies when he enters into an exchange relationship. In effect this means that two people exchanging goods with each other will continue to trade until the point is reached where the "ratio of exchange" is equal to the ratios of the final degrees of utility of the goods used, to the traders. To stop before this point would mean a loss in possible pleasure, and to go beyond this point would mean a loss of utility.

For the individual it means that he will try to spend his income in such a way that the utility or pleasure derived from the last unit of each commodity is exactly equal to that of the last unit of every other commodity. Then he is at "equilibrium."

Jevons, who was convinced that he had made an outstanding original contribution to the study of economics, was badly disappointed on two counts. He received very little recognition from contemporary students of economics, and, after his book was published, he discovered that Hermann Gossen, a German economist, had developed a substantially similar theory of marginal utility as early as 1854. Gossen's book failed to attract any interest and he had all but one copy destroyed. When Jevons accidentally came across this copy, he was generous with his praise, saying, "It is quite apparent that Gossen has completely anticipated me as regards the general principles and method of the theory of Economics."

Although Jevons did not generate a large number of disciples, the few that did follow him, namely, Philip Wicksteed and F. Y. Edgeworth, did become influential economists in their own right. Jevons' writings also exerted considerable influence on the Fabian socialists, including the Webbs, G. B. Shaw, and H. G. Wells, who were looking for a way to discredit the cost-of-production analysis of value. They were happy to accept Jevons' utility concepts. Finally, perhaps the greatest compliment paid to Jevons came about when Alfred Marshall in 1890 united his utility analysis with Ricardo's cost analysis into a "neoclassical" synthesis, which is still the basis of much of the economics taught today.

Jevons did not live long enough to perfect his theories, but his fertile imagination applied to a wide range of interests assures him a permanent place among the great thinkers of the world. It was said of him that, "he was a creator of patterns which showed the way to more thorough analysis and refinements leading to a verification of the whole subject matter of economics."

FURTHER READING

Jevons, H. S. *Letters and Journal of W. S. Jevons.*
Wicksteed, P.H. *Common Sense of Political Economy.*

————Ramakrishna————
[Also known as Sri Ramakrsna]
[1834–1886]

WHEN RAMAKRISHNA, the saintly Hindu religious leader who had personally experienced all the great religions of the world, was asked which was the true path to God, he replied: *"Ekain sat viprá bahudhā vandanti"* ("So many religions, so many paths to reach the one and the same goal"). To a world in which religious differences caused ill will,

hatred, and even bloodshed, his message was simple and
clear: "There is only one God, but limitless are his aspects
and limitless are his names. Call him by any name and worship him in any aspect that pleases you."

Ramakrishna was born to a Brahman family in Kamarpukur,
a small village in West Bengal, India. His parents were of
moderate means but pious and interested in learning. As a
schoolchild, Ramakrishna was precocious, gifted in speech,
with a retentive memory, but he did not like arithmetic. When
Ramakrishna was seven, his father died, and his brother,
Ramkumar, undertook to support the family. Years later Ramkumar, who was an eminent Sanskrit scholar, wanted Ramakrishna to live with him in Calcutta to prepare to become a
translator. But Ramakrishna had been touched by mystical
revelations that beckoned him to a religious life, and so he refused. However, when Ramkumar became the priest of a new
temple dedicated to the Mother of the Universe and built at
Daksineswar on the Ganges River near Calcutta, Ramakrishna
joined him there. After his brother's death, Ramakrishna became the priest of the temple.

It was here that he had his first theophany or divine vision.
He became dissatisfied with his daily performance of rituals
and developed an intense and pervasive desire to envision the
Divine Mother of the temple. And then it happened. In his
own words: "House, walls, doors, the temple—all disappeared into nothingness. Then I saw an ocean of light, limitless, living, conscious, blissful . . . and I lost all awareness of
outward things." From time to time he had other revelations;
indeed his strange conduct caused many to regard him as
mad.

In 1861, his temple at Daksineswar was visited by a holy
nun named Yogeswari, or Brahmani, who was learned in
Vaishnava and Tantric literature. Brahmani supported Ramakrishna's religious faith and taught him the sixty-four spiritual
disciplines of the Tantras and the meditation for achieving
the samadhi, the state of spiritual bliss, infinite grace, and
identification with the Divine Mother of the Universe.

Then the Brahmani taught him the practices of Vaishnavism: the worship of God as a personal being in the form of
Vishnu. The Vaishnavas believe that Vishnu visits the earth
from time to time and that the worshiper can unite with God

in his form of Rama or Krishna by reaching out in the highest form of love: as of parent to child, as of child to parent, as of servant to master, and as of lover to beloved. Vaishnavism was the religion of the great Hindu leader, Ramanuja.

A year or two later, the temple was visited by Tota Puri, a Vedantic monk of the order of Samkara who had experienced Brahma. Tota Puri taught Ramakrishna the Vedanta and the Upanishads and the identity of Atman with Brahma. Now Ramakrishna sought by meditation to achieve unity with the Brahma. He thus described the culmination of this experience: "I withdrew my mind from all objects and became absorbed in contemplation of the Atman, . . . then my mind soared beyond all duality and entered into nirvikalpa, the nondual, unitary consciousness." Tota Puri marveled at the ability of his saintly disciple to achieve Brahma after so short a time, for he himself had required forty years of training and discipline to achieve it. Ramakrishna remained in this state of union with Brahma for six months, being fed only enough for sustenance. He described his experience in these words: "It was as if on the ocean of Brahma, that infinite ocean of existence, knowledge, and bliss, a stick was floating."

Later in his life, Ramakrishna experienced Buddhism, Islam, and Christianity. Once he was asked why he had followed so many paths. His answer was, "I have practiced Hinduism, Islam, Christianity, and in Hinduism the different sects. I have found that it is the same God toward whom all are directing their steps, though along different paths." At another time he said: "The tank has several ghats. At one, the Hindus draw water and call it jal; at another Muhammadans draw the same liquid and call it water. The substance is one though the names differ. . . . But do not say your religion is better than that of another."

Ramakrishna had been betrothed to a Hindu girl, Sarada Devi, when she was five years old and he was twenty-three. They had not seen one another, but when he was thirty-six, she came to the temple to live with him, as disciple to teacher. After his death she was known as the Holy Mother, the guiding spirit of the order founded in Ramakrishna's name.

Many disciples and students came to Ramakrishna in his maturity, as his saintliness and wisdom became known. One of his disciples said of him: "His hard-earned jewels of spirituality, for which he had given three-quarters of his life, were now ready to be offered to humanity."

Ramakrishna taught understanding, reconciliation, and friendship. Just as in thirteenth-century Europe, Thomas Aquinas had sought to unify religion and philosophy, reason and faith, so, in nineteenth-century India, Ramakrishna sought to compose the three Vedantic schools of thought: dualism, qualified monism, and nondualism. He said that they were not mutually exclusive but that they were successive steps for the aspirant seeking oneness with God. Thus, too, in our time the ecumenical movement seeks to remove religious antagonisms.

Essentially Ramakrishna was a mystic, but paradoxically a pragmatic mystic. As to philosophy, he said, "I see the truth directly: what need have I to philosophize?" and again, "To reason out the truth of God is one thing, and to meditate on God is another. When illumination comes through the grace of God, then only is the truth of God known and experienced."

Ramakrishna did not believe in withdrawal from the world. His two ideals were self-liberation and service to God in man. He said, "The true hero is he who can discipline his mind by devotional exercise while carrying a heavy burden on his head. Similarly the perfect man can keep his gaze constantly fixed on God while carrying the burden of worldly duties."

When Ramakrishna died in 1886, his disciples honored his memory by founding the Ramakrishna Math and Mission dedicated to "our own salvation and the good of mankind."

FURTHER READING

Isherwood, Christopher. *Ramakrishna and His Disciples.*

——Henry George——

[1839–1897]

WHEN HENRY GEORGE died in 1897, more than 200,000 people passed through Grand Central Palace in New York City, where his body lay in state, to pay their respects and to say farewell to an individual who had devoted his entire adult life to working for the betterment of the ordinary man. Since that time the message he left in his writings has been translated into practically every language in the world. A painting of Henry George hangs in the Metropolitan Museum of Art, and more than three million copies of his best-known book, *Progress and Poverty*, have been printed and sold. In fact, sales of Henry George's books far exceed those of any other American economist, living or dead, and, with the exception of Adam Smith and Karl Marx, of all European economists.

Today the Georgist movement is still actively promoted in New York City by the Henry George School, which was founded in 1932. It maintains twenty-four branches in other large cities, and issues publications all over the world. The school, which also teaches by correspondence, claims to have students in every county of the United States and in every country of the world. In fact, the basic idea advocated by Henry George, the national taxation of land values, was actually introduced on a large scale in Denmark.

Henry George's achievements are all the more remarkable when we note that he ended his formal education at the age of fourteen and never was enrolled in any systematic curriculum of economics or government. He was a self-made man who was able to impress millions of his contemporaries throughout the world by his understanding of basic principles and by his devotion and sincerity in the cause of justice and social reform.

Henry George, the seventh of ten children, was born in Philadelphia on September 2, 1839, to an English father and a Scottish mother. His father, Richard Samuel Henry George, was a publisher of Sunday-school books and the family enjoyed a middle-class standard of living. The elder George was a devout member of the Protestant Episcopal church and raised his large family according to strict religious precepts. Each morning a portion of the Bible was read before the daily activities began. On the Sabbath, services were attended by the entire family, mornings, afternoons, and often evenings.

The family life was pleasant but quite simple. The children had to provide their own entertainment since, as strict church members, they were not permitted to play cards, to attend dances, theater, or parties. They did not have a piano and there was little interest in music, but there was a great deal of discussion of books in their home, particularly of books dealing with history, travel, and poetry.

Before being sent to a private grammar school, Henry George was tutored by his mother and aunt, both of whom had been schoolteachers. After grammar school he was enrolled in the Episcopal Academy, which he was permitted to attend at reduced tuition because his father was a publisher of church books. When the business proved unprofitable, the elder Mr. George took a job in the Customs House, where his salary was $800 per year, a small sum even in 1852 for so large a family.

Young George, realizing he was no longer entitled to the reduced tuition, begged to be taken out of the academy to lighten the financial strain on the family. His father reluctantly agreed but insisted on obtaining the services of a private tutor who instilled in young George a love for methodical study. Thus, when Henry entered high school at the age of thirteen, he was able to make rapid progress. However, as the oldest son, he felt an obligation to help support the family, so, although he had not yet reached the age of fourteen, he left school to go to work. He never returned to any kind of formal schooling after that, but continued his education by constant reading of books—obtained mostly from the Franklin Institute Library in Philadelphia.

Henry's first job was that of an errand boy for a china shop, where he was required to work twelve hours a day for two dollars a week. He was very unhappy at this job, especially since he could not spend any time at the wharves watching the ships come and go. Ever since Henry George had learned that his grandfather had been a sea captain, he had constantly yearned for an adventurous life at sea and spent all his free time at the docks watching the sailors and listening to their thrilling tales. Noticing how restless young Henry was and fearing that he might run away from home, Mr. George placed Henry in the custody of a good friend, a Captain Sam Miller, master of the ship *Hindoo,* then loading for a trip around the world.

At the age of fifteen, Henry George, putting his childhood aside, set out on the first of many adventurous and difficult journeys that he was to make during his lifetime. The trip lasted about fourteen months and touched such cities as New York, Melbourne, and Calcutta, giving Henry George an opportunity to see how people worked and lived in different parts of the world. It was also on this trip that he learned of the tyrannical powers over the lives of his sailors that the captain possessed, and of the terrible conditions under which the men were forced to live and work. As a result, Henry George was to become a lifelong champion of sailors' rights.

The seventeen-year-old young man who returned home from this great adventure was quite different from the young boy who had left to see the world. He was huskier and possessed more self-reliance; his skin was deeply tanned and his red hair was bronzed. He basked in the admiration of his family and friends who loved to listen to his tales of far-off places and hear him sing sailor songs in his high, off-pitch voice.

After several months at home, Henry George obtained, with the help of his father, a job setting type in a publishing house. His father hoped by this action to keep Henry at home, to give him a trade, and to teach him how to spell. This job came to have a pronounced impact on George's later career because it was here that he first became fully aware of the important political and economic issues dividing the pre-Civil War nation. The material he set in type provided him with much information, and his association with other printers led to long arguments and discussion over historical dates and facts. Once they were probing the reasons why wages were lower in older, industrialized countries, where population and progress were greatest, than in new, thinly settled countries. No one seemed to have any answers.

Later on, while living and working in California, when George thought he had discovered the answer to this question, he set down his reply in his first book, called *Our Land and Land Policy*, published in 1871. Here he attacked the governmental policy of giving large land grants to the railroads, which were privately owned. Here, also, he expounded his ideas on the relationship between land and labor, and he developed what later came to be called the "single-tax" theory.

According to George, wages in new parts of a country were high because the land was free. In older, more settled places, the land was monopolized and therefore wages were low and poverty acute. George's suggested remedy for this situation was to place on the landowner just *one* tax equal to the value of the land, and to remove all other taxes from the products of labor. This was a new approach to an economic problem, as far as Americans were concerned, and this first book did not sell well. George determined that he would have to reformulate his ideas in more convincing fashion, with more thorough economic reasoning, in order to command the attention he believed the theory deserved.

George had been a financial failure in almost everything he had tried. In 1861, when he had eloped with a young lady whom he had met in San Francisco, he had no job and only fifty cents in his pocket. He tried to join the gold rush but arrived in the fields too late. He worked as a typesetter for several newspapers but always had to leave because of disagreements with editorial policies or with foremen. Once, when he did manage to save a small amount of money, he purchased mining stocks that proved to be worthless. His diary entries of this period reflected his discouragement: "I have been unsuccessful in everything" and "am in very desperate plight" and "don't know what to do."

Making the best use he could of his enforced leisure, George studied and practiced writing, hoping for a regular position on a newspaper. As his style improved he was able to sell several essays and sketches to local magazines. With several partners, he started the *San Francisco Daily Evening Post*, which existed for about four years. In 1876 he was fortunate in being appointed to a job as a state inspector of gas meters. The job ended three years later, when the opposing party won the next election, but it had served a very useful purpose. It enabled George to complete his most famous work, *Progress and Poverty*, which was published in 1879.

Much of what appears in this work is the result of Henry George's firsthand experience and observation. From the time he came to California in 1858 until 1879, George had held numerous jobs and had experienced long periods of unemployment and poverty. During this same period, however, he noticed that huge fortunes were being made by land speculators, who had been able to induce both the United States and the new state of California to make land available to them at very low prices. These lands were neither used nor sold by the owners until artificially high prices, caused by the tremendous influx of population seeking gold, could be obtained.

A newspaper in San Francisco reported that with each ship arrival, land values tended to increase greatly. In one example, the price of a vacant lot bordering on the water went from $5,000 to $10,000 in one day with the arrival of a boatload of immigrants from New York. At the same time, George was very distressed to note that, while land values were constantly rising, wages and employment opportunities were diminishing. For example, in 1849 a carpenter in San Francisco could easily obtain $16 per day; in 1856 this had fallen to $5, and in 1862 to $4. Observing these facts, George was convinced that the practice of land monopolization by speculators, the unwise granting of large tracts of land to privately owned railways, and the graft and corruption which this involved, all conspired to keep the average man from obtaining a foothold on the land, which in turn significantly held back the development and progress of the state. The increasing social injustice, poverty, and vice that George saw developing in the fast-growing cities he believed to be traceable to one cause: "the pursuance of a wrong policy in regard to land."

George theorized that all land is a free gift of nature and belongs to all mankind. As population increases, all the land of a country is occupied and those who come later are forced to settle on inferior sites. As more and more land comes under private control, the working man is kept in a state of poverty because he is required to pay for the use of the land on terms fixed by the landowner. Furthermore, while the improvement in technology helps increase production, "all the advantages gained by the march of progress go to the owner of land."

The remedy, as it appeared to Henry George, was simple: Deprive the landowner of his rent. However, George was not advocating confiscation of the land, but a governmental tax on the full annual rental value of a piece of land. The landowner still could retain title to his property. George believed that this "single tax" would be so productive in income that all other taxes could be abolished. Among other benefits that George claimed his theory would produce were the following: all vacant land would come into productive use, people deriving their support solely from rent would be forced to go to work, the tax would be easy to collect and could not be shifted, the income of all communities would be greatly increased through the improvement of production, inequalities in the distribution of wealth would be minimized, and unemployment and recurring depressions would disappear once and for all.

The enthusiastic reception *Progress and Poverty* received in the first several years after publication, especially in Europe, was an indication of the great importance attached to the question of land distribution and taxation in many parts of the world. The poor, obscure printer soon became a well-known figure, and the increasing circulation of his book brought him an international reputation as the writer of "one of the most important contributions yet made to economic literature." It is ironical to note that this all-time best seller originally could not find a publisher either in New York or California. The original author's edition of five hundred copies was paid for by George himself!

Professional economists have criticized George and his theory for lack of originality and for not considering the inflexible nature of the single tax, the administrative difficulties in distinguishing between land and the capital improvements on land, the unjust discrimination against land ownership as opposed to other forms of property, and the fact that no one tax can be regarded as the single remedy for modern social and economic problems.

Yet, despite these professional objections, there is general agreement that the single-tax movement started by Henry George has had a great impact in stimulating public interest in economic problems, and in helping to stir public opinion about needed fiscal and social reforms. For example, it is now generally accepted that unearned increments on land (as well as on other forms of property) should bear a greater share of the tax burden and that taxing power may properly be used as an instrument of social reform. In addition, Henry George was the first to direct attention to the importance of conserving our national resources, by objecting vigorously to governmental indifference to the squandering of the nation's land, forest, and mineral wealth. Finally, antipoverty programs of recent years may be traced back to Henry George, whose most vital message was the urgency of social reform and the duty of a nation to "extirpate poverty and to lighten the burdens of those compelled to toil."

The widespread success of *Progress and Poverty* convinced George that his ideas were sound and should be put into effect. He turned to politics as a method of accomplishing his goals. In 1886, the Central Labor Union of New York City nominated George for mayor. The candidates of the Democratic and Republican parties were Abram S. Hewitt and Theodore Roosevelt, respectively. The campaign attracted nationwide attention. Mr. Hewitt was elected, as expected, but George, without the support of a political party, surprised the politicians by coming in second, ahead of Roosevelt. One byproduct of this campaign was the formation of the United Labor party, offshoots of which have continued in existence to the present time. Again, in 1897, George was a candidate for the office of mayor of Greater New York, but he died five days before the election. His last major work, *The Science of Political Economy,* was completed and published after his death by his son Henry George, Jr.

Henry George is buried in Greenwood Cemetery in Brooklyn, New York, where the following words from *Progress and Poverty* are inscribed on his tombstone:

> The truth that I have tried to make clear will not find easy acceptance. If that could be, it would have been accepted long ago. If that could be, it would never have been obscured. But it will find friends—those who will toil for it; suffer for it; if need be, die for it. This is the power of Truth.

FURTHER READING

Barker, C. A. *Henry George.*

———William James———
[1842–1910]

A SINGLE INCIDENT, a chance meeting with a person, or the reading of a passage in a book may have a profound effect upon the life of an individual. On April 30, 1870, William James made the following entry in his notebook:

> I think that yesterday was a crisis in my life. I finished the first part of Renouvier's *[French idealistic philosopher, 1815–1903] Essais* and saw . . . his definition of Free Will—"the sustaining of a thought because I choose to, when I might have other thoughts." . . . My first act of free will shall be to believe in free will.

Up to this time James had led an unsettled and inexplicably unhappy life that had included periods of despondency, a nervous breakdown, and feelings of uncertainty about his life-work. The reading of Renouvier, as he tells us, was an inspiring experience that gave him faith in himself and the determination to build his own future, not in the medical profession, a career for which he had prepared without zest, but in the academic world of ideas—philosophy and psychology. In these fields he became one of the greatest thinkers that America has produced.

William was born in New York City, the eldest of the five children of Henry and Lucy James. He had the advantages of a wealthy home and a father who moved in intellectual circles, who had written a number of books, and who liked to discuss philosophy and religion with his children. The family often traveled to Europe. As a result, William's formal education was obtained in various private schools, supplemented by tutors.

While this life had undeniable advantages and rich experiences, his career was rather unsettled. For a while he thought of becoming a painter; then he enrolled in the Lawrence Scientific School at Harvard. At twenty-two he entered Harvard Medical School. He remained a year and then joined the great Swiss-American naturalist Louis Agassiz on a scientific expedition to the Amazon River. His duties of observing and cataloguing were less glamorous than he had thought and, when his health turned poor, he returned to Harvard for a year.

In 1867, he went to Germany, where he studied under the scientists Helmholtz and Virchow, and immersed himself in the philosophy of Hegel, Kant, Spinoza, and Schopenhauer. Here, also, his despondency led to physical infirmity; he suffered a breakdown and even contemplated suicide at one time.

In 1868, he returned home and managed to complete his medical degree at Harvard the following year. However, he did not practice medicine; in fact he lived a life of semi-invalidism until his inspirational contact with the work of Renouvier.

At the age of thirty-one, in 1873, William James became a member of the faculty of Harvard, where he taught physiology, psychology, and finally philosophy. At last he had found the creative work that satisfied him. In 1878 he began a long and happy marriage to Alice Gibbens, a relationship that contributed further to the stability and self-confidence he needed to free his talents for analytical, vigorous thinking.

The same year he began a book on psychology that was to emerge, after twelve years, as a two-volume compendium called *Principles of Psychology*. This book summarized and clarified contemporary knowledge in the field and presented James's own "functional approach" in psychology, which stressed the practical and experimental more than the theoretical and which stressed the relationship between physiology and psychology. He also established the first demonstration laboratory for psychology in the United States.

During these years James continued to teach at Harvard,

where his classes were very popular because of his clarity of presentation, his interesting applications of ideas, the vigor of his speech, and his startling challenges to traditional thought. Tanned by the outdoor sun and dressed in informal tweeds, James caught the imagination of his students. He had a talent for analyzing the most difficult concepts and making them comprehensible. This talent carried over so well into his writing that a critic once said of him that, whereas his brother, Henry James, wrote fiction as though it were philosophy, William James wrote philosophy as though it were fiction.

It was about seven years after his book on psychology that his next book, *The Will To Believe* (1897), appeared; thereafter there were many publications in the fields of religion and philosophy. For a long time James had thought about the nature of God, the question of determinism versus free will, the immortality of the soul, and the ethics of humanity. He followed an empirical approach in his attempt to understand the religious experience, an approach that included observation and reflection. The results of his intensive study he published in *Varieties of Religious Experience*.

William James believed that there is no evidence of any life after death, but he accepted the existence of a divinity as being established by the inner reachings of mankind for help during times of stress. However, James rejected a monistic view of the divinity, leaning in the direction of ancient pluralism. "Why search for unity in the world?" wrote James. "Why is *one* more excellent than *forty-three* or than *two million and ten?*" In place of a universe, his concept was a "multiverse." In his view there was not one God, but one force among many, "one helper in the midst of all the shapers of the great world's fate."

In his illuminating essay "The Dilemma of Determinism," William James cast aside the old-world, static determinism that he believed concomitant with monism, and declared for free will, with each person having "a vote" toward his own future. According to James, if there is one all-powerful, all-knowing God, then human beings are merely puppets, working out a predetermined existence. To James, such a monistic world is a dead world in which everything has been decided, whereas the pluralistic world is a world in the making, a world where each person has an opportunity to shape his own future and that of society: "There belongs to mind from its birth upward, a spontaneity, a vote. It is in the game and not a mere looker-on. . . ."

James then considered some of the eternal questions of philosophers: What is truth? What is reality? During the years he had spent in Europe, he had drunk deeply the abstract, metaphysical potions of the German and other European philosophers. He rejected the obscure "Absolute" of Hegel, the pessimism of Schopenhauer, and Spencer's mechanical concept of mind. James's philosophical concept of mind, reality, and truth is based on the dynamic spirit of individualism that he had espoused in his pluralistic view of the universe.

So far as reality and truth are concerned, James stated, "The knower is not simply a mirror floating with no foothold anywhere, and passively reflecting. . . . The knower is an actor, and coefficient of the truth . . . he registers the truth which he helps to create." In other words, truth and reality are not coldly objective things but humanly conceived notions that vary with an individual's interest and preference, not necessarily "at any given instant, but as shown by the total upshot of experience." This was his famous philosophy of pragmatism. He talked about the "utility" of truth, its "cash value" in life, the manner in which truth has differed in different eras and altered circumstances. According to James, "Truth is *one species* of good, and not . . . a category distinct from good, and coordinate with it."

William James, the pragmatist, turned away from the abstract, the absolute, the so-called objective, and recognized the importance of the subjective, the changing values, and the living perceptions of individuals. The pragmatist has great respect for the individual, great hospitality for new ideas. He judges the truth of ideas by viewing their practical consequences. The truth is not the noumenon, or ultimate reality, of Kant that cannot be perceived by experience. The truth, according to James, is meaningful only through experience— satisfying and efficacious experience.

James's pragmatism was criticized severely as a "philosophy for philistines," materialistic, a debasing application of marketplace values and terminology to philosophy, an oversimplification. But James's ethical standards for society and individuals were as high as any. He declaimed against materialism and "the bitch goddess, Success." He worked actively to improve the lot of the underprivileged. He believed that every person had "reserve energies" that should be brought forth for the common good. He pointed out the dreadful waste of war.

William James championed the cause of democracy and the nobility of the common man. He extolled the individuality of the poet Walt Whitman and the "strenuous life" of President Theodore Roosevelt. James regarded life as a perpetual challenge and spiritual adventure. In his essay "On a Certain Blindness in Human Beings," James urges us to have "regard to the feelings of creatures and people different from ourselves," and reminds the intelligentsia that "life is always worth living. . . . But we of the highly educated classes (so-called) . . . are trained to seek the choice, the rare . . . and to overlook the common. We are stuffed with abstract conceptions and glib with verbalities and verbosities."

William James was one of the first American philosophers to win recognition upon the world scene. He brought modern philosophy within the reach of the common man, defining it unpretentiously as "only thinking about things in the most comprehensive possible way." His most famous book, *Pragmatism* (1907), and his later ones, *A Pluralistic Universe* (1909) and *Some Problems of Philosophy* (1911), were read and discussed in the capitals of Europe.

The surge and vigor of American expansion, democracy, and individualism were reflected in James's philosophical thinking. His challenge to traditional beliefs, his highlighting of "consequences of actions" rather than of "abstract absolutes" undoubtedly influenced the thinking of writers like Whitman and Emerson, and statesmen like Theodore Roosevelt and Woodrow Wilson. There is a kinship between Darwin's theory of evolution and the contemporary scientific view of a world in constant motion and flux, and James's idea of ever-changing values.

James loved the give and take of discussion and was a widely sought lecturer. Even when he retired and went to Europe for his health in 1910, he could not keep out of the stream of academic and philosophic discussion. However, while abroad his health failed rapidly and he returned to Chocorua, New Hampshire, where he passed away on August 26, 1910.

William James realized that he had not succeeded in answering the philosophers' eternal questions. But he knew that in his writings, in his many lectures in this country and in Europe, and in his many conversations with students, he had stimulated a strong new way of thinking.

FURTHER READING

Perry, Ralph B. *Thought and Character of William James.*

—————Alfred Marshall—————

[1842–1924]

"POLITICAL ECONOMY, or Economics, is a study of mankind in the ordinary business of life; it examines that part of individual and social action which is most closely connected with the attainment and with the use of the material requisites of well-being." Until Alfred Marshall wrote these words in 1890, economics was generally thought of as the "science of wealth." Marshall's definition was an attempt to focus attention upon human behavior as it is affected by economic motives, forces, and environment. Today it is quite commonplace in all of the social sciences to emphasize the importance of the human personality in the particular discipline from which it is viewed.

A careful and methodical worker in all that he did, Marshall's writings served as textbooks and reference works for several generations of British and American students of economics. To the present time writers and economists have been engaged in modifying, expanding, and interpreting what Marshall said. Even those economists who disagreed with or were critical of his concepts used his work as a point of departure.

Alfred Marshall was born in Clapham, England, on July 26, 1842. His father, William Marshall, a cashier in the Bank of England, was a devout member of the Anglican Church. At the age of nine, Alfred was sent to the Merchant Taylors School in London to obtain instruction in the classics. In time, however, his interests turned to mathematics, and when he completed secondary school, he refused a scholarship at Oxford because it meant more work in the classics and eventually ordination in the Evangelical ministry, the lifework his father had planned for him.

Instead, with the help of a loan from an uncle, Marshall was able to enter Cambridge to study mathematics, in which he soon excelled. Graduating in 1865 with high honors, he became a lecturer in mathematics and began to study molecular physics. The intellectual climate at Cambridge was very stimulating for Marshall and he soon found himself drawn into the society of a group of men deeply interested in philosophical studies. Recalling this period later, Marshall stated that his interest in mathematics and science slowly began to give way to "a sudden rise of deep interest in the philosophical foundations of knowledge, especially in relation to theology." Thereafter he began to pursue the study of social ethics.

Despite his having rebelled against his father's wishes that he follow the ministry, Marshall still maintained a great deal of "religious humanitarianism" within himself. As he looked about the industrial cities of England in the 1860's he was appalled at the poverty and terrible working conditions he saw. He believed that the solution of economic problems was the highest use of man's intellect because "the study of the causes of poverty is the study of the causes of the degradation of a large part of mankind." So Marshall resolved to do what he could to improve the material well-being of the ordinary working man, and he set himself the task of mastering the subject of political economy, or "economics," as he preferred to call it. Marshall is credited with being the first to establish the use of the word "economics," at least in the English-speaking world, by including it in the title of his famous book, *Principles of Economics*, published in 1890.

Alfred Marshall started his study by reading John Stuart Mill's *Political Economy* and Hegel's *Philosophy of History*, and then went to Germany to review the work of the German economists. As a result of these studies, he was appointed to a special lectureship in Moral Sciences at St. John's College in 1868. In 1875 Marshall toured the United States for four months, visiting Harvard, Yale, and talking to leading citizens and businessmen from New York to San Francisco. He was much impressed with the economic development of America and was particularly interested in studying the conflicting views on protective tariff, on which he wrote a paper, "The Problem of Protection in a New Country." It is indicative of his thoroughness and great attention to detail that when he had finished this study he was able to write to a friend in relation to protectionism for the young country, "I shall really know the whole of their case; and I do not believe there is or ever has been another Englishman who could say the same."

Returning to England, Marshall firmly resolved to devote the rest of his life to the study of economics because, as he later stated in the *Principles,* the only possibility of human progress "depends in a great measure upon facts and inferences, which are within the province of economics; and this it is which gives to economic studies their chief and their highest interest."

Thereafter, except for the eight years from 1877 to 1885, when he lectured at Bristol and Oxford, Marshall held the professorship in political economy at Cambridge until his official retirement in 1908. He continued to see students and carry on independent research at the university right up to the time of his death, July 13, 1924, two weeks before his eighty-second birthday.

As a result of Marshall's work, Cambridge became an outstanding center for economic study and instruction in England, attracting for more than a generation a large proportion of the intellectuals in the country. It is no accident that the most brilliant and lasting works on economics have come from his former students, who include John Neville Keynes, Arthur C. Pigou, C. R. Fay, and the outstanding economic theoretician of the twentieth century, John Maynard, Lord Keynes. In addition to his duties as teacher, administrator, and writer, Marshall frequently presented evidence before royal commissions, especially in the fields of fiscal policy and currency reform. Some of Marshall's most lucid writings are contained in these reports.

Marshall set as his goal the development of "a modern version of old doctrines with the aid of the new work and with reference to the new problems of our age." In other words, Marshall did not reject the economic system so carefully constructed by Smith, Ricardo, and Mill. Instead, he selected the best parts of their work and the work of those who criticized these classical economists, and synthesized them into his own "neoclassic" system, which has been called a "masterpiece and *as a whole* has probably never been surpassed as an explanation of economic life."

Alfred Marshall was especially conscious of the changed social and economic conditions of the times, conditions that made it imperative to view economic problems differently than had his predecessors. Malthus's theory concerning increasing population seemed to be contradicted by a decline in the rate of increase in many countries. Ricardo's theory of rent was in disfavor because of the serious decline in agricultural land values throughout Europe. Other factors, such as the sharp movement from prosperity to depression during the 1870's and 1880's, the rapid growth of monopolies, increasing trade barriers, and the development of systematic regulation of all economic activity by government, required a new interpretation of the fundamental aspects of economic theory.

Marshall was convinced that there was an underlying "principle of continuity" of economic and ethical forces. For economics to be scientific in character, it must discover the regularities of action of these forces, which according to Marshall had only one standard of measurement, money. Therefore, the scientific approach to economic life revolved around the study of prices. Marshall recognized that there might be many other influences pressing upon a given economic situation, but he excluded them from his conclusions unless it could be demonstrated that they have an effect on prices. It is clear that Marshall was influenced by the prevailing feeling of the physical scientists of his day that the prime function of the scientist was to extract law and order from the world at large.

To analyze correctly the forces at work at any particular time, Marshall concluded that it is necessary to establish a normal pattern of action of those forces that fix prices. He believed that the values of commodities are relative, since they express the exchange ratio they command to one another at any given time. Prices are fixed by the interplay of the forces of demand and supply, representing the combined strength of the consumers and producers. Prices tend to move in the direction of *the point of equilibrium*, which is where prices coincide with production costs. As soon as any deviation from equilibrium occurs, forces in the market place are set into motion to restore it. Marshall thus gave recognition to the fact that day-to-day prices are under pressure from a variety of forces which cause them to vary from the "normal price." However, the tendency is for prices to cluster around the normal price, and thus the normal-price concept is the result of influences that operate over a long period of time. Marshall was the first economist to emphasize the interplay of supply and demand in the determination of prices and to indicate that the movement toward equilibrium is present in all phases of economic behavior. He completely avoided the one-sided emphasis of his predecessors who argued that either cost (supply) or utility (demand) is predominant in fixing prices, and to prove his own point, Marshall used a pair of scissors as an illustration. It is impossible to determine which blade is more important in the cutting function, since the two blades are indispensable to each other. However, he did recognize the merits of studying the long-run forces which help determine demand and supply, respectively, and concluded that "the value of a thing tends in the long run to correspond to its cost of production."

Following this reasoning, Marshall saw the distribution of income to be the prices paid by the business community for the uses of the factors of production. These prices are also determined by the interaction of the forces of supply and demand, as are the prices of commodities. The unity within the economic system, as Marshall saw it, is maintained by forces that attract and repel each other, resulting in a "sort of solar system of counterpoise and balance."

Marshall was responsible for the introduction of many new terms and concepts into the language of economics. For example, in discussing methods of production, he speaks of the "representative firm" as being the one able to remain in business by charging prices that cover normal expenses, which include the costs of management. The term covered all business firms that set their prices at or just above their costs of production, and are, therefore, typical of business as a whole, since lower-cost firms are few in number and exceptional, and higher-cost firms tend to be eliminated in the competition of the market place. Another essential concept developed by Marshall relates to his insistence that, since economic activity extends over time, supply cannot be thought of as a *stock*, but must be regarded as a *flow* of goods. It is, therefore, extremely important in analyzing prices to be very conscious of three periods of time: (1) market periods, in which the capacity to produce cannot be altered; (2) long periods, in which there is enough time to introduce and use a new supply of the factors of production; (3) very long periods, in which long-range changes in population, capital, technology, and wants are able to affect the trend of prices.

Other concepts introduced by Marshall deal with "consumer's surplus," which is the gain a consumer obtains when he purchases a good at a price less than the price he would have been willing to pay; "quasi rent," which is the yield on an investment in capital goods above the current market rate of interest; and "consumer's goods," which are commodities that directly satisfy a human want. Consumer's goods may be durable—that is, usable over a long period of time—or nondurable—usable for a short period of time. A companion expression is "producer's goods," which are goods that satisfy human wants indirectly: that is, the raw materials, machinery, and factories that are used to make consumer's goods.

Finally, Marshall was fully aware of the fact that a static approach to a dynamic or changing situation would not prove useful or desirable. In order to avoid this pitfall, Marshall set forth certain assumptions that serve as a foundation for his entire economic structure, and which indicate a realistic awareness of the ever-changing, practical world. This structure, Marshall made clear, applies to the real world to the extent that the assumptions are true. His basic assumptions are the following:

(1) Freedom of enterprise will continue as the predominant aspect of economic organization.

(2) Property rights will remain unchanged.

(3) Population and capital will increase slowly, and at approximately the same rate, and both are capable of moving and being motivated by the possibility of gain.

(4) Technology and organization will change slowly.

(5) The pursuit of economic activity will chiefly be motivated by the desire to satisfy human wants, and will be limited by the fatigue and distastefulness of prolonged labor.

(6) Present and future buyers and sellers will be reasonably well informed as to the state of the market, and that their bargaining power is and will remain relatively equal.

Marshall worked very carefully and deliberately to develop a new and dynamic body of economic theory, which extended and modified the classical doctrines of Smith and Ricardo and synthesized the views of conflicting theorists. As a result he was able to exert more influence upon American economic thought than any other writer, with the possible exception of his most outstanding student, John Maynard Keynes. In the words of Keynes, he created "a whole Copernican system, by which all the elements of the economic universe are kept in their places by mutual counterpoise and interaction."

FURTHER READING

Keynes, John M. *Essays in Biography*.
Pigou, A. C. *Memorials of Alfred Marshall*.

——Friedrich Nietzsche——
[1844–1900]

As THE SIMPLE COFFIN was lowered into the German soil of the village of Röcken, Peter Gast said of Friedrich Nietzsche: "Holy be thy name to all future generations." It was this same Friedrich Nietzsche, dead at the age of fifty-six, who had said in *Ecce Homo*, his last major book, "I have a terrible fear that one day my name shall be pronounced Holy."

Peter Gast's brief funeral oration was to be neither the last irony nor the last misunderstanding to be associated with the name of Nietzsche. Perhaps the greatest of all ironies was that this philosopher died at the threshold of a century of titanic struggles, many of which he had foreseen. Surely the greatest, if most willful, misunderstanding was to occur in this same twentieth century when the Nazis distorted and adopted Nietzsche as *their* philosopher.

For the beginning of the life of this strange man, we have but to take a short walk from the cemetery in Röcken, and return to the year 1844, when Friedrich Wilhelm Nietzsche was born into a family composed of a long line of Lutheran theologians. From his very christening, he was provided with two ironies: this greatest critic of Christianity was the son and grandson of clergymen, and this "European" opponent of German chauvinism was named after the then King of Prussia, Friedrich Wilhelm IV.

Upon the tragic death of his father, the child, then only five, was moved to Naumburg, where he was brought up in an atmosphere dominated by women, piety, and provincialism, three things he was to detest later in his life. Admitted on a scholarship to the famous boarding school in Pforta, where Fichte, Ranke, and the two Schlegels had preceded him, he excelled in classics and literature but did poorly in mathematics. At twenty he entered the university at Bonn, but when William Ritschl, a philologist with whom he had become friendly, was transferred to Leipzig, Nietzsche followed him there the next year.

It was at Leipzig that he encountered the two most vital influences of his young life, for it was here, in a secondhand bookstore, that he came upon a copy of Schopenhauer's *The World as Will and Idea*. And it was here that he became personally acquainted with the composer Richard Wagner, then at the height of his fame. Without Schopenhauer, Nietzsche's philosophy could not have taken the form it did, for it was to some extent a rebellion against Schopenhauer's pessimism, although initially he had been greatly impressed by Schopenhauer's criticism of traditional thinking. And it was the encounter with Wagner that convinced Nietzsche of the possibility of creative genius existing in nineteenth-century Germany.

Nietzsche was a brilliant student. So great was his mastery of philology that in 1868, at the very young age of twenty-four, and before he had even received his doctorate, he was offered the chair of classical philology at the University of Basel, where he taught until 1879 when severe ill health forced him to retire. Ill health plagued Nietzsche throughout his life. During the Franco-Prussian War he served as a hospital orderly and contracted both dysentery and diphtheria, which severely aggravated his already poor health and led to his subsequent collapse. Nietzsche, however, was a firm believer that suffering ennobled the character, and he even attributes the brilliance he poured into *Thus Spake Zarathustra* to his final overcoming of both the spiritual and physical sickness within himself.

In 1872 Nietzsche published his first book, *The Birth of Tragedy*, with a dedication to Richard Wagner. In it, he presented the thesis that the development of tragedy by the Greeks was merely their way of avoiding pessimism and affirming the value of life as adventure and struggle against odds. His Greek hero was Dionysus (Bacchus), the god of revelry, whose joy in action was extolled in early Greek tragedies. The friendship with Wagner was not enduring. At first he had joined with Wagner and had written papers urging a revival of the dynamic life spirit of pagan antiquity and criticizing the lack of German culture. Though, when he realized that Wagner was in reality glorifying what Nietzsche regarded as the decadent virtues of humility and self-abasement, as exemplified by Parsifal, and that Wagner was in fact creating a static, romantic mythology that catered to German chauvinism, Nietzsche broke with him, and subsequently denounced him publicly in *Nietzsche Against Wagner*.

The break with Wagner occurred in 1879, and the next year Nietzsche's health failed, forcing him to leave Basel and commence years of solitary wandering from one health resort to another in search of relief.

The years from 1880 through 1889 were intellectually the most fruitful for Nietzsche, for they witnessed the publication of all his mature writings. In contrast to the intellectual excitement, his personal life was ordinary and, in fact, spent mostly in solitude, for Nietzsche, despite the great value he attached to friendship, was not able to retain many friends. A touch of the madness that later was to overwhelm him was noticeable in his manner. He began to regard his own opinions as incontrovertible and, more and more, his writings were egocentric expositions beginning with *"ich"* ("I"). His thick black hair, brushed straight back from his taut forehead, his walrus mustache, and his bony brows, accentuating the dark, piercing eyes, gave him a tense and intolerant appearance that was communicated in his conversation.

During this decade it can truly be said of him that he lived with his brain. His greatest achievement during this time was *Thus Spake Zarathustra*. He says the book was conceived "six thousand feet beyond man and time," and it is certain that it was written in a white heat of creative passion, ten days being spent on each of the first two parts in 1883, and another ten days on the third part in 1884. Part four was added later in 1884. *Thus Spake Zarathustra* is in every sense a remarkable work. For its style and brilliant use of aphorisms alone, its fame would be assured. Nietzsche was a master of German prose, and in *Thus Spake Zarathustra* his use of language frequently borders on pure poetry.

The book is also the cornerstone of Nietzsche's philosophy. He chose Zarathustra, a variant name for the ancient Persian philosopher Zoroaster, as his spokesman because he regarded Zarathustra as the first moralist. Feeling that all previous Judaic-Christian morality was a life-denying, negativistic creed and that his own was a bold, new philosophy, he considered Zarathustra to be the ideal narrator through whom to convey his message.

Nietzsche's bold new philosophy, as enunciated by Zarathustra, began with a denial of all traditional virtues, religion, morality, and hopes for an afterlife. He asked, "What is the greatest experience you can have? It is the hour of your great contempt. The hour in which your happiness turns to disgust and likewise your reason and your virtue."

In place of the decadent virtues, Zarathustra urges individual freedom of assertion, vigorous living, and self-perfection by reaching out beyond the confines of traditional mores. He says, "I love him who is of free spirit and free heart," and again he declares, "I teach you the Overman [translated by some as 'Superman']. Man is something that is to be surpassed. What have you done to surpass man?"

He has no patience with the "herd man," the man who lives the peaceful, comfortable life of acquiescence. On this Zarathustra says that "one must have chaos within oneself to give birth to a dancing star. I ask you: do you still have this chaos?" Nietzsche was not a "systematic" thinker, and the symbolism in *Thus Spake Zarathustra* is at times confusing. In fact, he realized that his message was an almost futile one in his own time, and so, through Zarathustra, he declared: "Now they look upon me and laugh; and as they laugh they also hate me. There is ice in their laughter."

In *Toward the Genealogy of Morals* (1887), *Beyond Good and Evil* (1886), and *The Gay Science* (1882 and 1886) he attacked both religion and science, asserting that "God is dead" because we ourselves have killed him, in our hearts and in our minds, with our rationality and our science. Nietzsche was merely recognizing the undermining of the traditional foundations of morality by science that had culminated in the nineteenth century. The problem, then, was to find new values, before being overcome by nihilism. Thus Nietzsche was primarily an ethical philosopher: his was a search for values, and this search for values embodied the transvaluation of values. It may seem paradoxical that he who called himself "the Immoralist" was primarily a moral philosopher, but this paradox occurred because Nietzsche's values were in direct opposition to Judaic-Christian morality. Nietzsche's attack on this morality was based on his feeling that it is a life-denying, ascetic morality of weakness. Thus he called believers in Judaic-Christianity "after-worldsmen," "despisers of the body," and characterized their morality as stemming from "a poor ignorant weariness, which no longer wants to want: That created all gods and after-worlds."

In short, Nietzsche's attack on Judaic-Christianity was based on his desire to reaffirm the value of life here and now, on earth, and not to deny it. And thus he called for a destruction of what he termed the old "life-denying" values and for a creation of new values that would be the exact opposite of the old, in other words, that would affirm life. He assailed the "good" that was called peaceful, meek, gentle, and patient; and he extolled the "good" that was bold, self-reliant, strong, cruel, and exuberant. Although Nietzsche was regarded in his own time as a rabid critic of society, an "antieverything" radical, and a nihilist, modern scholars now realize that he was indeed a creator and an affirmer; it is the supreme irony that sometimes he who wants to create must first destroy, that he who wants to affirm must first deny. In this sense Nietzsche thought of himself as a nineteenth-century Socrates, a gadfly attacking the evils of his time.

Nietzsche was a realist, not an idealist. To find a new set of values he focused on what was for him the greatest of all realities, the very essence of life: the "will to power." Nietzsche was also a psychologist, and as a psychologist he had formulated a theory that every animal is motivated by a brutal and raw force, a will to power. In its raw form this will is animalistic and destructive. However, in man, this will could be, and must be, sublimated. That is, the highest man must sublimate the raw will to power to a will to create. He must *overcome himself*. That is what Nietzsche meant by the doctrine of self-overcoming: man must overcome the raw and destructive will to power with *his* will to power. Once he has achieved this sublimation, he is a creative being. And it is the Overman, the *Übermensch*, who can achieve this sublimation to the fullest.

Nietzsche's doctrine of the *Übermensch* has been too often misunderstood. Literally translated, the term means "Overman," not "Superman," and it may be best to use the former appellation since it contains the idea of self-overcoming. The *Übermensch* is a metaphor for the moral superman who is able to liberate himself from the ascetic, life-denying morality and who is able to affirm all there is in life with supreme joy; he possesses the will to create, and he finds the value of life in life itself. He is emphatically not the Nazi Aryan who, while claiming adherence to Nietzschean principles, unleashed his animalistic, destructive impulses in an orgy of terror spawned in the most selfish of motives. The *Übermensch* of Nietzsche is an unselfish, life-giving prophet who is able to accept the reality of life, even the tragic realities, without sinking into either despair, nihilism, or pity.

Nietzsche admired the rebels and strong leaders of the world. He despised the leveling process of democracy, "this mania for counting noses." Of this he sarcastically said: "No shepherd and one herd! Everyone wants an equal share, everyone is equal: whoever feels otherwise voluntarily enters a madhouse." He attacked socialism, the feminine-rights movement, and pacifism as leading to national enfeeblement. He even denigrated marriage as "fettering" the creative man. He believed that a countermovement to the leveling process was inevitable, and he prophetically foresaw an era of vast struggle in the twentieth century, saying, "The democratization of Europe is at the same time an involuntary preparation for the rearing of tyrants."

Nietzsche's delineations of the national characteristics of the people of Europe are interesting revelations of his political naïveté, his propensity for attacking idols, and his excessive generalizing. He regarded the French as the most cultured, although hampered by the destruction of their aristocracy in the French Revolution. He praised the Germans' perseverance and industry but deprecated their stolidity of mind and their glorification of military over philosophical ascendancy. He admired the autocratic government of Russia under the czars and the fatalism of its people. The English provoked his wrath and ridicule most of all because of their democratic ideals. Of them he said, "Shopkeepers, Christians, cows, women, Englishmen, and other democrats belong together."

Thus Spake Zarathustra was followed by the elucidatory *Beyond Good and Evil* and *Toward the Genealogy of Morals.* There Nietzsche diverged for a while to attack Wagner. His last major work was the autobiographical *Ecce Homo* (1888), in which lucid explanations appear side by side with fantastic and somewhat egomaniacal claims of his own infallibility and brilliance that presaged his impending madness. By 1889 Nietzsche was hopelessly insane. In January of 1900 he collapsed in the streets of Turin, and was later taken to the asylum at Jena. He died in 1900 in Weimar, the city of Goethe.

In *Ecce Homo*, Nietzsche asked: "Have you understood me . . . ?" To a large extent, the answer would have to be "No," for out of his philosophical treatises have come misunderstandings, interpretive disagreements, and the grossest perversions. Much of this occurred because of the contradictions and the intemperate expressions of opinion that appeared at different times in his own writing. Recent scholars, such as Otto Manthey-Zorn and Walter Kaufmann, have determined that some of the difficulties stemmed from the misrepresentations of some of his relatives who survived him and that there was a good deal of perversion by later propagandists who took some of his aphorisms out of context and used them for their own purposes. For example, as has already been stated, the Nazis used such Nietzschean phrases as "master race," "elite leadership," and "subservient humanity" as a propagandist cover for their barbaric atrocities that included genocide. Thus, until recently, Nietzschean philosophy was believed to advocate tyranny, violence, and even racism. However, due to the efforts of these modern scholars, there is now a better understanding of Nietzsche's philosophy as basically an affirmative philosophy of life and joy, conceived amidst sorrow and the annihilation of life-denying, traditional creeds.

It is not to the Nazis that we must look to see Nietzschean influence in the twentieth century, but rather to such liberal humanists as Albert Camus and to the pyschologist Alfred Adler, who incorporated many of Nietzsche's ideas about the will to power. On an even larger scale, a significant tone of intellectual thought in the twentieth century was foreseen by Nietzsche. Nietzsche was seeking for authenticity in existence, and his philosophical contributions are acknowledged as influences by Sartre, Jaspers, and Heidegger, three leading proponents of existentialism (a philosophy in which individual freedom and choice are stressed).

In the historical development of philosophy, then, Nietzsche occupies a significant place because he marks a sharp break with German idealism; he follows Hegel and inaugurates a new, challenging spirit in philosophy. But, above all, the significance of Nietzsche is that, in a time when science had destroyed or undermined traditional values, he had the courage and will to seek new ones and at the same time affirm the value of life.

FURTHER READING

Danto, Arthur C. *Nietzsche as Philosopher.*
Jaspers, Karl. *Nietzsche and Christianity.*
Kaufmann, Walter, ed. *The Portable Nietzsche.*
Manthey-Zorn, Otto, ed. *Nietzsche: An Anthology of His Works.*

——John Bates Clark——
[1847–1938]

UP TO THE TIME of John Bates Clark, almost all American economists based their writings on the ideas developed by European economic theorists. However, Clark became the "master builder" of American economic thought and was the first economist in the United States to come close to founding a new school of economic thinking. He devoted most of his life to trying to show that the distribution of the income of society is "controlled by a natural law, and that this law, if it worked without friction, would give to every agent of production the amount of wealth which that agent creates."

The development of the marginal utility theory in economics, by which is meant the addition to total utility or usefulness added by the last unit of a good, is generally credited to three outstanding European economists: William Stanley Jevons, Karl Menger, and Léon Walras. Yet Clark, at approximately the same time, was formulating the same theory quite independently in the United States. Clark used the term "effective utility" to denote the additional usefulness of the last or marginal units. It was the application of this new concept to the traditional set of value theories that brought Clark to the immediate attention of his contemporaries and foreshadowed his role as one of the great theoretical writers of the early twentieth century.

John Bates Clark was born in January 1847, in Providence, Rhode Island, to Yankee parents in whom the Puritan tradition was a vital daily force. His mother, the daughter of a minister, knew many hardships but willingly made personal sacrifices for the benefit of others. His father, extremely well-thought-of by his neighbors, operated a dry-goods store until illness forced him to move to Minnesota in search of a more suitable climate.

455

In Minnesota his father pioneered in selling plows to farmers.

After a short stay at Brown University, Clark transferred to Amherst, entering with the class of 1869. Unfortunately, his course was interrupted twice, once by his father's illness, and the second time by his father's death. During the period of his father's illness, John Clark carried on the plow business and discovered that in the frontier community it was easy to sell plows but hard to collect for them. After his father's death, Clark returned to Amherst and graduated with the class of 1872. He was a brilliant student and his maturity and work experience stood him in good stead, so that despite the many interruptions in his studies, he finished first in his class. He early cultivated an independent mind. Once, when he was asked to enter a contest which would require him to defend a particular viewpoint, he refused on the ground that his own viewpoint was different.

Clark majored in political economy, in which his independent thinking soon convinced him that the instruction and the texts were far from adequate to explain a subject that he believed to be supremely important to the welfare of man. He set for himself the goal of filling in the gaps that neither teacher nor textbook had been able to fill for him.

At the age of twenty-five Clark went to Germany to spend the next three years studying under the direction of Professor Karl Knies of Heidelberg University. He was one of the first of the large group of American students who went to Germany to study in the 1870's, and who later did outstanding work in the United States. Upon his return in 1875, he married Myra Smith, also of New England ancestry, and joined the faculty at Carleton College. At Carleton, Clark was able to help a brilliant but troublesome student named Thorstein Veblen, who later became one of America's most creative thinkers in the fields of economics and sociology.

In 1881 Clark accepted a position at Smith College, then newly organized. While at Smith, he published his first book, *The Philosophy of Wealth* (1885), which immediately marked him as an original and forward-looking economic thinker. From Smith he moved to Amherst for a short time, and finally, in 1895, he accepted an offer from Columbia University to be a member of its newly formed graduate faculty.

He continued to write and teach and to influence a large number of students. The threat of war disturbed Clark a great deal because to him it represented a dreadful obstacle to the attainment of a higher standard of living for mankind. In 1911, Clark became director of the Division of Economics and History of the Carnegie Endowment for International Peace, whose purpose it was to develop objective studies of war and militarism on an international basis. He joined with William H. Taft and Elihu Root in the "League To Enforce Peace" which supported the establishment of the League of Nations.

Clark remained at Columbia until his retirement in 1923. He was one of the founders of the American Economic Association, and served as its third president in 1894. He had the unique privilege of seeing his son, John Maurice Clark, himself an outstanding economic theorist, succeed to his chair at Columbia University in 1926.

In *The Philosophy of Wealth*, Clark was still exploring in his own mind the problems of economic theory and organization, so that a number of his ideas are somewhat vague and sometimes self-contradictory; yet the book gives evidence that fertile ideas were in the process of development in the mind of a very original thinker.

Clark criticized some major assumptions of the classical economists because he believed them to be contrary to the truth. For example, Clark was not convinced that man is motivated only by material self-interest, a fundamental classical view. Instead, he held that moral principles and unselfish motives are just as important factors in man's behavior as an insatiable desire for personal esteem. Clark felt that man's innate sense of what is right is "the supreme motive in the market place as elsewhere," and is "the centripetal force in economic society." Throughout his works, Clark insisted that all economic theory must be based upon an accurate and correct view of human nature because the voluntary interaction of men is the basis of economic law.

The classical view which extolled competition was also criticized by Clark. Under a modern market mechanism, he declared that competition tends to become self-destructive because it resolves itself into an "ignoble struggle for personal profit." The more Clark studied the market place, the more he became convinced that its basic immorality, added to the inequality of those engaging in a bargain and the absence of any adequate code of behavior, made it impossible for competition to produce justice. To correct these shortcomings,

Clark advocated more reliance on the development of moral law and systematic governmental regulation of economic activities. Later, Thorstein Veblen was to base part of his attack on contemporary society on the same reasoning as that advanced by Clark.

Clark's major contribution to the field of pure economic theory, and the one on which his reputation as a great thinker rests primarily, was his work on *The Distribution of Wealth* (1899). It was the first major effort of American scholarship in the field of theory, and has been called, even one half century later, "one of the greatest works in pure theory yet produced in any language."

The subtitle of the book was "A Theory of Wages, Interest, and Profits"; its purpose was to show clearly that there is a set of underlying forces that control the distribution of society's income in such a way that fair and equitable compensation can be awarded to each factor of production in proportion to the contribution that each factor makes in creating the income.

Before proceeding with his analogies, Clark introduced the following three postulates: (1) Society is comparable to a biological organism and therefore the economic relationships of individuals are to be found in organic social laws. (2) A proper understanding of "dynamic," or changing, economic forces can only be obtained by first isolating and analyzing "static," or permanent, economic forces. (3) The natural laws of economic science may be considered valid only when they obtain the moral approval of mankind. Clark developed his theory within the capitalist framework which includes free enterprise, private property, the profit motive, and some governmental regulation to protect the individual. He acknowledged certain "frictions" in the economy, such as monopolies, trusts, and unions, that adversely affect the smooth functioning of the distribution of income to the factors of production, which, to Clark, are only labor and capital.

This "static" society which Clark used as a point of departure in the hope that it would lead him to a fuller understanding of a world full of constant change is very similar to the "normal equilibrium" society developed by Alfred Marshall. Stated in another way, Clark proposed to examine the "natural" way the economy would tend to operate if "labor and capital were to remain fixed in quantity, if improvements in the mode of production were to stop, if the consolidating of capital were to cease, and if the wants of consumers were never to vary."

Under these circumstances, Clark felt that all productive factors would receive a share of the national income corresponding to what they had contributed to the creation of that income. All forms of capital, including factories, tools, machinery, and money, were lumped together into an abstract concept called "social capital." The distinguishing characteristics of capital are its permanence, its mobility, and its homogeneity. "It is a sum of productive wealth." However, "capital goods" are different. They are made to be destroyed or used up in the process of creating goods to satisfy the consumer. Land, considered a basic factor of production since earliest times, was seen by Clark as a special form of capital good in which capital is embodied. It is the only kind of capital good that does not have to be destroyed in order to serve its purpose.

In a similar fashion, all laborers were lumped together in productivity units called "social labor." Proceeding further, Clark then applied the doctrine of marginal utility to the price of labor and capital. In his systematic presentation, Clark was saying that just as the values of all other goods are fixed by the values of the last or final (marginal) units of those goods, so the value of labor and capital is determined by the worth or value of the last or final (marginal) units of labor and capital. In other words, the return on the investment of capital is limited to the productivity of the marginal unit of capital, and wages are determined by the productivity of the marginal laborer. Clark went one step further to point out that the marginal worker is not necessarily the last worker hired or the least efficient, as Clark assumed that all the workers are of equal efficiency as are all units of capital. Thus every unit of capital and every unit of labor is completely interchangeable with other units in its class.

As a further indication of his great ability to understand human behavior as modified by economic forces, Clark reasoned that under these circumstances, each employer in his attempts to maximize his profits would continue to hire and employ additional units of capital and labor until the marginal revenue derived from the sale of the last unit was equal to the marginal costs incurred. In other words, the marginal unit of labor or capital is the one that produces just enough income to pay for itself. Under the principle of diminishing productivity, which indicates that each successive unit adds something less to the total product than the preceding one, if the employer adds one more unit beyond this point, he will sustain a loss on that unit. Under the pressure of pure competition, the employer is forced to add additional units of capital and labor until he reaches the marginal product. The same pressure will force the marginal worker to accept a marginal wage, and marginal capital to accept a marginal rate of return.

In order to sustain the internal consistency of his theory, Clark had to reverse his earlier evaluation of competition. In *The Philosophy of Wealth,* he thought of competition as a harmful and possibly dying force. In all his later works he accepted competition as a permanent and indestructible institution and one that performed many beneficial services. Thus, in the theory of final productivity, which, Clark stated, determines the earnings of men, all workers everywhere would receive "what would be lost to the employer if any one man now in the labor force would stop working." In other words, competition forces the marginal return everywhere to be equal to the level of the marginal producer or worker everywhere. Clark was saying that the marginal worker who changes his employer in the hope of obtaining a greater income will be disappointed, for under competitive conditions in the static society, his wages will remain the same. But what about the actual, dynamic world, where nothing stands still? Clark was very conscious of the nature and rate of change in modern industrial society. He believed that every phase of economic activity is greatly affected by the pressure of both static and dynamic forces. In his own words, "static forces set the standards, dynamic forces produce the variations." Clark hoped to be able to devise a method to measure the dynamic forces, once the static relationships were isolated and known.

A troublesome but very realistic set of elements that prevented the early measurement of the dynamic forces in the economy are the "frictions" which tend to obstruct the operation of pure economic laws. No friction exists in the static state, but it is found everywhere in the dynamic world. For example, a large number of frictions prevent labor from moving to areas and occupations where wages might be higher. These frictions might be caused by the worker's unwillingness to move from family and friends, or by his desire to allow his children to remain in the school in which they started, by the expense of moving, or by fear, uncertainty, or inertia. In any event, frictions such as these prevent the actual rate of wages from remaining at the theoretical level.

To add to the complexity of the problem, Clark recognized that the rate of change is increasing rapidly and that it is practically continuous. For example, the population is "exploding," capital funds are increasing and becoming more efficient, technology produces new and faster ways of doing things almost daily, workingmen are better organized and stronger, and human wants are changing in quality as well as in quantity. Toward the end of his career, Clark expressed the belief that human wants were also subject to discoverable laws. However, he made no attempt to formulate any of these laws, saying that this was a job for future generations.

Clark published several additional books, among them *The Problem of Monopoly* (1904), in which he tried to indicate how potential competition would tend to reduce the growth of industrial combinations and monopolies, and *Essentials of Economic Theory* (1907), in which he held that the dynamic laws of society are based upon, and very similar to, the static laws he had previously developed. In effect, Clark was indicating that there was a reasonably optimistic outlook for the future of American economic society, because his static analysis was essentially based on a system of social and economic harmonies. This results from the forces of competition, which tend to eliminate conflicts of interest and injustices and to give to every productive unit not less than what it produces. In this sense, Clark was refuting the Marxian exploitation thesis, which held that the capitalist gives the worker only enough to live on and "steals" for himself the surplus the worker produces.

Clark was later criticized for his overenthusiastic defense of the competitive forces inherent in the business world of the capitalist system. Even today, Clark's statement, to the effect that "If nothing suppresses competition, progress will continue forever," would require substantial modification to be acceptable to economists. Unsuppressed competition, like unsuppressed monopoly, is no longer a workable concept in our mixed economy.

Today some of Clark's work appears to be dated as modern

economists move into new fields of inquiry, and his "static society" is nonexistent. However, in his time, Clark's originality and independence of thought did a great deal to advance analytical thinking in economic science. His development of the marginal-utility theory of value and the marginal-productivity theory of wages was used in all the leading textbooks; and his division of economic analysis into "statics" and "dynamics" is an indispensable modern-day technique. His description of the mutual interdependence of factor prices and commodity prices, as well as the nature of distribution and production, is basic to an understanding of the concept of normal versus natural prices. Finally, his insistence on the social nature of the state is still considered valid today.

The esteem in which Clark was held by his fellow economists perhaps can best be seen in this line taken from *Economic Essays in Honor of John Bates Clark* (1927): "Clark's work as an economist has been both the creative activity of a philosopher and the specific service of a scholar."

FURTHER READING

Dorfman, Joseph. *The Economic Mind in American Civilization.*

———Knut Wicksell———

[1851–1926]

IN RECENT YEARS, as translations of the writings of Swedish economists have been made available in America, it has become evident that there has been a strong and vigorous "Swedish school" of social scientists with important ideas to contribute, especially in the fields of economic theory and policy. It is generally agreed that the founder of the so-called

Swedish or Stockholm school of economics was the complicated but brilliant personality Johann Gustaf Knut Wicksell.
When Wicksell finally settled down to a serious study of economics he mastered all the theories of the great economists
of the past as well as the then current writings of such
great thinkers as Léon Walras, Alfred Marshall, and Karl
Menger. Later John Maynard, Lord Keynes, was to utilize
Wicksell's works on interest theory and price levels as a guide
to his own masterful and revolutionary theory and policy suggestions.

Wicksell's career is yet another example of a great mind attracted to the study of economics late in life, after exploring
other fields. He did not begin to study economics seriously
until the age of forty-one, after he had obtained one degree in
mathematics and philosophy and another in physics. The fact
that he was able to complete his work toward one degree, let
alone two, is itself remarkable since both his parents died
when Wicksell was fifteen years old.

Wicksell was constantly troubled with emotional and religious problems, and seriously concerned with the unhappy
living conditions of the mass of the working classes around
him. As a young man, Wicksell saw a basic change take place
in his homeland, caused by the increasing world demand for
Sweden's natural resources of iron and timber. The demand
for labor increased rapidly and brought with it the evils of the
factory system: long hours, child labor, safety hazards, and unsanitary conditions. Wicksell believed that the best way for
the working class to improve its lot was to limit family size,
and at the end of a lecture on another subject advocated the
use of birth-control measures. The speech created a scandal
(the first of many), and involved Wicksell in recurrent debates. It was during these debates that he realized how badly
informed he was and that he needed to know much more
about economic and social problems in order to defend his
views. As a result he left the University of Uppsala in 1884,
after fifteen years of attendance, to study the social sciences
and to travel.

For the next five years he visited England, France, Germany, and Austria, meeting the leading economists of the day
and reading the works of the classical writers in the field. In
1895, he obtained the Ph.D. degree, but could not obtain a
university position, partly because of his advocacy of unpop-

ular views, and partly on the technical ground that economics was taught in the faculty of law and Wicksell did not have a law degree. His law degree was completed in 1899, and in 1900, at the age of fifty, Wicksell was appointed an assistant professor of economics at Lund University. Considering his complete disregard for authority, his outspoken views on a wide range of subjects, and his dedication to truth as he saw it, it is a wonder that he was able to obtain any position at all in a university. For example, in 1908, in a lecture to a socialist group, he made some remarks which offended religious and conservative groups and was sent to prison for two months.

In 1916 he retired from Lund University and continued his work in economics at home. He was a friend of the working-class movements, but did not hesitate to criticize their theories and actions when he believed them to be wrong. In some respects he was like Doctor Stockmann in Ibsen's *An Enemy of the People.* Wicksell died in 1926 at the age of seventy-four, leaving behind him a long list of books that were later generally acknowledged to have broken new ground in the fields of value, money, and interest. He was the recipient of many honors and awards, including an honorary membership in the American Economic Association.

Wicksell began his serious writings in economics with a book called *Value, Capital and Rent,* which he published in 1893, and with his *Studies in Finance Theory,* which appeared in 1896. His style of writing is quite lucid, although his mathematical training is evident in the somewhat terse and formal sentence structure. Later books included *Interest and Prices* (1898) and *Lectures in Political Economy,* translated into English in two volumes, *General Theory* (1934) and *Money and Credit* (1935).

Wicksell was concerned with a theory of output as a unified whole. Starting from the premise that the price of a good is determined by the interaction of those who want it (demand) and those who have it (supply), he asked, What causes the price to rise? One answer states that prices rise when the demand increases relative to the supply. However, Wicksell believed that another answer could be found in the fact that, at times, all prices—that is, the general price level—also rise. This was in effect a refutation of "Say's law," which stated that supply creates its own demand. It also was an attempt to refute the then accepted idea that the theory of relative prices and the theory of money were two entirely separate concepts. Wicksell's work in this area led, much later, to a unified theory.

Although Wicksell was not the originator of the theory of marginal productivity, his treatment and further refinements of the marginal principle mark him as a pioneer in its development. Wicksell regarded the marginal principle as applicable to all facets of the modern economy and closely related to exchange production, distribution, and capital. Furthermore, he saw its usefulness in all types of economies, including individualistic and collective societies. For example, in dealing with the problems of exchange, Wicksell utilized the concept of "marginal utility," which refers to the added amount of satisfaction that is derived from an additional (or the last) unit of a good. Following Adam Smith, he accepts the idea that water has high value in use but little value in exchange, while diamonds have little value in use but high value in exchange. Wicksell was not content to stop at that point. Instead, he shows that for a buyer, value in exchange cannot be larger than value in use, while for a seller, value in exchange cannot be lower than value in use. The point Wicksell made was that the same commodity can have a different degree of usefulness for different individuals, and therefore the relationship of values in use at any one time can "be greater or less than the relative exchange values for one or other of the exchanging parties respectively." The logical conclusion of this idea was that the actual determination of the exchange value of a good is the amount of utility it possesses at the exact time the trade is made, without reference as to whether the utility it has for the trading parties is related to a present or future need. With his new formulation Wicksell was able to break away from the ancient concept that what one individual gained in an exchange, the other lost. Instead, he in effect demonstrated that it was possible for both to be gainers.

Thus, the "marginal utility of a commodity" combines two things: the least important need which is satisfied by obtaining the good, and the most important need, which will not be satisfied if smaller amounts of the good are obtained. In Wicksell's words, "Marginal utility becomes the degree of utility at which consumption of a commodity must cease precisely because of its *scarcity*." In a free society operating under competitive forces, each person will attempt to limit his demand for the goods of others, and regulate his supply of his own goods in such a way that the marginal utility of all goods for him will be proportional to its price, or stated in another way, the marginal utility of all goods is the same for this individual.

At the time Wicksell propounded these ideas they were original and a genuine contribution to the field of economics. Today we recognize that other forces enter into trade relationships, such as goodwill, altruism, philanthropy, and governmental considerations. Further, we know that free competition is rarely achieved, thus creating additional obstacles in exchange activities. However, as an approximation of a sound approach to the basic explanation of the formulation of prices in the market, Wicksell's theories remain unequaled.

Another outstanding contribution made by Wicksell, and one that was later developed and extended by the great John Maynard, Lord Keynes, centered around the nature of money and interest and their effects on general economic equilibrium.

Wicksell was the first to clearly state that there was a direct, close relationship between money and the demand and supply of goods. Money itself was both a quantity and a "commodity" as well as a store of value. Thus, at a given price level there existed a need for people to hold as a "cash balance" a given amount of money. If serious disequilibrium developed as a result of too much demand or supply, these dislocations could remain indefinitely if costs or technology changed during the period in question. Wicksell's solution to cure this situation was greater control over the supply of money, including the use of discount rates and open-market operations, devices currently employed by the Federal Reserve System of the United States.

In discussing interest, Wicksell believed there was a "normal" rate of interest to be found in the market place. This rate is such that there is no reason for the general price level to change from its present position. However, if the "money" rate of interest (the rate charged by the banks) is lower than the "normal" rate, prices will tend to rise, and conversely, if the "money" rate of interest is higher than the "normal" rate, prices will tend to fall. He was concerned that stability of prices be maintained, but stated that any "permanent discrepancy between the actual rate" and the "normal" rate would have a "progressive and cumulative influence on prices." The value of this analysis was that henceforth the natural, or actual, rate of interest and the money rate of interest would not be thought of as being the same thing. Instead, the money rate of interest now would be viewed as a separate and distinct variable which would have to be watched. Thus, the effects of money on prices were broadened to include the supply of credit, the tendency of people to save, and the interest rates charged by banks.

Later in life, Wicksell urged a complete revision of the Swedish system of taxation. He favored a progressive income tax in place of taxes on consumption, and urged universal suffrage as a means to achieve it. He opposed monopolies and thought that inherited property should be taxed heavily.

In recent years, Wicksell's ideas have been criticized because they apparently placed too much reliance on the money mechanism. Yet he is considered one of the really great thinkers in the field of modern economics, and his works and ideas are still influential in England, Germany, Italy, and Japan, as well as in the United States. In the Scandinavian countries, of course, his influence was tremendous, both in governmental circles and in the universities. Recently an author praised Wicksell for his many seminal ideas by stating that the work of the Swedish school was "the most remarkably sustained intellectual performance in any of the social sciences in recent decades."

FURTHER READING

Uhr, Carl G. *Economic Doctrines of Knut Wicksell.*
Wicksell, Knut. *Selected Papers on Economic Theory.*

——Sigmund Freud——

[1856–1939]

THE MEDICAL WORLD was rocked to its very foundations during the last decade of the nineteenth century by a
young instructor of neurology at the University of Vienna,
Sigmund Freud. He had the temerity to claim that many
symptoms of mental illness and disturbed personality could be
traced back to suppressed memories of childhood experiences.
He felt that mental disturbances were similar to purely physical maladies in that both could be treated by getting to their
causes. This young upsetter of tradition believed that the vic-
tims of hysteria and hysterical paralysis were not to be treated
with contempt as malingerers just because some of them
seemed to develop and lose their symptoms with dramatic
suddenness on occasion. His greatest medical and social heresy
was to claim that the sex impulse existed in infants—in other
words, long before physical maturity had occurred—and that
its misdirection could be the principal cause of later mental
disturbances. Yet Sigmund Freud's theories about human behavior have deeply influenced social and philosophical trends
in our times.

Sigmund Freud, the oldest of the seven children of Jakob
and Amalia Freud, was born in Freiberg, Moravia, on May 6,
1856. Amalia was the second wife of Jakob Freud, being
twenty years his junior. This resulted in Jakob's children by
his first wife being older than their stepmother. Thus one of
Sigmund's playmates was his own nephew, who was a year
his senior. When Sigmund was four years old, his parents sold
their small textile business and moved to Vienna, where he
remained until he was forced to flee from the Nazis in 1938
because he was born of Jewish parents.

Sigmund Freud could easily have been lost to the scientific

and philosophical worlds, for he had great difficulty in select-
ing a vocation. He was interested in many diverse areas of
learning as a young student, including philosophy and the history of culture. Young Freud even translated one volume of
the German edition of John Stuart Mill's collected works. Although he had a great liking for and keen interest in chemistry, Freud shifted his later efforts into the fields of physiology
and anatomy, in which he did some original research work.
With these early aptitudes and interests Freud finally chose
the study of medicine, as many famous physiologists had done
previously.

This choice might seem strange, as Freud subsequently
wrote, with his customary frankness, in an autobiographical
sketch: "Neither in my youth nor later was I able to detect in
myself any particular fondness for the position or work of a
doctor." Significantly, he adds, "I was rather, spurred on by a
sort of itch for knowledge, which concerned human relationships far more than the data of natural science." Since the
University of Vienna had no department of "human relationships" and there was the necessity of earning a livelihood, Sigmund Freud finally secured his degree of Doctor of Medicine
in 1881 at the age of twenty-five.

At this point in the history of medicine, the medical profession was firmly convinced that all mental disorders were the
result of unhealthy changes in the nervous system. Thus study
and research in psychology was conducted exclusively in the
anatomical and physiological laboratories of the various universities. Freud spent the next few years in anatomical and
physiological research, both with the famous E. W. von
Brücke, and later with T. H. Meynert, a leading authority on
the anatomy of the brain. Each of these experts was quick to
recognize his protégé's skill and talents for research and wanted him for a permanent collaborator. Yet he was compelled to
refuse them, solely for economic reasons, particularly after he
had decided to get married. Instead he secured an appointment as an instructor in neurology at the University of Vienna
and began his medical practice as a neurologist.

Freud's future was now both bright and secure; he could
look forward to becoming a professor in due time and to increasing his private practice. For most of his colleagues this
happy result would be a certainty, but one could never be
sure when it came to such an independent soul as Sigmund

Freud. Yet all that was required of him was to follow the example of his older colleagues. At this time the leading neurologists were anxious to conceal from themselves, their patients, and their associates that the treatment of psychogenic symptoms by measures designed to reverse unhealthy changes in the nervous system was practically useless.

Shortly thereafter, in 1885, Freud took a leave from the University to observe and study with a French neurologist, Jean Martin Charcot, who was experimenting with the use of hypnotism in the treatment of some mental disorders. Charcot so impressed Freud that he later named his first son Jean Martin—a most unusual Austrian name! On Freud's return to the University, he dutifully reported on what he had observed firsthand in Paris. At first he was chided by his colleagues for having been taken in by a hoaxer. When Freud refused to admit that his observations were in error and held to his original opinions, he completely destroyed his assured future and economic security. Thus the dissenter of the University of Vienna never rose any higher than assistant professor and even this promotion occurred seventeen years later, and only through the intervention of a well-to-do lady patient. When the scientific world was according Sigmund Freud his well-merited acclaim more than a quarter of a century later, the medical people at the University still could not fully accept him.

Freud was so impressed with what he had observed in Paris that he began to treat some of his own patients with hypnotic suggestions. It was his good fortune to find a potential collaborator in Josef Breuer, a successful Viennese physician and thinker who had also had an extraordinary medical experience—he had helped cure one of his patients of the symptoms of hysteria by getting her to remember the circumstances of their origin and to express while still under hypnosis the emotions accompanying them. Breuer and Freud published their observations and conclusions in 1895 in *Studies in Hysteria*, in which their "cathartic" method of treatment was first announced to the medical world. This was the direct forerunner of what later became known as "psychoanalysis."

Sigmund Freud was not completely satisfied with this radical innovation and chose to go much further than Breuer by completely dropping hypnosis as a tool and replacing it with "free association." This change better enables the therapist to isolate and study the phenomena of "resistance" (in which the patient tries to hide unpleasant experiences of the past) and "transference" (the patient's emotional ties with his analyst).

Freud proceeded to develop new theories, terminology, and techniques. He conceived of the "id" as a vast primordial reservoir of energy derived from the two primary life and death instincts and comprised of the crude appetites and impulses, loves, and hates, especially those connected with what he termed the "Oedipus complex" (the infant's craving for the exclusive possession of the parent of the other sex). The "ego" is a part of the id. It works toward the survival of the individual, and hence it tends to repress the antisocial impulses of the id which are at variance with so-called civilized behavior. As the child matures, he develops a "superego" (conscience) which determines what is acceptable to the ego and what must be repressed.

If the ego, poised between the id and the superego, maintains the equilibrium, all is well; but should the ego throw its weight on either side, unbalancing the scale, neurosis develops. The urges of the unconscious id, repressed, create powerful disturbances and reassert themselves by appearing in symbolic disguise, resulting in a variety of neurotic symptoms.

Freud distinguished between hunger and love as representing instincts that aim at self-preservation and reproduction of the species, respectively. Thus he called the force by which the sexual instinct is represented in the mind of an individual "libido" (sexual longing). Much of his research and subsequent publications dealt with the interpretations of dream symbolisms, forgetting, the unconscious, sublimation, and slips of speech that uncover repressed wishes (often called Freudian slips). He believed that the latter originate during infancy with the undirected sexual experiences, which cannot be expressed because of social taboos. Thus they must be repressed into the unconscious. Through the use of psychoanalytic techniques in the hands of a highly skilled therapist, these repressed feelings can be released by giving the patient insight into their true nature.

In 1911, two of Freud's closest colleagues, Alfred Adler and Carl Gustav Jung, dissociated themselves from Freud's school of analysis. This split was largely the result of their strong disagreement with its sexual conception of motivation. They then proceeded to develop their own systems of psychology. In spite of these major defections and the original opposition of conservative medical authorities over the greater part of two decades, Freud's pioneering work in psychoanalysis is now widely respected. Thanks to this great original thinker, who refused to accept what he knew to be incorrect and untrue in the field of neurology, medical scientists and those interested in human behavior now have a much greater understanding of normal and abnormal behavior.

FURTHER READING

Costigan, Giovanni. *Sigmund Freud*.
Freud, Martin. *Sigmund Freud: Man and Father*.
Jones, Ernest. *The Life and Work of Sigmund Freud*.
Zweig, Stefan. *Mental Healers*.

——Thorstein Bunde Veblen——
[1857–1929]

THE CAVERNOUS LECTURE HALL at Stanford University was empty except for Professor Thorstein Veblen and his three students. The professor seemed unperturbed, however, as he droned on in his colorless fashion. After all, his thesis seminar had only *one* student in it, so that the three hardy souls in his course on economic factors in civilization were practically a crowd. The story was the same at his previous post at the University of Chicago, and it would be the same at the University of Missouri and wherever else Veblen would travel in the years to come. Students who had heard of his fame registered for his classes in substantial numbers, but after one or two bewildering lectures they usually dropped the course. It was common knowledge that as a teacher Thorstein Veblen was an unqualified failure.

Occasionally, however, a listening student would see the glorious rainbow that lay behind the fog of Veblen's language. Occasionally the polysyllabic words, the tremendous erudition, the corrosive irony, the stinging wit, and the dazzling intellect would illuminate the pageant of economic history, and the perceptive student would be rewarded for his patience.

Veblen did not seem hurt by his lack of success as a teacher, or if he did, he did not show it. The careful control of emotion was a trait he had inherited from his father, a Norwegian immigrant who lived as a farmer in this country but who possessed the first-rate mind of a true intellectual. In 1857, Thorstein was born on a Wisconsin farm, and he lived there with his eight bilingual brothers and sisters in an atmosphere that encouraged scholarship. The pioneer life was rugged and austere, but his mother taught him Icelandic lore and read to him from the Norwegian sagas; his father provided the books as well as the encouragement of the reading habit.

By the time young Veblen was ready to enter Carleton College Academy in Minnesota, it was obvious to those who knew him that he was lazy, irreverent, rebellious, and brilliant. His teachers quickly labeled him as a misfit, but they were wary of tilting with the sharp-tongued farm boy. Any student who chose to speak on "A Plea for Cannibalism" to a class of prospective Lutheran missionaries was too much for the ordinary professor to cope with.

After graduation he transferred to Yale, obtaining his Ph.D. there in 1884. A man with a doctorate from Yale should have had little trouble in securing employment, but such was not the case with Veblen. There were job interviews, of course. But the deans with whom he spoke were not eager to hire an unkempt young philosopher who stared at them with cold, piercing eyes and who confessed to being an agnostic. His icy remoteness made the deans uncomfortable, and his Norwegian reserve was taken as a sign of disrespect by some men to whom protocol and respect were important.

Without a job, Veblen returned to Minnesota and for a period of seven years practically withdrew from the world of men. Far from being wasted years, they were the profitable years of self-education and of quiet reflection. He read everything he could find—philosophy, history, economics, politics, psychology, fiction, anthropology, mail-order catalogues, poetry, hymnbooks, everything. Furthermore, what he read, he remembered. In the ensuing years, his lectures, essays, and books would reflect the riches that his mind had absorbed during those seven years of retirement and contemplation.

One of the ironic features of Veblen's life was the attraction he held for women. It was difficult for other men to see why any woman might become enamored of this introvert with the scraggly beard who was as unconscious of his personal appearance as he was about the gallantries ascribed to wooing a woman. But love him they did! In 1888, Veblen married one of the girls who had pursued him most energetically, the beautiful Ellen Rolfe, a college president's niece. Ellen's relatives tried to help Veblen get a teaching position, but they were subsequently repelled by his lack of religious faith, his aloofness, and his disdain for material wealth.

The year 1891 was one of decision for Thorstein Veblen. He turned from philosophy to economics, and attended Cornell University as a teaching fellow. When the new University of Chicago hired the head of Cornell's economics department, Veblen went along with him. It was there in the exciting and bustling Windy City that Veblen began to shine. Economists read his articles and were astounded by the author's insights and his virtuosity. Although his style tended to be obscure at times, requiring the utmost concentration, it was emblazoned with references to literature, philosophy, mythology, and history. Reading Veblen's essays in the scholarly journals was a rich experience, and the professionals looked forward to his first book.

In the final year of the nineteenth century, Veblen's book did appear. It was *The Theory of the Leisure Class,* a landmark in economic history and, surprisingly enough, an appealing book for the intelligent layman. Veblen's work was widely discussed; to be ignorant of its thesis was unthinkable.

What kind of book had the eccentric Norwegian written? Some saw it as an acidulous attack on the aristocratic class, a corrosive analysis of the shenanigans of the wealthy. Others viewed it as a thoughtful indictment of our social order.

The Theory of the Leisure Class made the following major points:

1. The rich are primarily concerned with wasteful expenditures in order to impress others with their material wealth. They busy themselves with "conspicuous consumption."

2. The activities of the moneyed class are given society's stamp of approval. Labor, by contrast, is regarded as undignified, even by the people who perform it.

3. Today's leisure classes are no different from the predatory feudal lords of past centuries. Their purpose is to seize the goods that have been produced by the blood and sweat of others.

The conservatives looked at Veblen with suspicion, pointing to the similarities between his theories and those of Karl Marx. Both men criticized the private ownership that characterized the capitalistic system. Both men declared that capitalism and war went hand in hand. It remained for Veblen to underscore the key difference in their philosophies—Veblen denied that the struggle between capital and labor was inevitable. The reason we will not have a revolution in America, he argued, is that the lower classes do not want to overthrow their managers, but to join them. According to one economist, in Veblen's explanation "lies the kernel of a theory of social stability."

Veblen's next book, *The Theory of Business Enterprise*, published in 1904, was a howitzer blast against the capitalists. He contradicted the accepted belief that capitalists were responsible for our economic progress. On the contrary, Veblen claimed, the men of wealth had little interest in the production of our factories; in fact, the capitalists were the chief saboteurs of the system. Wheeling and dealing in dummy corporations, holding companies, power grabs, stock swindles, mergers, cartels, and market manipulations occupy all the creative energies of the capitalists, leaving them bored by the mundane production of goods.

Veblen forecast the eventual demise of these parasitical robber barons, and he predicted that they would be replaced by a technocracy in which an elite group of engineers would operate the factories. This new, antiseptic army of technocrats would bring science, efficiency, and dedication to their work, unlike the absentee owners, whose sole concern was self-aggrandizement.

Other books by Veblen found appreciative audiences. In *The Higher Learning in America* (1918), Veblen was caustic in his appraisal of conservative college officials who lacked the boldness, courage, and resourcefulness of American explorers, pioneers, and inventors. College administrators, according to Veblen, were blinded by their fund-raising activities and by the need to field good football teams. As a result, education was suffering.

In *The Instinct of Workmanship* (1914), Veblen mourned the loss of the artisan's pride in his work, a pride whose origins could be traced back to the days of the caveman. The businessman's drive for "bigness" and for the accumulation of wealth, said Veblen, leaves no place for pride in workmanship because the emphasis is on quantity rather than on quality.

Although Thorstein Veblen's star was at its height, his personal problems were painful. The authorities at the University of Chicago, unhappy to learn of some difficulties in his personal affairs, dismissed him. The president of Stanford University, however, was eager to have a "name" professor, and Veblen accepted his gracious offer to teach in California. But it was no different at Stanford—he alienated the faculty, gave every student the same passing grade, was a hopeless lecturer, and his personal difficulties continued. After three years his contract was abruptly terminated.

The next stop for the wandering professor was the University of Missouri. By this time the long-suffering Ellen Rolfe had divorced Veblen, and he had married a divorcee with two children. Their relationship was a disastrous one, punctuated by a near scandal. His second wife eventually went insane and had to be institutionalized.

Veblen's remaining years were downhill. A frustrating stay in Washington, D.C., during the First World War was terminated at the government's request. The officials had rejected most of his suggestions, and they had suppressed others. Disgusted with what he regarded as shabby treatment, Veblen then came to New York to edit the *Journal of Political Economy* and *Dial* Magazine, and to lecture at the New School for Social Research. These ventures were very disappointing for Veblen. Yet his work had a profound influence on a new group of economists who were developing an "institutional approach" to economics, a school of economics that taught that "group behavior," not price, should be the central concern of economics. This conception of economics was the basis of Franklin D. Roosevelt's New Deal of the 1930's.

Old, rumpled, and ill, Veblen returned to the warmth of California and a rustic setting, which he had grown to like. His spare frame, clad in rough work clothes, could be seen by his neighbors as he shuffled in and out of his cabin. Curiosity-seekers spied mounds of dirty dishes lying in his sink, the unmade bed, and a pyramid of packing cases filled with his precious books. There, in 1929, Thorstein Veblen died. Ironically, it was the same year in which many of the financiers whom he had attacked took their lives when the stock market collapsed.

Even in death the maverick economist sought to isolate himself from the world. His will specified that there be no tombstone, obituary, or tablet for his cremated body. Veblen also requested that no pictures of him be circulated, that no biographies be written, and that all traces of his existence be blotted from the record of history.

But the contribution of Thorstein Bunde Veblen to the history of our times was too large to be erased by the whim of a bitter man. Lewis Mumford accurately described him as "one of the half-dozen important figures in scholarship that America produced since the Civil War . . . a stick of dynamite wrapped up . . . to look like a stick of candy."

FURTHER READING

Dowd, Douglas. *Thorstein Veblen.*
Riesman, David. *Thorstein Veblen.*
Rosenberg, Bernard. *Thorstein Veblen.*

——— John A. Hobson ———

[1858–1940]

JOHN A. HOBSON has been called the "intellectual godfather of the British Labour party" because so many of its aims and programs were inspired by his long list of writings. During his lifetime, Hobson published more than fifty books in which he consistently stressed the pressing need for social re-

forms in the England of his day. Unlike most critics and dissenters, who merely attacked existing institutions, Hobson
offered a new body of economic theory which he hoped would
have a practical impact on public policy. In today's economic
terminology, Hobson would be called a "welfare" economist,
one who wishes to harness the laws of economics for human
welfare rather than for the profits of the entrepreneur.

Hobson was born in Derby, England, into an upper-middle-
class family. He received a good education in the Derby
School, and later at Oxford University, where he studied the
classics. After completing his degree at Oxford in 1880, he
spent the next eight years teaching classical languages in well-
known English boys' schools, such as Exeter and Faversham.
Apparently he was not completely satisfied teaching Latin and
Greek to these boys; for in 1887 he accepted an assignment as
an extension lecturer in the workers' schools to teach English
and economics.

Up to this period, Hobson had not given any evidence of
being seriously concerned with the nature of the social order.
His entire existence favored a complacent acceptance of the
existing system. His family was well-to-do, and, in his background, order, respectability, status, and the rights of the
wealthy were taken for granted. The wretched conditions of
the poor were held to be the result of their own unwillingness
to work and provide for their families. Only at Oxford had
Hobson begun to feel that somehow the widespread misery
of the working classes was wrong and not of their own doing.

A good part of this uneasiness in Hobson's thinking was due
to the interest in reforming society which was generated by
the lectures of John Ruskin and Arnold Toynbee (uncle of the
contemporary historian) at Oxford. Utilizing moral earnestness
and the historical approach, they made it very clear that the
multiplying social evils of the society were a direct result of
England's industrial expansion, and that the increasing discrepancy between the growing wealth of the empire and the
continuing misery of the people was not going to be solved
by a *laissez faire* policy. Hobson was also influenced by Henry
George's *Progress and Poverty*, in which George attacked the
privileges enjoyed by landed property owners in the United
States. Unfortunately, like George, Hobson alienated the
academic powers by attacking the status quo, and thereafter,
also like George, was never able to obtain a formal academic

position. Hobson decided to devote himself to the economic
education of the working classes, and, because he was quite
disturbed at the tremendous amount of economic inequality
that he saw before him, to attempt to reshape the system of
economic organization in order to promote social welfare.

He was not alone in devoting his efforts to the alleviation
of the poor and downtrodden. Many in his generation, including the Fabians and the radical liberals, were also active in
the struggle. However, Hobson was the only one who sought
the solution to the problem in the realm of economic theory.
With this in mind he published his first book, *The Physiology
of Industry* (1889), in which he and his coauthor, A. F. Mum-
mery, first introduced the heresy that thrift and saving were
no great social virtues. In fact, they said that too much saving
would result in a serious decline in purchasing power, sure to
cause increased unemployment.

Other ideas in this work dealt with the relationship of investment, demand, and production in the various sectors of
the economy, and with the importance of inventories in periods of economic crises. Although these ideas are fully recognized and accepted by economists today, they were about half
a century ahead of their time, and were received with hostility
by the professional economists of the period. Hobson was
simply saying that too much savings and capital increase in-
variably lead to an accumulation of inventories, which current demand cannot absorb in time to prevent a rise in
unemployment. Even when John Maynard Keynes introduced
similar concepts in the 1930's, he was credited with having
created the "Keynesian revolution" in economic thinking. As
a result, shortly after Hobson's book appeared, the London
Extension Board refused to allow him to continue teaching
economics in the extension lectures, and an invitation to address the Charity Organization Society was withdrawn. Assisted by an independent income, Hobson then became a
journalist, writing books, pamphlets, articles, and newspaper
stories on a wide range of subjects. In addition, he traveled
extensively, visiting South Africa, the United States, and
Canada, where he had the opportunity to interview such leading world figures as Smuts, Kruger, and Rhodes, and to speak
to such literary figures as Lincoln Steffens, Henry Lloyd, and
E. A. Ross. He thus was able to reach a much wider audience
than most of the professional economists who criticized his

work. During the last forty years of his life, Hobson, a frail and mild-mannered man, constantly concerned with the condition of his health, turned out scores of pamphlets and hundreds of newspaper and journal articles, as well as fifty-odd books. When he died in 1940, the *London Times* paid homage to his modern ideas and lamented the fact that his contemporaries had failed to recognize his value.

Starting with the underlying premise, based on his years of personal observation, that the existing social and economic institutions did not automatically guarantee human well-being, Hobson traced the historical development of the capitalist system to try to determine why this was so. In his work *The Evolution of Modern Capitalism* (1894), which was to become a standard work for students of economic history, Hobson developed the theme that modern technological methods and machinery had succeeded in increasing productivity and the importance of the capitalist but that the position of the worker had been completely overlooked. The once independent and self-sufficient individual had been separated from the tools of production and had become totally dependent on the capitalist for survival. Unlike other economists and writers of the period, Hobson saw his function as including a prescription of what "ought to be," not only as describing "what is."

In his *Work and Wealth: A Human Valuation* (1914), Hobson treated the processes of producing and utilizing goods and services in a modern industrial economy from the viewpoint of human welfare. In effect he was saying, "Let us see what human costs are incurred in the production of goods." Then he would analyze the utility of these goods, including the satisfaction that could be derived from them, and would weigh the costs against the utility, to see how the balance came out. Human costs are defined as the sacrifices involved in the work of the artist, scientist, inventor, professional, entrepreneur, industrial manager, and manual worker. The landowner is not included because he is not undergoing any human cost when he rents out his property.

In evaluating these categories, Hobson found that the work of the artist, scientist, and inventor, and the professional and managerial classes produced more utility and satisfaction than their work cost. This work, including the joy of discovery or creation, was so pleasurable, varied, and interesting that no

outside motivation or incentive was required to further stimulate them. All they really need is the cost of their upkeep.
However, the situation of the manual worker was quite different. He was constantly subjected to excessive muscular
and nervous strain and fatigue. Hobson made this clear by
stating that "machine tending at a high pace, for a long working day is in itself the most 'costly' type of labor, and, in so
far as a machine controls the sort and pace of work done by a
human being, these costs accumulate." In other words, Hobson's thesis was that of all the activities that economists of his
day lumped under the heading of labor, those that revolved
around the artistic, scientific, managerial, or planning side of
industry were relatively costless, while the activities of the
greatest majority of workers, who actually carried out the
plans and produced the goods, were very costly and involved
great strain. Heavy human costs were also involved in unemployment, child labor, and the labor of older people and
women, in terms of damage to their health or disruption of
their homes.

Hobson then turned his attention to savings. Here again he
calculated the human costs involved in saving according to
the types of people who did it. A considerable portion of the
nation's saving was done by people with large incomes or by
corporations with surplus funds. This type of saving was
largely automatic and hardly incurred any human costs because there was no sacrifice involved. Savings accumulated by
the comfortable middle classes were rationally planned with
due regard to present and future benefits. In fact, as long as
their present needs were satisfied, savings for the middle
classes represented an increase in future utility and security.
The situation of the poorer classes was quite different. Here
savings for the future could only be accomplished by stinting
on current necessities and comforts. Very likely it is done at
the expense of the worker's children, in the sense that the
savings could be used to provide better medical care and education for them in the present. Not satisfying present needs in
order to save meant that the human costs of this type of
saving were very high. Hobson believed this type of saving to
be socially wasteful because "it is literally a coining of human
life into instrumental capital," and under a sounder social
structure would be unnecessary.

The last aspect of human welfare analyzed by Hobson deals

with the utilities of consumption. He found that although consumption is the final use to which all economic activity is directed, economists tended to neglect it in favor of the study of production and exchange. Hobson was greatly disturbed by what he observed in this area. There are three factors in the standard of consumption: the first factor is physical needs; the second factor is industrial needs, by which is meant the special requirements related to a person's work; and the third factor is conventional needs. Many of the conventional needs are without human value because they represent human vanity, extravagance, waste, and ostentation.

Furthermore, Hobson believed that the economy was organized not to satisfy socially desirable wants but only those wants that could be satisfied at a profit. Moreover, due to the unequal distribution of wealth, the standards of consumption were further debased. The wealthier classes, recipients of an "unproductive surplus," consumed without regard to their social responsibilities. It may be noted that Thorstein Veblen also criticized the upper classes for their "conspicuous consumption" patterns. Other classes in society tended to imitate the idle rich and thus contributed to the production and use of harmful or undesirable goods. Hobson saw the use of surplus funds, which could have served to improve standards of living for all, being poured into drink, tobacco, sport, sham culture, and useless display. To Hobson this meant that, "from the standpoint of pecuniary expenditure, the misdirection of the surplus income into empty or depraved modes of recreation, culture, religion and charity is the largest of all economic wastes." Consumption of goods according to this pattern involves very large human costs.

To overcome this misdirection of income, which prevented a large segment of the population from obtaining the essentials of a satisfactory life, Hobson proposed a "human law of distribution," which would try to eliminate all the unnecessary human costs in the then-current method of distribution, and would increase human utilities by a more systematic consideration of the needs of individuals and society. Although his proposals called for "distribution according to needs," the reduction of excessive incomes, and the implementation of equality of opportunity, Hobson did not consider them part of communist doctrines. Instead of stressing the conflict inherent in society, Hobson called for two types of reform that would emphasize cooperative elements in the social structure. The first called for creating, through the educational process, a new understanding of the social nature of industry and its dependence on social harmony. The second reform was "the substitution of direct social control for the private, profit-seeking motive"; Hobson believed that social and economic reconstruction could lead to more efficiency, elimination of profiteering, higher wages, and the required conditions leading to a "good life."

Hobson's views can be said to be a mixture of freedom and controls, very much like the direction in which England has moved since the end of the Second World War. It is a kind of modified socialism in which heavy taxation of "unproductive surpluses" and "excessive income," plus the revenue obtained from certain nationalized industries are used to pay for better educational facilities, housing, parks and playgrounds, improved transportation, and universal low-cost medical attention.

In other parts of the world as well, the claims of labor and labor groups are receiving more attention along the lines Hobson advocated. For example, he was among the first to point out, through his scale of "human costs," the damage to wage earners caused by increased standardization, monotony, loss of initiative, and regimentation, as well as by irregularity and uncertainty of income. Hobson was also insistent in his demand that labor not be regarded as simply a commodity to be bought and sold. Instead, he felt that wages and salaries should be regulated "on the basis of the human needs of a family living in a civilized country." To this end he advocated the establishment of a legal "living wage," the limitation of the hours of work, and the creation of old-age pensions as a matter of right for the workers.

Hobson was a firm believer in the power of mankind to shape its own destiny and to achieve the "great society" in which all divergent interests will harmonize for the benefit of the whole. At the same time he was anxious to allow the greatest possible expression of the individual personality. The community must not be allowed to displace the individual from those areas in which he can develop fully by his own efforts. He constantly emphasized the underlying unity in the social structure. He was a social reformer who was able to suggest many practical concepts and ideas. In his analysis he

attacked the existing economic theorists and forced them to
acknowledge the barren nature of their science, since it failed
to give adequate consideration to the problems of human welfare. He made it quite clear that the "subject-matter of economics is human beings" and that their improved welfare has
the first claim on the thinking of all social scientists.

FURTHER READING

Seligman, Ben B. *Main Currents in Modern Economics.*

————Henri Louis Bergson————
[1859–1941]

HENRI BERGSON'S LIFE WAS, for the most part, un-
marked by dramatic episodes. Extremely talented as a young
man, he was very successful both in school and in his career
in philosophy. He moved from one university to another, always advancing, and his lectures and books were sensationally
successful for philosophical works. Indeed, his name had become known over the whole intellectual world before he retired in 1921. He was awarded the Nobel Prize for Literature
in 1927 when in retirement and suffering from chronic illness.
As philosophical interests shifted, his popularity began to
wane, but in 1941 he was suddenly recalled to the public
mind. When the Vichy government promulgated laws remov-
ing Jews from educational positions and requiring them to
register, it offered Bergson, then a venerable and venerated intellectual figure, exemption from these laws. He refused the
offer and voluntarily suffered these indignities during the last
days of his life.

Bergson is the one continental European philosopher of the
nineteenth and twentieth centuries to whom the greatest

American philosophers of the twentieth century admit indebtedness. James, Dewey, and Whitehead all paid respect to Bergson, pointing to him as the first man to see how the problems of philosophy had to be approached in our time. Bergson had great popularity, both among philosophers and among the literate public in the early part of the century, but this popularity has since declined, especially among professional philosophers. The source of both his reputation and its decline is found in his view of science and its place in understanding the world.

Recognizing the usefulness of science for making predictions and for dealing with practical problems, Bergson questioned the completeness and accuracy of its grasp of reality. Like Whitehead after him, he saw the basic flaw in the scientific apprehension of reality to be its use of abstractions. In his *Introduction to Metaphysics* (1903), he pointed out that science necessarily uses abstractions, since every concept is an abstraction and since science strives to understand the world by means of its concepts. But reality is not abstract; it is concrete. In opposition to the positivistic view that the scientific understanding is the only true understanding, he claimed that it was possible for human beings to grasp reality in all its concreteness. This power of the mind to grasp reality as it is, by a kind of intellectual empathy, he called "intuition." Metaphysics, for him, was the "science" which uses intuition. While all men have this power of intuition to some extent, in artists it is highly developed. It tends to atrophy to the extent that man deals with reality in terms of abstractions, so that it is likely to be weakest in scientists.

One basic limitation of intuition as a means of apprehending reality is that its results cannot be reported. Any account of an intuition would have to be formulated by means of abstractions. The concrete whole would have to be reduced to those few aspects of itself that can be grasped by concepts. Thus in one sense there are no metaphysical results; indeed, he described metaphysics as "the science which claims to dispense with symbols." In this respect, art brings us closer to reality as it is, because art, by creating a concrete object, creates a situation in which the audience might grasp the intuition which was the artist's apprehension of reality.

The main characteristic of reality as we confront it in experience is the continuity of the flow of events through time, process, or flux. Bergson distinguished between real time and the abstraction "time" used by scientists. The latter is simply a one-dimensional movement, a line on a graph, or a variable t which can take on as values various specific numbers. The real time, from which this is an abstraction, is richer and more complex, yet it is something which every man experiences in his inner life as "duration" *(durée)*. A precise definition of duration is impossible; it refers to that which is immediately given in human consciousness.

The aim of science, Bergson said, "is to enlarge our influence over things." (By designating action as the purpose of scientific thought, he earned the praise of the pragmatists James and Dewey.) This aim is reached by the deliberate selection of certain aspects of the world as we experience it, substituting signs or symbols for them, and manipulating the signs by the use of mathematics. But, he continued, although this method has proved most fruitful in achieving one aim of science, mastery over nature, it has been a failure insofar as science has the coordinate aims of apprehending and understanding nature.

In *Creative Evolution* (1907) he said that "the intellect represents *becoming* as a series of *states,* each of which is homogeneous with itself and consequently does not change." Thus the scientific intellect misses both the continuity and the cumulative character of becoming, change, or evolution. To take the results of science as a final and complete account of the world is to understand the whole in terms of merely a preselected part. Bergson sought for metaphors and analogies to express his intuition. His best known is the one which compares the scientific account of the world to a motion picture. The motion picture gives the impression of movement by flashing on the screen a series of still pictures in rapid succession. In the same way science gives an account of motion in terms of a succession of unmoving states.

In applying his insight to other areas of man's experience, e.g., to life and society, Bergson produced some of his most influential ideas. The liberation of man from complete bondage to the products of his intellect means for him a liberation of the human spirit from bondage to the dead mechanism of a mechanically conceived universe. Evolution is important to him because it means freedom from the causal chain. Evolution is a creative process and creation is freedom.

In his *The Two Sources of Morality and Religion* (1932), he developed the moral and social implications of his approach. The religion and the morality of necessity are contrasted with the religion and morality of freedom. The former are dominated by the demand for conformity to law. The latter are oriented toward the imitation of a model of perfection. This distinction leads to the recognition of two types of societies, closed societies and open societies. All finite societies of men based on systems of law are closed societies and necessarily so. When humanity itself comes to be thought of as a society of beings working together creatively to realize ever and ever higher ideals, we shall have what may properly be called an open society.

The decline of Bergson's reputation has been concurrent with changes in science. What he said was relevant to the somewhat limited mechanistic concepts of nineteenth-century science. As science has evolved, his criticisms have become less pertinent. Yet John Dewey's remark in 1912 is still just: "No philosophic problem will ever exhibit just the same fact and aspect that it presented before Professor Bergson invited us to look at it in its connections with duration as a real and fundamental fact." Two currently strong movements in philosophy, phenomenology, and existentialism confirm Dewey's judgment in their debt to Bergson's attempt to come to grips with the immediacy of experience.

FURTHER READING

Kumar, Shiv K. *Bergson and the Stream of Consciousness Novel.*
Larrabee, Harold A., ed. *Selections from Bergson.*

─── John Dewey ───

[1859–1952]

ARTISTS OF CARTOON HUMOR are heavily indebted to John Dewey, the father of progressive education. They are fond of drawing school situations in which so-called Dewey techniques of modern instruction result in an Alice-in-Wonderland world of madness. In one such cartoon we see a teacher apologizing to a visiting school-board member for the unusual behavior of one of her students, a lad who is quietly reading a book. "You'll have to excuse him," she explains, "as he has only been with us for one week."

But the artists are really not to blame for poking fun at the progressive educational concepts of John Dewey. Long before they took pen in hand, his friends and disciples were doing an adequate job of distorting his theories so that they were ripe enough for satire. Few men in modern history have been so abused by their well-intended followers as John Dewey. Perhaps he is somewhat to blame, however, for he dealt with general principles which were vulnerable to misinterpretation when put into practice by zealots. Those responsible for translating Dewey's ideas into administrative realities often did in Dewey's name things which were not consistent with the great philosopher's doctrines. As a result, therefore, Dewey was a controversial figure throughout his lifetime, and the arguments continue even after his death.

Archibald Dewey was the proprietor of a general store in Burlington, Vermont, and it was there in 1859 that John Dewey was born. Mr. Dewey's dry Yankee wit was reflected in the sign he placed over the entrance to his store: HAMS AND CIGARS—SMOKED AND UNSMOKED. John inherited that homely cracker-barrel wit, and kept it for the entertainment of his intimate friends. His early school record was undistin-

guished, and it was not until his junior year at the University of
Vermont that John Dewey began to show that he had exceptional ability.

It was his interest in a physiology text by Thomas Henry
Huxley, a Darwinian, that awakened Dewey's intellectual
curiosity and set him searching for answers. He read widely
in the sciences before turning to philosophy to help himself
resolve the conflict between science and dogma. This was the
beginning of his interest in human behavior and social progress, as opposed to abstract metaphysics.

After his graduation in 1879, Dewey taught algebra, natural
science, and Latin at a small high school in South Oil City,
Pennsylvania. There some of his ideas about educational reform began to take shape. When the opportunity for a graduate fellowship at Johns Hopkins arose, Dewey took it with a
view toward concentrating on the psychology and philosophy
of education. For the next seventy years he was to travel that
road, becoming the most famous figure in twentieth-century
education.

Dewey's first book, *Psychology,* published in 1886, helped
him obtain an appointment to the philosophy department at
the University of Minnesota. Soon his articles in scholarly
journals stamped him as a rising young philosopher. The University of Michigan invited him to head their department, and
there he continued to add to his reputation until, in 1894, he
was brought to the University of Chicago to supervise the combined departments of psychology, philosophy, and education.
Since he had attained eminence in all three fields, he was the
ideal choice for this coveted position.

It was at Chicago that Dewey organized the famous Experimental or Laboratory School, called by Sidney Hook "the
most important experimental venture in the whole history of
American education." There Dewey revolutionized pedagogy,
turning his back on the classical, authoritarian methods and
instituting a curriculum based on experience as the ultimate
authority. The principles which guided him there shocked
many professional educators but they made sense to the thousands of fascinated observers who flocked to Chicago to take
the grand tour of Dewey's classrooms.

The highlights of Dewey's pedagogic creed, which were
preached in his writings and practiced at the Experimental
School, can be summed up briefly in ten basic points:

1. The only true education comes through the stimulation of the child's powers by the demands of the social system in which he finds himself.

2. The school is a *living* school building. Part of each child's day is spent in coping with subject matter under the direction of several teachers; the rest of the time is given over to physical activities, dramatizations, music, folk dancing, cooking, and socializing.

3. The school is run democratically. Each youngster is responsible to committees within which there are interaction and cooperation.

4. Subject matter is important, but it is only a means to achieve the primary objective—living. "Learning? Certainly, but living primarily," wrote Dewey.

5. Learning is individualized, with each student being encouraged to work up to his maximum.

6. The teacher is no longer solely responsible for maintaining discipline. Each member of the living school community disciplines himself and receives the respect due to him.

7. Through the new education the child develops the capacities to control his environment, not just adapt to it.

8. The inductive scientific method is the best one for teachers and pupils to pursue. Experimental science can be brought into play to help us solve our moral and social problems. Books are less important tools of learning than experiences and experiments.

9. We learn by doing things rather than talking about them. Knowledge, in order to have any lasting value, must be functional rather than conceptual.

10. The ideal lesson begins with a recognized problem, travels through experimentation and analysis to a homemade hypothesis, which enables the pupil not only to understand the world in which that problem arose but to "control and refashion it."

Book after book by John Dewey appeared in the ensuing years, and most of them were translated so that his influence was felt abroad as well. *How We Think, Art as Experience, Liberalism and Social Action, School and Society, Education and the Social Order, Democracy and Education*—all added to Dewey's stature and helped one school system after another to change its way of doing things.

From 1904 until his retirement in 1930 Dewey was a pro-

fessor of philosophy at Columbia University. During those
years he was in great demand as America's unofficial intellectual ambassador, visiting China, Japan, South Africa,
Mexico, Russia (where he praised the educational reforms of
Lenin and Trotsky), and Turkey (where he reorganized the
school system). He followed his own precepts by taking an
active part in civic movements and in trying to improve his
world. If one glances through the newspapers of the 1920's
and 1930's, he will find daily references to Dewey's activities.
He was organizing the Teachers' Guild, signing petitions for
prison reform, protesting the injustices in the Sacco-Vanzetti
case, helping to found the American Civil Liberties Union,
supporting the socialist Norman Thomas in his presidential
campaigns, warning the world about the dangerous growth of
fascism, and meeting with politicians who could aid education
in America.

Ironically, Dewey himself was a poor teacher. He would
enter the lecture hall and begin musing out loud about a
problem he had been facing. Irwin Edman, who took Dewey's
courses at Columbia, thought it miraculous "that so dull a
lecturer could have influenced so many students." Oliver
Wendell Holmes provided us with a memorable description
of Dewey's oral delivery: "So, methought, God would have
spoken had He been inarticulate, but keenly desirous to tell
you how it was."

Over a period of thirty-five years, Dewey wrote on the topic
of logic. His concepts of logical theory must be grappled with
if one is to understand his general philosophical position. In
a major work, *Logic, the Theory of Inquiry*, Dewey describes
the five-step process of problem-solving through inquiry:

1. *The indeterminate situation.* In a given situation, the
equilibrium between an organism and its environment may
become disturbed and indeterminate. In order to restore that
equilibrium, inquiry is introduced.

2. *The institution of a problem.* The inquirer institutes
the next step in the process when he becomes aware of the
indeterminateness of the situation and visualizes it as a problem requiring his attention.

3. *Setting up a hypothesis.* The inquirer observes the problem, senses the discord, and anticipates what will happen
when certain forces are brought to bear upon the disturbance.
The symbols with which he expresses his idea, or hypothesis,

become the conceptual elements in this fresh pattern of inquiry.

4. *Reasoning.* The deductive elaboration of the hypothesis then follows. In order for it to be successful, it must work in tandem with scientific experimentation and testing.

5. *The construction of judgment.* With this last phase, the inquiry is concluded as the equilibrium is restored. A situation which had become indeterminate is now rendered determinate by means of the solution of the problem.

In addition to education, logic, human nature, and dozens of other topics, Dewey was also interested in aesthetics. He believed that aesthetic experiences are not confined to the rarefied atmosphere of museums where select numbers are enraptured by works of art. As a matter of fact, Dewey thought that aesthetic experiences are unlikely under such conditions because of the isolation from ordinary human activities. A true aesthetic experience, the philosopher contended, is the one enjoyed by an intelligent workman who does a job well and finds pleasure in the process.

The aesthetic experience is a cooperative one, requiring an interaction between the spectator and the art product. In those situations where the interest of the spectator is sufficiently aroused to marry with the artist's interest, a communication is achieved which, in effect, is the highest form of an aesthetic experience. To pursue this line of reasoning is to admit that so-called "inferior" works of art can give rise to an aesthetic experience if the viewer is personally affected. However, truly great and enduring art has a way of establishing that rapport over a span of centuries and in different cultures, communicating with the effectiveness of a Shakespeare, a Rembrandt, or a Beethoven.

Dewey's writing style is involved and difficult. His sentences are tortuous and the rhythm of the prose is so unappealing that it takes complete concentration to follow it. Those who wade through his numerous books, however, find a consistent philosophy which has four major branches:

1. *Pragmatism.* An idea must be judged by how it works. All thinking is directed toward definite ends, and the truth of an idea lies in its practical effects. In his pragmatism, Dewey was of the school of William James. Dewey had no patience with philosophy that was lost in metaphysics. He

was not interested in "states of consciousness" but in improving human responses to the practical difficulties of life.

2. *Instrumentalism.* Ideas are battle plans that arise in response to a problem and then serve their purpose by solving the problem. Ideas are "instruments" in the reconstruction of experience.

3. *Radical empiricism.* Things *are* what we experience them to be. To ascertain the meanings of things, one must observe how they are depicted in experience.

4. *Experimentalism.* Ideas must be exposed to experimentation for verification. No matter how sure we are of a "fact," our certainty can always be altered by the new evidence that experiments and experiences can furnish.

Dewey lived his philosophy, and that accounts for his active participation in politics and world affairs. It was his belief that freedom lay in the exercise of man's will and in the cultivation of man's intelligence. It is not enough to be pure in heart if such innocent purity leads to inaction and blindness to environmental problems. There is no absolute good. The truly good man is the one who, regardless of his past errors, is now becoming better through an application of his intelligence and social awareness.

One cannot be a disciple of John Dewey's philosophy and at the same time retreat from the world into a parochialism that worships knowledge for knowledge's sake. According to Dewey, "The task of future philosophy is to clarify men's ideas as to the social and moral strifes of their own day. Its aim is to become, so far as is humanly possible, an organ for dealing with these conflicts."

It is too early, perhaps, to judge Dewey's full effect upon twentieth-century society, but historians, philosophers, social scientists, and many educators already regard him as one of the true earthshakers of our time. But others attribute most of the shortcomings in today's school systems to Dewey's pernicious influence. They claim that the schools began to decline when Dewey's "child-centered" philosophy replaced the traditional "subject-centered" curriculum.

Although there are frequent skirmishes in the war between the progressives and the traditionalists, it is apparent that Dewey's forces carry the day. New teachers are firmly steeped in the philosophy and techniques of progressive education for democratic living. The training has been scientific, as John

Dewey wanted it to be, with more scientific understanding of the learning process and of the child's nature and growth. Today's teachers have been making use of the scientific, inductive, democratic, and cooperative approaches to developing the whole child. In so doing, they are following Dewey's lead toward "a system of education that best recognizes the dignity and worth of all individuals, that allows every individual to develop to his fullest, and that teaches the virtues of democracy by establishing a democratic atmosphere."

On John Dewey's ninetieth birthday, admirers presented him with a gift of $90,000, which he turned over to his favorite educational projects. Three years later, in 1952, he succumbed to pneumonia after a brief illness. His voice was stilled, but its echoes continue to reverberate throughout our culture.

FURTHER READING

Brickman, William W., ed. *John Dewey's Impressions of Soviet Russia and the Revolutionary World.*
Geiger, George R. *John Dewey in Perspective.*
Nathanson, J. *John Dewey.*
Roth, Robert J. *John Dewey and Self-Realization.*

——John Rogers Commons——
[1862–1945]

EVERY READER of this selection is likely to be affected by laws dealing with minimum wages, child labor, unemployment compensation, civil service, workmen's compensation, public-utility regulation, social security, or consumer protection. Yet very few know that the author of the first types of legal protection in these areas was a mild-mannered, soft-spoken, and self-effacing college professor named John Rogers

Commons. Professor Commons devoted his life to an exploration of the nature of economic institutions in the United States, in order to influence the makers of public policy and laws. His sole purpose was promoting the welfare of his fellow man. In so doing he left a legacy of practical ideas that have been incorporated into law on the state and federal levels in this country and copied in many other countries of the world. The school of thought called "institutional economics," by which he meant the "collective action to control individual action," also owes its growth and development to Commons.

Professor Commons had a long, active, and varied life and career. He was born in 1862 in the town of Hollandsburg on the border between Ohio and Indiana. His father was a Quaker whose family had moved north of the Ohio River because they could not tolerate the institution of slavery. His mother, who came from New England, had graduated from Oberlin in 1853, at a time when it was the only coeducational college in the United States. She was a very industrious woman, determined to see that her three children would also go to college. As it turned out, only John Rogers was able to finish college. His brother and sister had to withdraw in the middle of their college careers because their mother's illness prevented her from earning the required tuition funds. Their father, who had strong literary interests, was a very poor businessman and never seemed to be able to show a profit from the several newspapers he owned and published. John R. Commons learned to set type in his father's country newspaper office and later used this skill to earn enough money during summer vacations to meet his college expenses. During one of these summer jobs, he joined the Typographical Union and got his first taste of "collective action in control of individual action."

Instead of going on to college after high school, Commons spent three months teaching in a country school. The experience was a very unhappy one, primarily because he could not maintain order in the classroom. When he resigned, he vowed never to try teaching again. Then, bowing to his mother's insistence, he agreed to go to Oberlin College in 1882, but his high-school preparation was considered so inadequate that he was required to spend one full year in Oberlin's preparatory department before he was able to gain admission as a freshman.

Periodic and prolonged attacks of illness, added to the necessity of using his time and energy to earn money to support himself, prevented Commons from completing his college work in the normal time. It took some six years for him to complete the degree requirements. Until his senior year he had planned to become a journalist, but he decided to study economics instead. His interest in economics as a field of study was aroused after he read Henry George's *Progress and Poverty*, which was creating quite a sensation among American workingmen and European intellectuals. Perhaps Commons felt a special attachment for George since he, too, had started out as a typesetter on his first job. He was so impressed with George's ideas that he organized a political economy club in the college.

Commons' academic career at Oberlin was unsuccessful primarily because he could not uncritically accept things printed in books or delivered from the lecture platform. Unless he could verify a statement by personal investigation, he was not satisfied. One of his chief complaints, for example, was that he could never find actual specimens to match the illustrations in the biology textbooks his professor gave him. This failure, he stated later on, caused him to be very skeptical of all scientists and their theories. He spent so much time trying to find out things for himself that he was always behind in his work and was never prepared for his examinations. He finally was permitted to graduate in 1888.

The only satisfying experiences Commons had at Oberlin came from his courses in economics which were taught by a Professor Monroe. With Monroe's encouragement, Commons applied for admission at Johns Hopkins University, after first arranging to borrow from two Oberlin trustees sufficient funds to pay for two years of study. Some fourteen years later, Commons finally managed to pay back these loans.

At Johns Hopkins, Commons had the good fortune to meet Professor Richard T. Ely, who had just returned from Germany where he had studied the economic theories of what later was called the "German Historical School." Under Ely, Commons began to study many practical problems, such as the nature and composition of charity organizations and building-and-loan associations. Ely's insistence on "finding the facts" first and then generalizing from them, or applying the inductive method to the study of economics, was in sharp contrast to

the deductive method, used extensively by American and
English economists of the time. Ely fought hard to have
his inductive approach adopted. His methods and humanitarian attitudes appealed to Commons mainly because they
closely approximated his own feelings and attitudes. He
resolved thereafter to study and stress only the practical
aspects of economics and economic theories.

Unfortunately, Commons' determination was not bolstered
by his ability to do the work required by his professors. After
two years at Hopkins, he failed the history examination and
became ineligible for the fellowship for the following year.
In effect this meant that he would not be able to continue his
studies for the doctorate. A few of his instructors, however,
believed in his ability and recommended him for an instructor-
ship at Wesleyan, where his salary was $1,000 per year. His
attempt at systematic teaching at Wesleyan was a failure and
before the end of the academic year he was informed that he
would not be rehired for the following year.

Once again his friends helped, and in the next few years
he taught at Oberlin, Indiana, and Syracuse universities, each
time obtaining a higher rank and a larger salary, in spite of
the fact that the officers of each university were glad to see
him leave. His unorthodox views constantly disturbed the
university officials. For example, in 1899, he organized a
cooperative and wrote an article defending Sunday base-
ball. This caused so much commotion in the local community
that the trustees at Syracuse promptly abolished his chair
at the university.

By a stroke of good luck he immediately received an offer
of a job from a politician who believed that the gold policy
of the government was depressing prices. Commons' job was
to construct a weekly index of the movements of wholesale
prices. This was the first time such an index was to appear,
and Commons was very pleased with the challenge it represented. As long as the index showed prices falling, his
employer, who was then an adviser to the Democratic National
Campaign Committee, was pleased. Unfortunately for Commons, the index began to move upward in the summer of
1900 and the propaganda value of the index disappeared, as
did Commons' job.

For the next few years Commons worked for the United
States Industrial Commission, where he produced a report

on immigration, and for the National Civic Federation, where he concerned himself with the maintenance of industrial peace. As a result of his experience in these two positions, his former teacher at Johns Hopkins, Richard Ely, now at Wisconsin, invited Commons to join the university to teach the labor economics courses and to help Ely complete a history of the labor movement. Commons' reputation both as a poor teacher and as an advocate of unpopular views was such that the administration at Wisconsin agreed to the appointment only on the condition that half of Commons' salary be paid from private sources. Ely took the gamble and it clearly paid off. Thus, at the age of forty-two, Commons began his permanent attachment to the University of Wisconsin, where he was to remain until illness forced his retirement.

It was to be an unusually rewarding position for Commons, and 1904, the year he joined the university, was particularly favorable for the exposition of the ideas he had been developing up to that time. In 1904 the state government, as well as the administration of the University of Wisconsin, was completely dominated by the progressive viewpoints associated with Robert La Follette. In all his previous positions, Commons had been an outsider advocating ideas that conflicted with the ideas of those in authority. Here, at Wisconsin, he was an insider whose special talents were sought after by those in authority. His desire to unearth all the facts in a problem, to suggest new goals in all areas of social-welfare activities, and to participate in the formulation of practical legislation to accomplish long-overdue reforms, fitted in precisely with the La Follette program. Commons had come into his own: "The man and the opportunity were well matched."

Commons immediately set to work on the vast collection of material Ely had accumulated and, in 1910, published *A Documentary History of American Industrial Society* in ten volumes, a work that has been called "our most important collection of sources for the history of labor in this country." This was followed, in 1918, by *The History of Labor in the United States*, in four volumes published between 1918 and 1935, a work that is considered a classic in its field and is often quoted even today. Its detailed coverage of the early years of labor history in this country has never been surpassed, and clearly established Commons' reputation as an outstanding labor economist.

Despite his duties as teacher and his heavy writing schedule, he always found time to advise and assist Governor La Follette on matters of importance to the entire state. In 1905 Commons drafted the Wisconsin Civil Service Law; in 1907 he wrote the Wisconsin Public Utility Act; and in 1932 he developed the first state unemployment-insurance program. All of these later became models for many other states. He also prepared the research documents that led to the formation of the Wisconsin Industrial Commission which, for the first time, placed the enactment and enforcement of industrial safety regulations under an administrative commission and which provided compensation for workers injured on the job. He was also active in the National Consumers' League, the Wisconsin Board of Public Affairs, and spent over eighteen months in revising and streamlining the administrative machinery of the city of Milwaukee. In 1918 he was elected president of the American Economic Association and in 1920, with the help of another great economist, Wesley C. Mitchell, he founded the National Bureau of Economic Research, an organization that pioneered in the study of business cycles and other national economic problems, and that is still functioning and performing very important work today.

Commons spent most of his life dealing with everyday practical matters, yet he did not overlook the theoretical implication of his method of approach to economic problems. In 1934 he summed up his ideas in his book *Institutional Economics*, which systematically analyzed the conflicting interests in modern economic society. According to Commons, in order to really understand modern economic life all economic activity has to be considered as a series of transactions.

The first of these is the *bargaining* transaction. This was the concept developed by most economists in the past. To Commons, however, there are not two parties involved but at least five. There is a buyer and a seller, both of whom make certain offers. In addition, there is always an alternate buyer and an alternate seller. Finally, there is, always present in the background, a court whose function it is to regulate the opposing interests of buyer and seller, and to uphold the existing rules of the society in relation to the bargaining transaction.

Secondly, there are *managerial* transactions, in which one party is the legal superior and the other party the legal inferior, as typified in the relationship between an employer and his worker in a factory.

Finally, there are *rationing* transactions, such as those carried out by a board of directors drawing up a budget for the corporation. Always in the background is the legal system, the courts, to keep all actions and activities within the established framework of the society. To Commons, in effect, this was the institutional approach to the study of economic behavior. Thus we have "collective action in control of individual action." Thorstein Veblen, another important institutional economist, defined an institution as a widely prevalent habit of thought and action. It would seem that Veblen's and Commons' definitions are quite different. However, habits of thought and action are acquired in the process of growing up, and result in standard reactions to the problems presented by a complex economic society. These standard reactions are very similar to the collective actions referred to by Commons. Basically, therefore, the two definitions are quite similar, although Veblen was less concerned about improving the lot of mankind.

With the development of the concept of the institution as the controlling mechanism in economic life, Commons indicates the role it is to play and the problems it must solve. In his highly theoretical and original work *The Legal Foundation of Capitalism* (1924), Commons emphasized the part played by the law and the courts in establishing the true economic base upon which capitalism rests. Using the historical method, he traced the concept of private property from the time of William the Conqueror to the present. In the earlier period there was no distinction made between property and sovereignty, since they were considered one and the same. Over the years, as a result of court actions and decisions, the principle was established that private property in land was quite different from sovereignty over the land. By extension, Commons also included in the concept of private property, intangibles such as promises to pay, bills of exchange, rules of fair competition, and the legal limitation of privileges and rights. Thus, the permanent existence of the concept of private property was assured by the courts, and in the capitalist system became the center around which all other aspects of economic activity revolved.

From his systematic review of legal and economic history,

Commons was convinced that the courts were extremely important in helping to eliminate the more destructive practices of the economic institutions developed within capitalism. The courts were constantly seeking to establish "reasonable" policies to be followed by the competitive forces in the economy. On this basis, Commons was convinced that it was possible to induce compromises based on "reasonable value" in labor disputes, taxation, public-utility rates, and prices in general. To Commons, "reasonable value" meant the "evolutionary collective determination of what is reasonable in view of all the changing political, moral, and economic circumstances and the personalities that arise therefrom to the Supreme Bench." Thus, the required flexibility needed in an ever-changing, complex industrial society was fortunately provided for within the framework of the capitalist system. Throughout his life and works, Commons continued to emphasize the paramount importance of compromising to establish the greatest good for the greatest number of people in the society. Commons' vision can be attested to by the fact that the courts have indeed made extensive use of the "reasonable" concept in decisions involving fundamental changes in our society.

Commons is best known for his work in the field of labor economics, yet few American economists had broader interests. He tried to be in close contact with every phase of American life as well as with the worker, the industrialist, the statesman, and the policymaker. In his own record of his life, called *Myself* (1934), he summarized his general approach as follows: "I was trying to save capitalism by making it good. I wanted also to make trade unions as good as the best that I knew." Not enough time has elapsed to judge how successful Commons was in saving capitalism, but among reasonable men it may be said he pointed in the right direction.

FURTHER READING

Commons, John Rogers. *Myself.*
Harter, Lafayette G. *John R. Commons: His Assault on Laissez Faire.*

───George Santayana───

[1863–1952]

IN THE AUTUMN OF 1951, while residing in the Convent of the Blue Nuns in Rome, George Santayana related his perplexing fears to a friend. Santayana, nearing eighty-eight years of age, said that "For the first time in my life . . . I am in mortal danger of being bored." His eyes and health were failing, and he feared that he would not be able to continue writing. He finally concluded that "if I go completely blind, I can translate Latin, French or Spanish poems I know by heart."

Santayana, an outstanding philosopher, was always engaged in intellectual activities. He lived in the world of ideas, retreating there as a young man because of his father's death, the marriage of his adored sister, and the death of a boyhood friend, whom he considered as a "younger brother—a part of myself." As a professor at Harvard University, he regarded himself as "harnessed for life like a beast of burden." Santayana "rendered external things comparatively indifferent." He once related to Bertrand Russell an incident occurring a few days before the Battle of the Marne when the capture of Paris was imminent. Santayana said that he had left some winter underclothes in Paris, and he desired to retrieve them before the Germans took them. He casually mentioned, however, that he had also left a manuscript on which he had worked ten years. Nonetheless, he was not too concerned about it!

What is the background of this man—philosopher, novelist, stylist, poet—who was so concerned with ideas and yet so unrealistic about the exigencies of life that he "desired nothing fixed, no place in society, no circle of prescribed friends, and engagements"?

Born in Madrid on December 16, 1863, Santayana was nine years old when he was taken to Boston. His Spanish-born parents, freethinking Catholics, met in the Philippine Islands. His mother's first husband, the Boston merchant George Sturgis, promised that the Sturgis children would be reared in Boston. Therefore, the Santayanas migrated to Boston. In kindergarten, Santayana learned English by ear, thus learning to speak English without an accent. Educated at Boston Latin School and at Harvard, having written his dissertation on the Chinese philosopher Lao-tzu under Josiah Royce's direction, he became an instructor of philosophy at the age of twenty-six. After a brief tenure, he went to England to study Plato and Aristotle. Plato greatly influenced the ideas expressed in his philosophical writings and he always admired the practical, commonsense solutions to problems offered by Aristotle.

Upon his return, Santayana joined the Harvard philosophers of renown—Josiah Royce, William James, and Hugo Münsterberg. At thirty-one years old, his first poems were published. During the next eleven years, he published *The Sense of Beauty*, which Münsterberg called the best book of aesthetics ever written in the United States, two more volumes of poetry, and *The Life of Reason*, his five-volume statement on naturalism —a view that the universe is explained in natural terms without benefit of supernatural control.

When *The Life of Reason* appeared in 1905, William James said: "I think it will probably be reckoned great by posterity. It has no rational foundation, being merely one man's way of viewing things: so much of experience admitted and no more. . . ."

As a lecturer, Santayana was quite popular, even though Harvard's President Lowell sometimes seemed overly concerned with the number of students in Santayana's classes. His students included T. S. Eliot, Conrad Aiken, Walter Lippmann, Felix Frankfurter, and Robert Benchley. The latter quipped that the music of Santayana's language fascinated him even though he did not understand Santayana's words.

In 1912, Santayana received an inheritance and resigned his professorship at Harvard, after having taught there for twenty-three years. He then left for Oxford, remaining there only a short period. Subsequently he lived in Paris, and in 1924 he settled for his remaining years in Rome in an obscure hotel and later at a Catholic nursing home. Ironically, Santayana could have purchased a château instead of living in

frugality. In his retirement he wrote extensively. He died in
1952 under the care of Catholic nuns. His life's writings consist of twenty-six volumes—indeed a prolific production.

After World War II, while residing in Rome, Santayana
would sit on a bench and hail the passersby. Anyone who
would take the time might be engaged in conversation by
Santayana. Since he could speak a number of foreign languages, he conversed with many people. The American GI's,
literate and illiterate, would equally partake in his conversations. One American, who conversed with him in the 1940's,
remarked that Santayana talked on any subject and that he
spoke the most beautiful and wonderful English. The remarks
indeed characterize the man.

Santayana was an outstanding and profound philosopher
who approached philosophy with the mind of a realist and
the pen of a poet. He is usually categorized as a "critical realist." In fact, in 1920, he contributed a chapter, "Three Proofs
of Realism," to *Essays in Critical Realism,* a work depicting
the viewpoint of some prominent critical realists. They maintained that the objective world exists independently of the
person. However, the knowledge of the objective world is
conveyed to the person by what Santayana called "essence"
(explained below). He accepted reality as his senses conveyed
it to his mind. In this he was rejecting Hume and the German
philosophers who considered reality merely as an untrust-
worthy figment of the mind. Accepting reality, Santayana
regarded reason as the illumination of reality and human behavior as the responses of individuals in a materialistic world.

A few remarks on some of Santayana's works will reveal the
breadth and depth of his philosophical writings.

Concerning the five volumes of *The Life of Reason (Reason
in Common Sense, Reason in Society, Reason in Religion, Reason in Art,* and *Reason in Science),* Santayana commented that
they were "a presumptive biography of the human intellect."
Regarding society, Santayana advocated "timocracy." This
Platonic society would be aristocratically governed by honorable men. "The only equality subsisting would be equality of
opportunity." Each citizen would progress according to his
own abilities. Santayana also pleaded for a world power and
religion, for a one world ruler would be better than many
feuding ones. He cautioned against the great evil of a state as

a warring machine. Santayana approved of science, saying that it contained "all trustworthy knowledge." Concomitantly, he was so steeped in his materialism (the belief that matter is the only reality) that he said "the soul is only a fine quick organization within the material animal . . . a prodigious network of nerves and tissues, growing in each generation out of a seed." Regarding religion, Santayana maintained some attachment to the beliefs and values of Roman Catholicism. He felt, nonetheless, that religion was a phenomenon of man, that gods were produced from the fear and imagination of man, and that initially Christianity evolved from Greek and Jewish religious concepts.

In 1923, he completed *Scepticism and Animal Faith*, which presented an introduction to his new system of philosophy, which he freely revealed was a restatement of the best of the ancient philosophers. However, he valued highly Democritus, a Greek philosopher, and Aristotle; he liked, according to one philosopher, the "plain blunt materialism of the first, and the unruffled sanity of the second." Of himself, Santayana said:

> In natural philosophy I am a decided materialist—apparently the only one living. . . . But I do not profess to know what matter is in itself. . . . I want the men of science to tell me.

He believed in being critical of accepted beliefs with a wholesome skepticism. Once establishing his natural (belief that all reality has an explanation in the laws of nature) philosophy, Santayana said:

> Scepticism is an exercise, not a life. It is a discipline fit to purify the mind of prejudice and render it all the more apt . . . to believe and act wisely. Thus a mind enlightened by scepticism . . . finds in the wilderness of essence a very sweet and marvellous solitude.

For Santayana, "essences" are "indispensable terms in the perception of matters of fact, and render transitive knowledge possible." Then to rely on essences is "animal faith." This was the faith that he advocated, faith in man's ability to understand and to make progress in the real world of his existence.

In *The Realms of Being*, he pursued the theme of man's knowledge. Throughout *Dialogues in Limbo*, a stranger, name-

ly Santayana, conversed on great issues with the spirits of
some great minds, including Socrates. In *Character and Opinion in the United States,* Santayana, an incisive critic, criticized American thinking. He, in *The Sense of Beauty,* was
concerned with "the nature and elements of our esthetic judgments." *Three Philosophical Poets* presented his views on
naturalism, supernaturalism, and romanticism in an impres-
sionistic analysis of Lucretius, Dante, and Goethe. In *Egotism
in German Philosophy,* Santayana exposed the extravagances
of German moralistic philosophy. His novel *The Last Puritan,*
a best seller in America, portrayed the moral conflict within the
American conscience because of the influences of puritanism.

Santayana, one who could speak the most beautiful and
wonderful English, was unique as a stylist of American letters.
Not only was he a great thinker, but he also was able to present his philosophy in stylistic prose. Since he learned English
in the late Victorian tradition, he imitated the styles of writing
of that period. His style contains abundant metaphors, rhyth-
mic sentences, humor which mingles overstatements with un-
derstatements, and delightful aphorisms. Incisive thoughts are
contained within this magnificent prose. Surely Buffon's adage
is apropos: "The style is the man himself."

Perhaps no American writer except Emerson has included
as many aphorisms in his works as Santayana. The astute reader notices the articulate phrasing and pointedness of his aphorisms. The following give some indication of his philosophy:

> The people we care for the most give us the most
> trouble.
> When women's opinions waver, it means that their
> hearts are not at rest.
> Chaos is perhaps at the bottom of everything.
> The young man who has not wept is a savage, and the
> old man who will not laugh is a fool.
> Fanaticism consists in redoubling your efforts when
> you have forgotten your aim.
> There is no cure for birth and death save to enjoy the
> interval.
> Those who cannot remember the past are condemned
> to repeat it.
> It is easier to make a saint out of a libertine than out
> of a prig.

Santayana also distinguished himself as a poet. Some of his first sonnets, appearing in the *Harvard Monthly* during his senior year in college (1885–1886), record his religious questioning of Roman Catholicism and his acceptance of naturalism. His outstanding poetical works include *Lucifer* (1889), a poetical drama, and *Poems* (1923).

Santayana's life was paradoxical: he was an American yet had European ideas; he seemed to be renouncing his Catholic faith yet he clung to some of his religious beliefs; he ignored the friendship of fellow Harvard faculty members yet befriended students; he was a profound professor yet disliked the position. However, Santayana has left his mark on American philosophy and literature. Philosopher, novelist, stylist, or poet—any one, and surely all, denotes the greatness of the man.

FURTHER READING

Butler, Richard. *Life and World of George Santayana.*
Cory, Daniel. *Santayana, The Later Years.*

———Sun Yat-sen———
[Also known as Sun Wen]
[1866–1925]

DR. SUN YAT-SEN, dressed like an English gentleman, was walking to church in London one Sunday morning. Soft-spoken, neatly groomed, and affable in manner, he gave no indication that he was regarded as a dangerous revolutionary by the government of his native China.

Suddenly a carriage drove up beside him. Several men jumped out, forced him into the vehicle, and drove off. Following a circuitous route, the carriage proceeded to the Chinese Legation, and the kidnaping victim was dragged into the building. Here he was imprisoned in an upstairs room. Sun Yat-sen knew that they intended to smuggle him out of the legation at night to a ship bound for China and certain execution. But luck was on his side. He was able to persuade a British servant employed in the building to carry a note to an influential Londoner, and the kidnaping story reached the newspapers.

Anger at the violation of British sovereignty reached such proportions in the press that the Chinese were forced to release Sun Yat-sen, who thereby became internationally famous. Thus did fate spare the life of the Chinese medical doctor who was to bring down the last of the Chinese dynasties that had ruled China for some four thousand years and who, ironically, was also to call for the abolition of the imperialism in China of the same British government that had saved his life.

Sun Yat-sen was born the youngest of three sons in the family of a poor tenant farmer of rice in the small village of Choyhung in Kwangtung province in southern China. His home was a mud hut with earthen floor, and the boy had to work hard assisting his father from early childhood. Yet there was time for the usual boyhood play and even for a little schooling. His father, who himself was illiterate, had converted to Christianity and saw to it that his son attended the temple school. Sun Yat-sen received the most rudimentary schooling, which consisted of memorizing and reciting the *Three-character classic*. Sun recalled his rebellion against memorizing without understanding, a rebellion that was put down by the schoolmaster's stick.

However, he was more fortunate than the other children of his village. His older brother, Ah Mei, had emigrated to Honolulu, where he had a successful farm and a general store. At the age of fifteen, Sun went to live with his brother. He helped his brother in the store but also attended an English school, where he learned mathematics, history, and English, and where he accepted Anglican Christianity. After two happy years in Hawaii, he returned in 1883 to his village in China.

Sun Yat-sen's experience abroad had wrought changes in him. He rebelled against the traditional mores, the ancestor worship, the reverence for idols, and other superstitions. On one occasion he even entered a Chinese temple and broke the idol of Pei-ti, the god of autumn, to publicly show his scorn of idol worship. To maintain peace in the village, his family sent him to Queens College, in Hong Kong. At eighteen he returned to be married to a girl of his village, but the magnet of emancipated life in Hong Kong called him back.

Now he became a leader of a group of revolutionaries who resented the degradation of their country by foreign exploiters and who blamed the weak, corrupt government of the Manchus for this predicament. To Sun Yat-sen the extreme poverty of the people, the illiteracy, rampant disease, ravages of civil war, periodic famines, widespread addiction to opium, and backward customs that permitted children to be sold into slavery were evils that could be corrected only by the deposition of the Chinese rulers. He declared that the world was not created for a fortunate few but that "the earth, the universe, belongs to everyone," a quotation he adopted from the ancient Chinese philosopher, Confucius. This thought was the foundation of his thinking.

He decided to become a physician as one way to help his people and so, from 1887 to 1894, he studied at a Hong Kong hospital and medical school, earning a medical degree.

Sun Yat-sen worked not only to cure the ills of his patients but the ills of his country. He was a leader in the Hsing Chung Hui, the Revive China Society, one of many secret societies organized in China which published pamphlets urging reforms, resistance to foreign exploiters, an end to corruption and civil wars, and a more democratic government. In one of their pamphlets he wrote, "The people are the foundation of a country; when the foundation is strengthened the country will be secure." When pamphlets and petitions availed them nothing, the Revive China Society decided on an armed uprising in Canton. But the watchful eye of the Empress Dowager, through her many spies, was on the young revolutionaries. The conspirators were arrested and executed. Sun Yat-sen was one of the few to escape, but he had to leave China. He now signified his break with Old China by cutting off his queue (long braid of hair), donning Western garments, and growing a mustache.

Beginning a long period of perilous exile, he traveled in Hawaii, the United States, England, and among the islands of the South Seas. In 1905 the Chinese Revolutionary League was organized with Sun as one of its principal agents. Everywhere Sun Yat-sen sought financial and other aid from overseas Chinese against the corrupt Chinese government, and everywhere there was danger for him. His country had put a price in excess of $50,000 on his head.

In England he spent much time in the British Museum reading the works of such reformers as Edmund Burke, Rousseau, Henry George, and Karl Marx, whose *Das Kapital* had been translated into English in 1887. He probably met Lenin and other Russian revolutionary exiles in England.

In 1898 he returned to China, and tried to unify the many anti-Manchu secret societies. In 1900 the Boxer Rebellion occurred, supported by the Empress Dowager as a diversion from her misgovernment. This uprising ended in further humiliation for Dr. Sun's China as she was forced into giving further concessions to foreign governments. Sun Yat-sen planned another armed rebellion against the Empress, but this, too, was put down. In 1903 the Empress issued an amnesty to the revolutionaries, but excluded Dr. Sun Yat-sen.

Sun was not discouraged but set out on another world tour to gather support and funds. He had developed a clarity and quiet fervor of speech that captivated his listeners as he talked of conditions in China and the need for reform. He was always gentle and sympathetic; yet he was steadfast in his Lincoln-esque principles that "the people are to have, the people are to rule, the people are to enjoy."

Dr. Sun Yat-sen kept in close touch with his homeland. From exile he organized the Tung Meng Hui, which later became the Kuomintang, a political alliance espousing nationalism, democracy, and socialism: (1) an end to foreign imperialism and domination, (2) a democratic form of government, and (3) the end of feudal landownership so that there might be a better sharing among the Chinese people of the wealth, profits, and resources of the country. These became known as the "Three Principles of the People." The ranks of the Tung Meng Hui grew, and Dr. Sun Yat-sen, though in exile, was made the president of the party.

In one of the publications of the Tung Meng Hui, Sun echoed the sentiments of the French Revolution as he wrote: "The revolution today is by the people. . . . The essence of revolution by the people lies in the fact that all the people possess the spirit of liberty, equality, and universal love, and all share in the responsibility of revolution."

In 1911 came the eleventh, and this time successful, rebellion initiated by rebellious troops at Wuchang. Every feudal warlord and general entered the struggle for power. Sun was in the United States on October 10, 1911, when news of the revolt reached him. Knowing the immense importance of foreign support, he immediately set out for England and France, where he succeeded in winning pledges of assistance. Now he was ready to return to China and, on January 5, 1912, at Nanking, he was made provisional President of the Republic of China. On February 12, the child Emperor abdicated in favor of a republican government. Chiang Kai-shek, who had graduated from a military school, was made commander-in-chief of the republican forces. In his first proclamation as provisional President, Sun Yat-sen broke with the ancient Chinese governmental tradition, pledging adherence to five "unities": unity of all the races of China, unity of territory, unity of military command, unity of internal administration, and unity of finance.

Internal frictions and schisms still persisted, and so Sun Yat-sen, believing that a more influential administrator acceptable to all groups was needed to unite the country, resigned the presidency on February 1, 1912. The man he selected for the post was Yuan Shih-k'ai. Sun realized the importance of communications if vast China were to prosper, and decided to devote himself to a plan for building a gigantic network of railroads. However, Yuan had his own ideas and ambitions, and the two leaders soon found themselves in opposition. Although Sun was the leader of the political party, the Kuomintang, Yuan controlled the army, and so Dr. Sun Yat-sen was again forced into exile, this time to Japan, in 1915. Yuan almost succeeded in uniting the country along more conservative lines, but when he declared himself Emperor, the leaders of many provinces would not accept him and revolted. Although Yuan died in 1916, the civil wars continued.

At this time Sun Yat-sen, now nearly fifty, married Chingling Soong, a graduate of Georgia Wesleyan College and daughter of his industrialist friend Charles Soong. Chingling's younger sister, Mayling Soong, was to become Madame Chiang Kai-shek. The three Soong sisters (the third was Eling) departed from the traditional Chinese role of feminine dependence and became influential forces in the emancipation of China.

One after another, Chinese political figures appeared on the scene, striving hopelessly for unity and nationalism. Most of these were willing to forsake the ideals of the Kuomintang and to compromise with tradition and foreign imperialism. Some were more interested in self-aggrandizement than in promoting the welfare of the Chinese people. Although Dr. Sun Yat-sen did not have extensive political authority in China, as the head of the Kuomintang party he remained the indefatigable inspiration for Chinese "nationalism, democracy, and socialism," and his ideas were passionately discussed throughout China. He never forgot his early belief that "the earth, the universe, belongs to everyone." These ideas were difficult to disseminate in a China that had been under the sway of authoritarian traditions and superstitions for four thousand years.

In 1921 Sun, aided by the powerful warlord Chen Chiun-ming, was restored to power in Kwangtung Province in southern China. But there was no end to the civil wars, to the agreements made and broken, or to the violence. It was not long before he broke with General Chen, whom he succeeded in defeating. Indeed several times Sun himself narrowly escaped assassination attempts. During this period he had the support of the intellectuals, the students, the peasants, and the workers, but he was bitterly opposed by the landowners and others of vested interests. In 1923 he declared that "henceforth our revolution can never succeed unless we take the Russian revolution as our model." For the first time in a life full of many discouragements, he seemed to feel bitter and disheartened and undertook extremist measures to force compliance with his goals.

Dr. Sun Yat-sen watched the "people's revolution" in Russia and, although he did not believe that Soviet communism should be established in China, he accepted Russian help and invited Soviet military and civil advisers into China. On the advice of the Soviet agent Michael Borodin, the structure of the Kuomintang was centralized and strengthened along the lines of the Communist party. Members of the party were to accept the discipline of soldiery. Also on Borodin's advice, members of the Chinese Communist party were now admitted into the Kuomintang.

In 1925, Sun Yat-sen went to Peking where supposedly a meeting was to be held with leaders of the warring groups in

an effort to establish unity. Sun Yat-sen never lived to attend
this meeting. He fell ill of what seemed to be a liver ailment
but turned out to be an advanced cancer condition, and died
on March 12, 1925. On his deathbed he signed a proclamation
urging adherence to the Three Principles of the People and
"unity with those peoples of the world who will treat us on
terms of equality."

For a while the struggle for nationalism and unity continued
successfully under Chiang Kai-shek. In 1927 Chiang expelled
Borodin and broke with the powerful Communist group. One
by one, rebellious warlords were brought under control, and
the republican dream of Dr. Sun Yat-sen might have been
achieved under Chiang Kai-shek. However, 1937 brought an
invasion by Japan, and then came the Second World War. In
1949, the Nationalist Government under Chiang Kai-shek was
no longer able to suppress the rising forces of the people led
by Mao Tse-tung, who established a Communist People's Republic of China; Chiang was expelled from the mainland to
the island of Formosa and several neighboring islands.

Whatever the future of China, it is certain that Dr. Sun Yat-
sen was the architect who envisioned a China of 800 million
people that would cast off its feudal chains, its corrupt government, and its subservience to foreign governments, and that
would advance to a democratic form of government in which
the people would share more equitably the fruits of civilization. He saw a China that would take a constructive place
among the family of nations. Sun Yat-sen, called the father of
the Chinese Republic, helped his country take the first giant
step in this direction.

FURTHER READING

Greene, Felix. *China: The Country Americans Are Not Al-
    lowed To Know.*
Linebarger, Paul M. A. *Political Doctrines of Sun Yat-sen: An
    Exposition of the San Min Chu I.*
Snow, Edgar. *Red Star over China.*

——Benedetto Croce——

[1866–1952]

THE LONDON *Times,* upon the death of Benedetto
Croce, the Italian who expounded about aesthetics, literary
criticism, liberalism, philosophy, and history, stated that Croce
achieved "an immense erudition, a wide and almost unleasing
production, the highest possible quality of scholarship and a
peculiar felicity in bringing learning into contact with life."
This man, orphaned at an early age, inheriting a fortune, and
ironically never receiving a professorship or being associated
with an educational institution, created an institution unto
himself. Croce's tenacious concern with life was partly stated
late in life in his guide for living:

> In the worst travail . . . a voice echoes within me: Do
> something. And so I go tenaciously doing what I must
> do, doing what my capacities and the education I have
> given myself have prepared me to do. . . . "Do something"
> is the advice I give . . . because while one is doing, one
> is alive and keeps alive the flame of life in the world
> which we feel. . . . But it will not . . . go to ruin and it
> demands and commands that *we do something of our
> own* to keep it whole.

Croce, exuding his greatest influence in aesthetics—a branch
of philosophy concerned with beauty and art—maintained
that art is created before an artist puts brush to canvas, or a
poet puts pen to manuscript. Indeed the Italian artists Michelangelo and Leonardo da Vinci and the English poet Percy
Bysshe Shelley held a similar idea. Michelangelo said, "One
paints not with the hands but with the brain." Leonardo da
Vinci is said to have been upset before painting *The Last Sup-
per* because an abbot, who commissioned the work, insisted

that Leonardo stop looking for days at an unpainted canvas. Leonardo once wrote, "The minds of men of lofty genius are most active in invention when they are doing the least external work." Shelley wrote in his *Defence of Poetry* that "the most glorious poetry that has ever been communicated to the world is probably a feeble shadow of the original conceptions of the poet. . . ." Croce's philosophy, as will be explained, is intricately associated with his aesthetics.

The Olympian Croce, the offspring of wealthy landowners, was born in southern Italy and spent his early childhood in Naples. While his grandfather was a high magistrate of the Kingdom of Naples, his father was not concerned with politics. At nine years of age, Croce, who was quarrelsome and studious, was sent to study at a religious boarding school run by priests. He was an avid reader. In early adolescence, Croce began doubting his Catholic faith, and he later wrote concerning it that "one day I remarked and said to myself clearly that I was altogether quit of religious belief."

In 1883, Croce was vacationing with his family on the island of Ischia when an earthquake struck, killing his parents and sister. He was buried by debris for twelve hours and was severely injured. His paternal uncle, Silvio Spaventa, a powerful statesman in Rome, requested that Croce, now a wealthy orphan, come to live with his family in Rome. Croce studied at the University of Rome, but was uninspired by its faculty or by the political environment in the Spaventa household. "These were the saddest and darkest years," he wrote, "the only ones in which often, as I laid my head on the pillow, I keenly desired never to wake again, and even had notions of suicide."

In 1886, Croce, dejected and depressed, returned without his degree to the family estate in Naples. After a few years, Croce was gaining some prominence for his research and publications on Neopolitan folklore, culture, and history. In 1895, Antonio Labriola, a professor from the University of Rome, showed Croce a manuscript about Karl Marx. Croce, gaining interest in Marx from this association, wrote articles on Marxian economic theory. In fact, he was called in print "Comrade Croce." However, he wrote that this "political enthusiasm, that faith, did not last." Croce, nevertheless, maintained that Marx's *Das Kapital* was not a theoretical work, that Marxism

has fallacies in its labor theory of value and in its falling rate
of profit, but that his theories offered new insights for the historian. Croce wrote that Marxism was "a kind of anthology of
all proletarian rebellions."

Around 1900, Croce illustrated his "true nature as a man
of study and of thought" in the initiation of his four-volume
work *Philosophy of the Spirit*. The first volume, *Aesthetics*,
completed in 1902, was followed by *Logic*, then by *Philosophy of Conduct: Economics and Ethics*, and finally in 1917 by
Theory and History of Historiography.

Croce's philosophy of the spirit is based on a sort of Hegelian idealism: the only true reality pertains to ideas, spirit, or
life existing in man's mind. Whatever man conceives in his
mind is reality. Croce wrote: "All philosophy . . . shows that
there is nothing outside the mind." The mind then performs
spiritual activities, and the activities, theoretical and practical, are what concern Croce himself. The theoretical activity
is synonymous with "knowing," and practical activity with
"doing." Each of the two activities has two divisions: the
theoretical has aesthetics and logic; the practical has economics and ethics. The task of philosophy is to explain how
these activities unite to construct the world of human experience. He believed that history is the concrete form of
philosophy. He praised Hegelian dialectic since it verified
that reality is "not static but living, not fixed but changing."

Croce's concept of aesthetics, commonly called "expression-
ism," is his great contribution to philosophy. Croce conceives
of art as a "complex of images and a feeling that animates
them." Art is something that exists only in the mind. Art is
not a poem, a painting, a musical composition, a building, or
a piece of sculpture. "Art is perfectly defined when it is simply
defined as *intuition*" or vision.

The poet realizes that his art, or all art, is not a physical
object—print on a page—but an idea in the mind. Art is not
a philosophy; it is "an unreflective intuition of being." Art
is not instructive or moral; it merely conceives of the association
of images and feelings, and does not attempt to instruct or to
give a moral evaluation of life. Art, however, is not the mere
conjuring of images. When the poet or artist has a strong
enough feeling, it must result in expression.

An image that does not express, that is not speech, song,

drawing, painting, sculpture or architecture—speech at least murmured to oneself, song at least echoing within one's own breast, line and color seen in imagination and coloring with its own tint the whole soul and organism— is an image that does not exist.

To Croce intuition and expression are one. When the poet *expresses* the words of the poem to himself, art is complete— *art exists in the mind of the poet.* When the poet says aloud the words of his poem for another's benefit, or when he writes his poem on paper, he communicates his intuition. Communication "is the fixation of the intuition-expression upon an object metaphorically called material or physical." In communication the poet enters a new stage of activity. He leaves the "aesthetic" activity and enters the "practical" activity. Croce associates technique with the communication of art. The technique pertains to the furtherance of the practical activity, the placing of words on paper, or the preparation of a canvas or panel.

"In the creation of a work of poetry," Croce wrote, "we are present, as it were, at the mystery of the creation of the world." The intuition in art is life, reality, or spirit. Similarly, a robin in early spring sings his song; the song expresses his whole nature, his very existence.

Croce does not give the artist the prerogative to be aloof to humanity or unaware of morality. The intuition of the artist does not have morality or instruction as its purpose; however, "the basis of all poetry is human personality, and since human personality finds its completion in morality, the basis of all poetry is moral consciousness." As a result, the poet must be aware of the drama of life; and if he is "aloof from contact with humanity," he "is no real figure but a caricature."

About the time *Aesthetics* was completed, Croce initiated a magazine, *La Critica,* which was published without interruption every other month from 1902 to 1943. Its publication resumed shortly thereafter, and it still appears irregularly. The magazine, the basis of Croce's renown in literary criticism, set out to evaluate the authors and philosophers of the nineteenth century. The initial editorial stated:

We intend to fight for a determinate order of ideas. Nothing is more harmful to healthy learning than a mistaken sentiment of tolerance, or, to put it more clearly,

of indifference and scepticism. . . . Liberty is better
served by presenting a clear target to one's opponents
than by joining with them in an insincere and useless
brotherliness.

Prior to World War I, Croce gained national recognition as
a philosopher, and he was given a life senatorship in Italy in
1910. Initially, he favored neutralism for Italy instead of being
allied with war propagandists in Europe. However, with Italy's
monarchy engaging in war on the side of the West, Croce
finally advocated the national cause.

After the war, Croce was appointed as Minister of Education. Upon the failure of Giolitti's government in one year,
Mussolini formed his government. Croce initially favored
Mussolini, leader of a socialist group and an advocate of
Italian patriotism; Croce believed that Mussolini was able to
rehabilitate the country and the working classes. It was not
until 1925 that Croce saw the ruthlessness of Mussolini's
regime, and wrote a denunciation, which was signed by
intellectuals of the country and which condemned Mussolini
and his Fascist government. In part it read that the government was "an incoherent and bizarre mixture of appeals to
authority and demagogy, of professions of reverence for the
laws, ultramodern concepts and moth-eaten bric-a-brac, abso-
lutism and Bolshevism. . . ."

Mussolini, the Italian dictator and Fascist leader, said of
Croce: "There is one man in all Italy whom I fear—Croce.
And I fear him because I do not understand him."

Subsequently, Croce joined the Italian liberal party and
much of his later writing was devoted to the concepts of
liberalism. Mussolini never fully extinguished liberal thinking,
and many have concluded that Croce was not suppressed so
that Mussolini might capture some of the support of the liberal
thinkers. Nonetheless, people who visited his home became
suspect, and though *La Critica* was being published it was
cautiously sold; his books were not allowed in the schools'
curricula. In effect Croce was tolerated (even though his
excellent library was ransacked), but his associates and
writings were not.

Upon the collapse of Fascism in 1943, Crocian liberalism
became the favored form of political thinking. The first political assembly, receiving the blessings of the Allies, elected

Croce as the spokesman. Many suggested that he head the
government, but he countered, "What Italy needs in this
crisis is not a tired old philosopher, but a vigorous and practical
man of the world." He, however, did effect the withdrawal of
King Victor Emmanuel III into private life because many felt
the latter was partly responsible for the country's problems
of the past decades. Croce argued that Italy should be allowed
to solve her internal problems outside the United Nations.
Concerning freedom Croce said: "I am often asked if I believe
that the future belongs to freedom. My answer is that freedom
has no need of the future—it already possesses eternity." A
contemporary commented that "thanks to his work, thousands
of young Italians who have been influenced by Fascist propaganda in their teens switched to liberalism in their university
years."

In 1946, Croce set up the Italian Institute of Historical
Studies so that he could lecture to youths. Each lecture was
published in *La Critica*. Croce's total writings up to 1944 num-
bered sixty-two volumes. When he died in Naples on November 20, 1952, one of his contemporaries described him as a
person "with the rugged face of a fighter and the sensitive eyes
of a saint."

Croce's neoidealism, a revolt against naturalism, spread
throughout Europe, and his idealism also served as a basis
for his concepts of history. History, as traditionally conceived,
concerns a narration of events disassociated from the present.
The historian then evaluates the events and attempts to determine the causes or the results of a series of events. Croce,
however, had an entirely different view of history. His concept
has two principles: (1) "All true history is contemporaneous
history," and (2) History is philosophy and philosophy is
history. In keeping with Croce's philosophy of the spirit, all
reality exists in the mind; history, then, is the most concrete
form of experience which exists in the mind.

Croce's first principle of history—history is contemporaneous
—is best realized if his concept of time is understood. In
Croce's world of idealism, the present is the "eternal present."
This is not the same as identifying the present with timeless-
ness. The eternal present is the present of existence, and no
existence falls outside it. Traditionally, the past is divorced
from the present. In the Crocian sense when man conceives of
a historical event—reality in the mind—all that has been

associated with the event is conceived in the present, the eternal present. In other words, the past is acting in the present. If, for an example, a historian contemplates the dropping of the atomic bomb on Hiroshima, he in the eternal present intuits all the history about the event in the present, and this concept in the present becomes reality or history. If the historian, a week later, contemplates the same event, bringing to bear what he contemplated previously in addition to what he contemplated since his last intuitive state, he conceives of history again.

Croce's second principle of history—history and philosophy are identical—is a natural result of his first principle. History is created in the present; as a result, it is changing and it is vital. When man makes a judgment about history, he is actually evaluating the past in light of the present. The past must be known in order to conclude rightly about the present. If a person, to illustrate that all judgments involve history, approaches a rock and wishes to "move" it, he realizes that his making noises will not make it fly away like a bird. The history of a rock, conjured in the eternal present, would indicate that rocks do not fly, but must be thrown, kicked, or rolled. So in making a judgment, history is philosophy.

Philosophy, in the Crocian sense, does not arrive at final answers to problems. The answers for one moment satisfy the problem for that moment only. History must be re-created, and philosophy must be devised to answer the problem for another moment. History, re-created each moment, is a continuous process of creation. As a result, the answers for one moment would not suffice for another.

According to Croce's views of history, the historian must always express history positively. The past acts as an operating force on the present, and, as a result, it should be expressed positively. Since history is a positive force, the writers of history must treat their work as an art; they must include feelings in their writings; their entire personality must be present. Croce stated: "It is necessary to be dispassionate at the threshold of philosophy, but not at the door of historiography."

Croce, as an outstanding modern-day thinker, influenced many aspects of culture. His aesthetics allowed every man to be an artist. Croce's exponent of aesthetics in the English-speaking world is R. G. Collingwood in his *Principles of Art*.

Croce's literary criticism instigated an intellectual spirit in Italy. His concepts of history helped the twentieth century to discover a way to understand the nature of man.

FURTHER READING

De Gennaro, Angelo A. *The Philosophy of Benedetto Croce.*
Orsini, G. *Benedetto Croce: Philosopher of Art and Literary Critic.*

———Mohandas Karamchand Gandhi [Also known as Mahatma Gandhi]

[1869–1948]

IN 1893, young Gandhi was visiting South Africa on legal business. Going to the railroad ticket window, he asked for a first-class ticket to Pretoria. Gandhi was dressed neatly in Western style, except for the Indian turban on his head. The ticket agent glanced at him peculiarly but sold him the ticket. When the train arrived, however, and he tried to board it, the burly conductor told him he would have to sit in the third-class section. When Gandhi held up his ticket and quietly remonstrated, the conductor told him to move. Apparently the Indian turban on his head and his swarthy color labeled him unacceptable for first-class accommodations. Gandhi refused to move and so the conductor shoved him bodily off the train. Gandhi picked himself up, dusted off his clothes, and walked back to the station.

Frustrated and angry, he thought of dropping the legal case he was on and returning to his native India. In his autobiography Gandhi recalls this decisive moment when he asked himself, "Should I fight for my rights or go back to India?"

He decided that it would be cowardice to run away: "The hardship to which I was subjected was only superficial . . . a symptom of the deep disease of color prejudice. I should try, if possible, to root out the disease and suffer hardship in the process."

He sat down to wait for the next train.

This was a turning point in Mohandas Gandhi's life. His determination to seek to improve the lot of the Indians in South Africa led him to remain there for some twenty years, and it was his efforts in South Africa that set him on the road to the leadership of India and the eventual reverence with which he was regarded by the entire world.

Mohandas Gandhi was born October 2, 1869, in Porbandar, a small town on the western coast of India, in Bombay Province. His father had a responsible position in the government and the family was in very comfortable circumstances, although they were in the third class of the Hindu caste system. (In the first class were the wise men and priests; in the second were the aristocrats and warriors; in the third were the merchants and tradesmen; and in the fourth were the workers. Lowest were the classless ones, the untouchables.)

Gandhi was brought up in the Hindu tradition. He was not permitted to eat meat or to smoke. In his autobiography he tells us that his brother once induced him to taste meat and to smoke and that he became ill from each experience. Mohandas's home life was affectionate and he had great admiration for his father, whose forbearance, kindness, and truthfulness deeply influenced his own personality. His intellectual life was enriched by the good books in his home, the discussions, and the playing of musical instruments.

Following the Indian tradition, a marriage was arranged between Mohandas and Kasturbai, the daughter of a neighboring merchant, when they were each about thirteen years old. Their marriage was a lasting one, with mutual understanding and affection through many trials and ordeals. They had four sons.

At nineteen, Mohandas went to England to study law. Photographs of this period (1888) show him in the meticulous attire of an English dandy, with starched white collar, striped vest, patent-leather shoes and spats, and carrying a cane and gloves. His black hair was slicked down and, because of his slimness and smallness of stature, his ears and pointed nose seemed larger than they were.

Gandhi was a serious student of law and, in 1891, after passing the bar examinations, he returned to India to practice law. In 1893 his law firm sent him on a short business trip to South Africa. It was here that he encountered the degrading discrimination against his people that made him determine to stay and combat it.

Gandhi's problems were to unite the Indians in South Africa under his leadership and to bring about reforms even though his people were an impoverished minority without political influence. He addressed meetings, wrote letters to newspapers and officials and, in 1894, organized the Natal Indian Congress. At last his voice was being heard and the British colonial government took notice of him as an "undesirable." But the more he was abused or mistreated by the government, the more followers flocked to him. The justice of his cause made Gandhi more eloquent than he had ever thought possible. The sincerity and unselfishness of his convictions won over individuals of all ranks and positions.

In seeking to bring about reforms, Gandhi developed a method of nonviolent civil disobedience which he called *Satyagraha* ("soul force" or "truth force"). More than a hundred years earlier, Edmund Burke, in urging the British to grant greater freedom to the American colonies, had declared that it is not possible to jail an entire nation for disobedience. The writings of Thoreau and the Russian Tolstoi taught Gandhi the strength of nonviolent disobedience.

To advocate *Satyagraha* in civilized countries in the second half of the twentieth century is difficult enough. To have applied it in a hostile country in the nineteenth century was even more perilous. Gandhi had as much difficulty in persuading his followers not to retaliate with riots and blows as he did to win public opinion. He and his followers were often abused, beaten, and jailed but they grimly refused to yield or to resort to retaliatory violence.

In 1907 a discriminatory law was passed in South Africa requiring all Indians to register and be fingerprinted. Gandhi urged his people not to obey, no matter what the consequences. For this, Gandhi was sentenced to jail. But the pressure of his followers did not cease, and he was released.

When questioned about his experience he said, "Jail is jail for thieves and bandits. For me it was a palace."

By this time Gandhi had become editor of a newspaper and had, through his law practice, earned a modest fortune. Most of this he now set up in a trust fund to help his people in South Africa. He determined to live simply, to eat the bare necessities of life—fruits, nuts, and vegetables; to perform, himself, the manual labor of the lowliest menial whether it was grinding flour by hand, spinning thread, or emptying the chamber pots; and to live as close to the soil as possible. In this respect he said he was influenced by the English author John Ruskin, who extolled the dignity of labor and deplored the effects of industrialization. Probably the greatest influence on his philosophy of life was exercised by the Hindu Bhagavad-Gita and the New Testament in which he found the ideals of forbearance, forgiveness and humility, love of one's fellow man, and the requiting of good for evil. Gandhi abandoned Western attire and began to wear the loincloth, sandals, and white toga which are part of our picture of him today. It was his belief that living a simple life and denying himself physical pleasures would strengthen his will and purpose and bring him closer to goodness and God.

When the Boer war broke out (1899–1902), Gandhi refused to turn against the British but instead, declaring a moratorium on civil resistance, he actually helped by organizing an ambulance corps.

Many of his followers disagreed with him, but Gandhi, with the shrewd political insight that he was to reveal on many occasions, was convinced that the best hope for redress of injustice would come from the democratic British government, and so he rendered support.

After the war, the civil disobedience campaign, the mass marches, and the strikes continued. In 1913, he led a huge protest march which was supported by a strike of miners and white railroad workers. The government finally yielded, and many of the demands of the Indians were met at last.

In 1914, Gandhi was asked by a representative of the Indian National Congress to return to India to help his native land win *swaraj* ("self-rule") from England. Here his problems were infinitely more complex. There were more than 250 million people in India, formed into different and often conflicting sects, such as the Muslims, Hindus, Sikhs, and Parsees.

Poverty, illiteracy, and corruption were widespread, and change was opposed by the superstitious and traditionalists. It seems almost unbelievable that this frail, idealistic man could have even hoped to unify the destitute, diverse people of India and win their freedom from the powerful British Empire.

Gandhi journeyed from place to place in India seeking to win justice for the Indian sharecroppers, for the Indian factory workers, for the Indian merchants, and for the Indian employees everywhere who were being treated unfairly by the British. At times he was threatened by the authorities and ordered to leave the vicinity, or was beaten and thrown in jail. He actually served more than two thousands days in jail in India.

Wherever Gandhi went, *Satyagraha*, nonviolent civil disobedience, was put into effect against the British. When the Rowlatt Acts were enacted in 1919, giving the government extraordinary powers to punish Indian dissidents, Gandhi called upon his followers to withdraw from all schools and government positions. A massive campaign of civil disobedience was begun. When violence was committed by his people, Gandhi deplored the acts and did public penance to demonstrate his disapproval.

In 1919, British troops fired upon unarmed masses of Indians at Amritsar (the Amritsar massacre), and Gandhi faced an almost impossible task when he sought to restrain his followers from retaliatory violence. His efforts were only partially successful and, when riots occurred, he was blamed and jailed from 1922 to 1924.

Now violence broke out between the Muslims and the Hindus, and Gandhi began a three-week fast to bring about peace. His efforts were successful, but only temporarily.

While, on the one hand, Gandhi was combatting the injustice of the British colonial policies, he was also seeking to raise the sights and standard of living of his own people. Wherever he went, he preached cleanliness, the avoidance of drugs, improvement of farming, the elimination of illiteracy, the dignity of manual labor, and the brotherhood of man. He opposed the caste system and the inhuman treatment of the "untouchables." To weaken the caste system, he would break the nonintercourse rule by sitting among the "untouchables" in the villages, and he even adopted an "untouchable" girl into his own home. Thus the saintly Mohandas captured the sympathy of democratic peoples everywhere.

In 1925, the British government extended a greater degree of self-government to India, and when the Indian National Congress decided to participate in the new legislature against Gandhi's advice, he retired from politics. However, in December 1926, a group of Indians, dissatisfied with the slow progress toward independence, broke away from the Congress and began terroristic bombings and shootings. This brought Gandhi back into political activity as leader of a new extended campaign of civil disobedience and strikes, called hartals.

In 1930, the British broke what seemed to be a promise of greater self-government for India, and so, in March of that year, Gandhi determined upon a major demonstration of civil disobedience. Joined by hundreds of followers, he walked for twenty-four days to the sea at Dandi where, in violation of British law, they gathered salt, which had been set up as a British monopoly. Again Gandhi was imprisoned but the organized disobedience continued.

The spiritual impact on world opinion of Gandhi's efforts on behalf of the disadvantaged Indian people led important leaders in England to call Mohandas to London for a conference with the King and Queen in Buckingham Palace. Gandhi provided an unusual contrast to the pomp and splendor of the palace by appearing in his usual loincloth, shawl, and sandals.

Home rule was promised in 1931 by one British cabinet but denied by their successors. Now the demand by many members of the Indian National Congress and by Gandhi was for complete freedom. The unrest in India continued, and Gandhi and his companions often found themselves in jail. His beloved wife died in 1944 while imprisoned with him.

While being persecuted by the British for his opposition, Gandhi also suffered because of the violent clashes between Muslim, Hindu, and Sikh factions. From 1946 to the end of his life, the interfactional killings sent him, though he was in poor health, walking from village to village in Punjab, Bengal, and other provinces pleading for peace and brotherhood. He began fasts and threatened to continue unto death unless peace was restored. So universal was the veneration of this saintly man that again he achieved his purpose.

At last Great Britian was ready to grant India freedom. The terms of the proposed independence included the partition of India into Muslim Pakistan, under Muhammad Ali Jinnah, and Hindu India, although there were many minority groups in each country. At first, Gandhi opposed the partition, but his practical political wisdom showed him that the alternative to this arrangement was long delay and continued civil strife, so he and the Indian National Congress agreed, and on August 15, 1947, independence was granted to India.

Gandhi was now past seventy-five and the years of deprivation and strain had taken their toll. He was little more than skin and bones, toothless, bald, and wearing steel-rimmed glasses. Yet there was a warmth of spirit that radiated from his face and he showed amazing stamina when the occasion required. He never spared himself, doing manual household chores, working on a spinning wheel, and speaking to thousands throughout the country. Sometimes, when he was too tired to speak, he would merely sit silently before the multitude, who somehow gathered strength and determination from his silence. But Gandhi's satisfaction was short-lived, for on January 30, 1948, in New Delhi, he was shot to death by a young Hindu fanatic who held Gandhi responsible for the separation of Pakistan from India.

More than a political leader, Gandhi was known to his countrymen as Mahatma, the "Great Soul." In an age when expediency, desire for personal power, and Machiavellian cynicism seem to have guided the rulers of governments, Gandhi stands out as one who was a symbol of truth and fearlessness in espousing the cause of truth. Indeed, he entitled his autobiography *The Story of My Experiments with Truth.*

Although he followed the Hindu religion (he spent two portions of each day in prayer) Gandhi believed that truth and God were synonymous. Where he saw injustice and oppression, he fought against them, not with the weapons of war, which serve falsehood as well as truth, but by marshaling the moral forces and conscience of mankind. His tolerance, understanding, and devotion to truth were such that he was willing to yield to his opponents when they were right, though it was disadvantageous to himself and his cause.

Although Gandhi seemed to oppose the industrialization of India, in fact he opposed rather the evils of the factory system of the early 1900's in which unskilled labor was exploited by greedy industrialists. His cure for these evils was a return to the soil and to universal hand labor. Some have believed that

he advocated socialism but this was not so, for he did not
believe in increasing government controls. His desire was to
change human nature so that men would cease their in-
humanity to other men, so that men would share their wealth
as he had done. Gandhi urged the world "to replace greed by
love."

Gandhi understood the basic elements of self-government
to be freedom of speech, freedom of assembly, and freedom
of the press. He described these freedoms as the "breath, the
food, and the drink of public life."

India is now a land of almost 500 million. In the lifetime
of one man—Mohandas Gandhi—these millions, because of
his magnificent example, moved without the bloodshed of a
military revolution from the primitive condition of political
illiteracy under colonial rule to democratic, independent self-
rule, and a place of dignity before all nations.

FURTHER READING

Eaton, Jeanette. *Gandhi*.
Fischer, Louis. *Life of Mahatma Gandhi*.
Gandhi, Mohandas. *Autobiography*.
Nanda, B. K. *Mahatma Gandhi*.

———Nikolai Lenin———
[Vladimir Ilich Ulyanov]
[1870–1924]

"LENIN IS ALWAYS WITH US" is a frequent statement
in the Soviet press. To this day he is respected and honored by
the Russians above all men—the champion of the proletariat,
the father of modern socialism in the Soviet Union, the inter-
preter of Marx, the great organizer of government.

When Vladimir Ilich Ulyanov (Lenin) was born in 1870,

Russia seethed with talk of revolution. This reached all the way to Simbirsk (now Ulyanovsk) on the Volga, the place of his birth. He was one of six children born to the family of Ilya Ulyanov. Lenin's grandmother was one of the Kalmucks, Buddhists of Asian Mongol background. On his mother Maria's side of the family, there was German blood. Maria's father was a physician and she seems to have inherited a progressive background which gave her an interest in strong and independent ideas. Ilya, the father, was a teacher of physics and mathematics promoted to Inspector of Schools in a wide area of the province of Simbirsk. His diligence led to his taking over this undeveloped school system and building it to a new and much improved condition. For this success, he was awarded all the rights and the title of nobleman.

This was a family of diligence and success. Only with difficulty could one believe that from it could come several revolutionaries. Papa Ulyanov played croquet with the boys. Vladimir Ilich himself soon grew to love chess and became quite an excellent player. He loved skiing. He graduated from the gymnasium (high school) at Simbirsk with highest honors. His boyhood seemed happy and secure. Though Maria, his mother, never attended school, she qualified as a schoolteacher, teaching herself English and French and a literary German and Russian. Under her guidance the children published a weekly handwritten magazine. She sewed their clothes on a Singer sewing machine, and the family had a piano which Maria taught the future Lenin to play.

Vladimir could have become almost anything he chose in that day: a doctor, a lawyer, or a merchant. He chose the law, but en route to his degree and examinations other developments influenced his life. His father died while Vladimir was still attending high school. It seems that the passing of the father lifted a subtle control from the boys and gave them a tinge of bitterness. Replying to a census questionnaire Vladimir wrote: "Nonbeliever [in God] since the age of sixteen." His older brother, nicknamed Sasha, was already a member of the People's Freedom Party, whose members had planted the bomb which had killed Czar Alexander II five years earlier. Now they were planning an attempt on the life of his son, the grossly overweight Alexander III. Sasha (Alexander Ulyanov), already a Marxist or near Marxist, now heir to his father's title of nobility, volunteered for the deed.

Before the plot made much progress, Sasha and several associates were arrested. At the trial, Sasha Ulyanov made no attempt to disguise his feelings or to deny his part in the plot. Rather he presented his theories to the court, apparently willing to die to make his views known. He wrote his own death sentence in his statements at the trial.

The death of such a talented young person in the spring of 1887 was a shock to his family and followers. To die in a hangman's noose, by order of the hated autocrat, made him a hero to Russians who had never heard of him before. He became a hero to his high-school brother Vladimir, who later adopted one of Sasha's former nicknames, Lenin. Later, as a university student, when Lenin was first arrested, a colleague in his cell asked what he would do after being released. He replied, "What is there to do? My path has been blazed by my older brother."

The times were ripe in Russia for revolution. The serf system was a system of oppression. Alexander II (Czar, 1855-1881) did introduce some reforms, the most important of which was the emancipation of the serfs in 1861. He refused, however, to allow a national constitution, and during his reign there was an increase in revolutionary thinking, especially among the educated classes. A terrorist group, the Narodnaya Volya, finally assassinated the Czar in 1881. The reign of Alexander III was harsh and there were absolutely no reforms. Thus the growing feeling led to the plot that ended in the death of Lenin's brother Alexander.

Unrest grew with the years. The nobility surrounding the Czar lived in luxurious splendor, while the illiterate peasants who tilled the huge estates and the workers in the factories lived in abject poverty and squalor. Famine, drought, pestilence, and injustice were rampant. An unsuccessful war with Japan (1904–1905) pushed Russia back from ports on the Pacific and caused greater unrest at home. There were student demonstrations, workers' strikes, peasant seizures of land, and occasional mutinies in the army and navy. There was little economic progress on the part of the poor, who were little better off than in their days of serfdom. Through his secret police and through deep-rooted traditions, the Czar, known as the "Little Father," continued to rule.

In this atmosphere of unrest and oppression, the young Lenin entered the University of Kazan but was expelled within a few months for participating in student demonstrations. He then began to read Karl Marx and, in 1889, he formed a small discussion group in Kuibyshev, where his family had moved. In 1891, he read for the law and passed the examinations at the University of St. Petersburg without actually attending. In his home city he spent more time in revolutionary activity than in practicing law.

Karl Marx had a profound influence on Lenin's thinking. Marx was not the first of the socialist thinkers but he became their spokesman. His *Das Kapital* became the bible of the Communist party, and Lenin adopted many of his economic policies: heavy income tax, nonallowance of inheritance, government control of railways, communications, production, an end to child labor in factories, and free education for all people in public schools. Lenin accepted Marx's belief that all history is controlled by economic factors.

Marx had died when Lenin was only a small boy, but Lenin developed and enlarged upon his ideas. It was Marx who claimed to have made socialism a "scientific" theory. He predicted that capitalism would follow feudalism, and socialism would succeed capitalism. He believed this succession was *inevitable*. This was what gave his followers, no matter how much they disagreed among themselves, absolute certainty in thinking that their cause would ultimately prevail. Part of this socialist doctrine is the theory of the class struggle between the proletariat, or working class, and the bourgeoisie, or employer class. Also involved is the materialistic view of history—the idea that material conditions under which man lives determine his ideals, his systems of law, and his ideas of right and wrong. Marx also believed, as did Lenin after him, that capitalism contains within itself many important "contradictions" which must inevitably lead to its downfall at the hands of a socialist working class. These basic theories of communism were Marx's, but it was the indefatigable Lenin who disseminated them, organized followers, and made plans to apply them in Russia.

In 1893, young Lenin, then twenty-three years old, moved to St. Petersburg to enter the revolutionary movement on a full-time basis. In a trip abroad he met George Plekhanov, known as "the father of Russian socialism," and was influenced by him. Two years later Lenin was arrested as an agitator and imprisoned. After fourteen months of preliminary imprisonment, he was deported to Siberia for three years. There, a year later, in 1898, he married Nadezhda Krupskaya, a fellow revolutionary exiled to the same village. In exile he wrote a book on the development of Russian capitalism.

In 1900, Lenin returned from exile. He was prematurely bald, had a broad forehead, wore a red Vandyke beard, appeared shabbily dressed, and had small penetrating eyes. His wife, Nadezhda, was calm, plain-faced, utterly devoted to her husband, willing to move with him from shabby apartment to unfurnished rooms, from city to city, from country to country. In the seventeen years from their return from Siberia to the 1917 revolution, they lived in London, Munich, Geneva, Brussels, Paris, Stockholm, and Zurich. It was a life of extreme hardship and danger. In those seventeen years Lenin and his associates wrote voluminously, argued vociferously, and little by little formulated the procedures by which the takeover would be put into effect when the opportunity came. Lenin became the editor of a magazine called *Iskra,* whose motto was "From Spark to Flame." The magazine was the spokesman of the revolutionary movement and was smuggled into Russia by underground methods. Lenin sought to win to his cause the peasants and the factory workers.

The story of the revolutionaries was one of intrigue and devotion. There were organized bank robberies, holdups of mail trains, and actual guerilla warfare to raise funds for their movement. There were arrests, deportations, escapes, reconvictions, and exiles. There were many people involved in the movement, but from the time of his return from Siberia in 1900, Lenin began to take the lead.

Lenin stood for unrelenting and absolute hostility to all other reform groups. There must be leadership by an uncompromising group of socialist leaders. They must be completely disciplined, dedicated, and trained to think and act together. In 1902 Lenin was joined by the brilliant young revolutionary Leon Trotsky. Trotsky wanted to broaden the base of their Russian Social Democratic party by including nonmilitants as well. Lenin refused and the party split, with Lenin leading the militant majority known as Bolsheviks, as opposed to the minority, the Mensheviks.

When the revolution of 1905 came, Lenin opposed having his Bolshevik group take charge. He knew the time was not yet ripe, his group not yet properly disciplined and their procedures not yet perfected. There were too many quarreling factions within the socialist camp. Lenin's strength of personality prevailed then as later in winning other revolutionary thinkers to his theories. He had a simple, direct, convincing style in expressing himself. Again and again he drove home two basic ideas: No man has the right to live by exploiting the work of his fellowman, and every worker has the right to enjoy the fruits of his labor.

When World War I came the socialist leaders throughout Europe declared their loyalty to their own countries and the war effort, but Lenin refused to join them. He thought this would be the great opportunity for workers in all countries to arise. The soviets (committees of workers) were to become the power group in the new communist government to be. He persisted in his hope that the imperialist war in which millions of Russians were dying could be turned into a civil war in which the worker committees would come into power. Conditions in Russia were now deplorable. The country was unable to maintain its army properly. The soldiers were ill-clothed and ill-fed. Profiteers were making fortunes, while the workers were in abject poverty. The ex-monk Rasputin was the "power behind the throne." Hysteria ruled. It was even rumored that Czar Nicholas was trying for a separate peace with Germany. In February 1917 there was a "five-day revolution" which failed. There was no organization to lead it.

Lenin, still in exile in Switzerland, knew he must get back to Russia. The consent of the imperial government of Germany permitted him to cross Germany on a train for Stockholm en route to Russia. He rode in the so-called "sealed car" at the end of the train, not permitted to alight anywhere in Germany. The German government felt that getting Lenin back into Russia would promote further revolution there and take Russia out of the war.

That is exactly what happened. But Kaiser Wilhelm understood little of what Lenin believed and never dreamed he was aiding a revolution that was to affect vast areas of the earth. Czar Nicholas had finally abdicated and the new Kerensky government was weak. Lenin had sent word ahead of him that there should be absolute distrust of Kerensky and non-cooperation with his government.

Once back in Russia, Lenin made his presence felt by the power of his personality in speaking and writing. He realized the weaknesses of the Kerensky government which had taken over after the Czar's abdication. This new government was frustrated by indecision. It could neither deal effectively with the industrialists, the merchant class, nor the workers. Lenin and his Bolshevik group knew their hour was near in that summer and early fall of 1917.

Soon the Kerensky government was seeking Lenin's life as a traitor. He fled to Finland, there to write constantly to the central committee with instructions, prodding, and reprimands. By October 22, 1917, he could stand isolation no longer. He shaved off his beard, acquired a wig, and even while hunted for treason he showed up among his followers in Moscow. In the "ten days which shook the world" in early November, the government fell, and Lenin, Trotsky, and their followers were in control of all business and government.

At a huge meeting the day following the fall of the government's Winter Palace, the crowd shouted itself hoarse and then Lenin spoke, saying, "We shall now proceed to set up the socialist order." The Bolsheviks were renamed as the Communist party. Reform followed reform in quick succession. All land remaining in the hands of landlords was to go to the peasants (but not yet to be communized). Production in all factories and distribution of all goods was in charge of workers' soviets. All railways, all foreign trade, all banks, and some major industries were nationalized. All existing laws and courts were abolished and in their place "people's courts" were set up. All inequalities based on religion, sex, class, or nationality were abolished. In the army all officers were to be elected. All illiterate citizens between eight and fifty were to attend "literacy schools." The war was to end at once.

These reforms sounded good in theory, but in practice they resulted in chaos. No Bolshevik leader had any experience in business or industry. Factory production fell to one-seventh of the already low output. Many trains did not run. Shop owners were outlawed overnight, and this led to a system of barter for goods and resulted in starvation in the towns and villages. Money ceased to have any value.

In order to get the tasks done, Lenin's government had to conscript labor, and all work was put under Communist commissars. When the Bolsheviks found themselves in the minority in the national assembly, they simply abolished the assembly and all other political parties. There were many small civil wars throughout the country and for a time it seemed that the Communist-conscripted army would be defeated by the "white Russians" (as the army of the nobles and upper middle classes was called), who were aided by their Western allies. However, in 1921, the Red army prevailed. Lenin and his followers were tenacious and dedicated men completely convinced of the justice of their cause.

A powerful speaker (not a great orator), Lenin won by force of argument in speech and written word. As President of the Republic after 1917, he accepted only the salary of a skilled worker. He slept in the Kremlin in a steel bed and his room was uncarpeted.

Lenin's pace of living led to his early death. In the spring of 1922 he suffered a stroke, followed in later months by two other such attacks. He was most unhappy as an invalid. He still dictated constantly, often when too ill to really do so. He attempted to prevent Stalin's following him in power, but failed. In less than two years he was dead. After his death he was practically deified in all the Soviet states. A large mausoleum holds his embalmed body and, to this day, thousands of people line up to visit his tomb. St. Petersburg was renamed Leningrad in his honor. His words even today are quoted over a third or more of the earth. Leninism became both a science and a cult. He was one of the few revolutionaries in all history who was an original thinker but at the same time a man of direct action. His thinking has influenced men of all the earth —both those who believe and follow his precepts and those who utterly disagree with and oppose them.

FURTHER READING

Brown, Nina. *Lenin.*
McNeal, Robert H., ed. *Lenin, Stalin, Khrushchev: Voices of Bolshevism.*
Payne, Robert. *The Life and Death of Lenin.*

——Bertrand Russell——

[1872–   ]

BERTRAND RUSSELL, the outstanding English philosopher and social reformer, has expounded on his divergent interests in more than sixty volumes. His philosophical interests, expressed in a clear style, include mathematical logic, history of Western philosophy, human knowledge, and analysis of the mind; his social and political interests include education, marriage, Bolshevism, pacifism, nuclear disarmament, and religion. In his longevity, he has changed or modified many of his early ideas. As a truly great philosopher, he has explained that these modifications of ideas have been for the purpose of coming closer to fundamental truths about the nature of existence and man.

Russell has associated with many great thinkers of the nineteenth and twentieth centuries. In fact, these associations help to account for his many divergent interests. In a sense, Russell seems to bridge the intellectual circles of the two centuries. Russell met and discussed Bolshevism with Trotsky and Lenin. Lord John Russell, Bertrand's grandfather, was England's great liberal prime minister who introduced the electoral Reform Bill of 1832. Russell and his first wife, Alys, visited the American poet Walt Whitman in his home. D. H. Lawrence, the English novelist and poet, exchanged with Russell numerous letters concerning pacifism.

Furthermore, G. E. Moore, the English philosopher, was Russell's classmate at Trinity College. Moore once remarked about Russell that "he was always talking." The essayist Logan Pearsall Smith, a brother of Russell's first wife, stayed at the Russell home for some time. Sidney and Beatrice Webb, the English economists and socialists, were house guests of the Russells, occasionally staying for three months. Ludwig Wittgenstein, the Austrian-born mathematician and philosopher, was greatly influenced by Russell, whose classes he attended at Trinity College. In addition, Russell claimed the following as personal acquaintances: the physicist Albert Einstein, the economist John Keynes, the English biographer Lytton Strachey, the English biologist and writer Julian Huxley, and the poet and critic T. S. Eliot.

The characteristics of Russell's philosophy have been summarized by Alan Wood in the very title of his work: *Bertrand Russell. The Passionate Sceptic.* Wood also said of him that his "ideas are so intertwined with those of other men of the age that a clever detractor could easily deny him much originality. . . ."

Russell, an orphan at the age of three, was by his father's will to be brought up as an agnostic. The courts ruled otherwise, and his education was handled by his grandmother. His early education was received at the hands of governesses and tutors. In October 1890 he went to Trinity College, Cambridge, where he studied mathematics and philosophy. He graduated in 1894 after achieving distinction in philosophy.

Russell first achieved fame as a logician with *The Principles of Mathematics* (1903), an outline for *Principia Mathematica* (1910, 1912, 1913)—a great three-volume work written in collaboration with Alfred North Whitehead. This latter work, extending the idea of symbolic logic of the Italian philosopher Giuseppe Peano, stated that the terms in mathematics can be reduced to those used in logic. Mathematics and logic are therefore identical. Russell, even at the age of eleven, had questioned the axioms of Euclid; he could not accept the concepts Euclid professed as self-evident. He challenged, for example, Euclid's axiom that a point has position but no magnitude. From his early questioning and his search for certainty, Russell developed his logic of relations and a theory of descriptions.

Russell maintained that the object of philosophy is the search for truth. However, any truth which man believes must be expressed in a statement or proposition. And for centuries logicians, including Aristotle, had stated that all propositions have a subject and predicate in common: for example, "Socrates is mortal." The subject is a class or an individual, and the predicate is a quality belonging to the subject.

Russell noted, however, that the Aristotelean schema did

not allow for relational propositions—a proposition that asserts a relation between two or more things: e.g., "London is bigger than Manchester." Russell then introduced his logic of relations which does show multiple relations do exist, for instance, as illustrated with his example of jealousy: "*A* is jealous of *B* on account of *C*." Russell's admittance of multiple relations suggested a new solution to a problem in the theory of knowledge.

Russell's theory of descriptions added an influential innovation to the science of logic. He wrote: "Every proposition which we can understand must be composed of constituents with which we are acquainted [perceived by means of sense data]." For example, "the author of *Waverley*" has no meaning alone, but it has meaning when it is associated with an object (Sir Walter Scott) with which one is *acquainted*. Thus the statement "The unicorn is a mythical animal" can be explained by the theory of descriptions by use of a known object, even though a unicorn is nonexistent: a unicorn is an animal having a horselike body with one horn.

One critic of Russell once commented that Russell produced a "different system of philosophy every few years." Since Russell is a prolific writer, and since Russell is willing to re-examine many philosophical problems, one receives the impression that Russell changes his philosophy. Upon closer examination of his works, one discovers that his outlook has shown little change per se, but perhaps a change of emphasis or interest.

In developing his philosophy, Russell at first adhered to Kantian and Hegelian idealism, which were fashionable when he attended Trinity College. However, because of the influence of G. E. Moore and because of his studies of Leibniz, Russell altered his views on absolute idealism. Through the influence of Peano, and in collaboration with A. N. Whitehead, he developed a mathematical logic. Russell used mathematical logic as a tool of philosophy for determining or developing his theory of "neutral monism," his concepts of perception, and the nature of truth.

Russell's development of philosophy was guided by two principles. First, science was consulted to see what was applicable in that area which could be applied to a philosophical problem. Second, Ockham's dictum was adopted as a principle. William of Ockham (c. 1300–c. 1349), an English scholastic philosopher, devised a dictum, and Russell stated it as:

"Whenever possible, substitute constructions out of known entities for inferences to unknown entities." The principle allowed a simplicity and an economy to prevail in developing his philosophy.

Russell applied the methods of the formal sciences of mathematics and logic in his development. First, he approached his subject with a skeptical mind. This attitude demanded a questioning of the basis of man's beliefs. Russell cautioned against an insincere skepticism. Second, Russell admitted, according to a commentator, "The tentative and provisional nature of his conclusions." He seemed to be rather cautious about assuming too much in his conclusions. Third, he did not set out to develop a system of philosophy, but he studied one philosophical problem at a time and allowed a system to build from one tested conclusion after another, as a scientist might do. This was his conception of the "new philosophy" one that "abandoned any claim to a special philosophic method" but that used the methods of science.

Russell's theory of "neutral monism" has been subjected to some criticism. Russell in his theory maintained that there is no basic difference in nature between "mind" and "matter" or between what is physical and what is mental. Russell believed that when man looked at an object, the sensations of man became associated with the object and with the person himself. Thus the same sensation existed in the same two places. Russell in *The Analysis of Mind* explained his version of monism.

For some years, Russell has been a critic of William James's pragmatic theory of truth. James maintained that truth arises from consequences of man's beliefs. Russell criticized: "Pragmatism holds that a belief is to be judged true if it has certain kinds of *effects*, whereas I hold that an empirical belief is to be judged true if it has certain kinds of causes." Truth then, to Russell, is something to be searched for but probably never to be attained. "All human knowledge is uncertain, inexact and partial. To this doctrine, we have not found any limitation whatever."

A development of Russell's philosophy is presented in *Our Knowledge of the External World* (1914), *Analysis of Mind* (1921), *History of Western Philosophy* (1946), and *Human Knowledge: Its Scope and Limits* (1948).

Besides his important work in philosophy, Russell has expressed his views concerning many social and political problems, namely those involving pacifism, Bolshevism, education, marriage, ethics, and nuclear disarmament.

However, H. W. Leggett wrote in *Bertrand Russell* that "it can hardly be said that the practical application of his views has had much effect." Moreover, his "influence was exercised chiefly on the attitude, the outlook" of his contemporaries. He used his philosophical aptitudes to cause men to think anew on contemporary problems.

Russell first achieved fame outside of philosophical circles with his stand on pacifism. Russell stated his position about war when he wrote at the start of World War I that "intellectual integrity made it quite impossible for me to accept the war myths of any of the belligerent nations." He became involved in the No-Conscription Fellowship (NCF), the main organization for pacifist propaganda. In spring of 1916, he addressed an NCF convention in London where he was greatly applauded. At that time, he was struggling to secure legal rights for conscientious objectors. He wrote a leaflet, published by the NCF, which furthered the cause of conscientious objectors. For this activity he was prosecuted and fined. His personal belongings and his library (he lost many books) were confiscated to pay for the fine. As a result, Trinity College dismissed him—an act he deeply felt. In 1918, he was sentenced to six months in prison for writing an article which portrayed the American army shooting down strikers. While in prison, he wrote his outstanding *Introduction to Mathematical Philosophy* (1919). It is noteworthy that Russell modified his views on war, recommending participation at the start of World War II.

In the spring of 1920, Russell visited Russia as an unofficial member of the Labour party delegation. When Russell stressed socialism at this time, he meant guild socialism—a system whereby industry is run by the men working in the industry, not by the state. During his tour, he had an interview with Lenin in the Kremlin. Lenin was amazed to hear Russell's belief that England could achieve socialism without bloodshed. Upon his return to England, Russell wrote *Practice and Theory of Bolshevism* (1920). In the book he presented favorable and unfavorable comments about Bolshevism. However, he correctly rationalized that the workman would have "little control over his work" when the state controlled industry. He maintained a hostile view toward communism. He declared after World War II: "Anything is better than submission" to communistic dictatorship. A Russian once described him as a "philosophizing wolf."

Concerning education, Russell outlined his views in *On Education* (1926). In 1927, Russell and his second wife, Dora, set up an experimental school because of an intense interest in their children's education. The school, consisting of twenty boys and girls between four and eleven years of age, followed the theory that the students should have freedom but not license. According to a biographer, Russell's four traits of an ideal character are "vitality, courage, sensitiveness, and intelligence." He maintained that the time to start moral training was at birth. At a later time, a child "will have to fight against contrary habits and will consequently be met by resentful indignation." His ideas are noteworthy in present tendencies to extend public schooling to earlier ages than kindergarten. One commentator said that the students played games, never received punishments, attended classes compulsorily, "bathed together, ran about unclothed in warm weather, and received no religious training." Students were taught to recognize their duties to others and to society. The school was not a success, and when Russell and his wife Dora started divorce proceedings, he left the school, which continued to hold classes until 1939.

For his views on marriage, Russell received notoriety in America. In 1940, he was invited to join the staff of the College of the City of New York. Upon the acceptance of his appointment, a protest against his appointment came from an Anglican bishop on the grounds that Russell was "a recognized propagandist against religion and morality . . . who specifically defends adultery." Next, a taxpayer's suit was filed in the New York Supreme Court to annul the appointment. Judge McGeehan delivered his verdict, annulling the appointment on three grounds, one of the three grounds being the "immoral and salacious doctrines" and the "filth" contained in Russell's books. In 1929, Russell had written *Marriage and Morals,* which advocated youth's better understanding of sexual matters and the freedom of husband and wife to have extramarital relations. Apparently this book influenced the judge in his verdict.

Concerning ethics and morals, Russell has published much, even though he has acquired lasting fame through his philosophical writings. To Russell, the ideal life is "one inspired by love and guided by knowledge." Love is necessary to appreciate the "desires" of another; knowledge is essential to determine the means whereby the wishes or desires may be accomplished and to discover whether the desires are at all contradictory to other desires. Russell does not concur with some moralists that some desires are good and others are bad. "Primarily, we call something 'good' when we desire it and 'bad' when we have an aversion from it." Russell recognizes that the "official" outlook on good and bad tends to be formed by early training and society, and that human nature tends to classify a large area as goodness and badness.

For his views on nuclear disarmament, Russell was indirectly sent to jail. As early as 1923, Russell predicted that the unleashing of atomic energy would give man the means to destroy himself. When a campaign for Nuclear Disarmament with which he was associated in Britain in 1960 proved too mild, he broke away and set up the Committee of One Hundred. This committee conducted sit-down strikes in front of Parliament. In September 1961, Russell led ten thousand followers to sit down before Parliament. For this action, he was indicted for not keeping the peace. Rather than being freed on good behavior, Russell and his fourth wife consented to be sent to prison for one month—they actually served only seven days.

Russell envisioned that if Britain had no nuclear weapons, Russia would not attack her. In a neutral position, Britain could negotiate a nuclear treaty between Russia and the United States. He asserted that even if Britain were armed with nuclear weapons, the Soviet Union could destroy Britain in half an hour with no guarantee that America would be involved. Therefore, Britain has everything to gain and nothing to lose in being neutral.

In October 1965, Russell resigned his membership in the Labour party after fifty-one years. Long an outspoken critic of American policy in Vietnam, he protested what he called the "so-called" Labour party's "complacency over the Vietnam atrocities."

Bertrand Russell, one who advanced the knowledge of man with his mathematical logic, one who fiercely fought for social reforms, one who delved fearlessly into the problems of modern society with "passionate rationality" and with objectivity, received the 1950 Nobel Prize for Literature "in recognition of his many-sided and significant authorship, in which he has constantly figured as a defender of humanity and freedom of thought."

When ninety, Russell wrote: "Like Cassandra, I am doomed to prophesy evil and not be believed. Her promises came true. I desperately hope that mine will not."

FURTHER READING

Fritz, Charles A. *Bertrand Russell's Construction of the External World.*
Russell, Bertrand. *The Autobiography of Bertrand Russell.*
Schilpp, Paul A., ed. *The Philosophy of Bertrand Russell.*
Wood, Alan. *Bertrand Russell: The Passionate Skeptic.*

———Wesley C. Mitchell———
[1874—1948]

THROUGHOUT THE WORLD TODAY, it is generally acknowledged that no country has done as much work in applying statistical techniques to the investigation of economic phenomena as has the United States. The chief credit for this belongs to a calm but indefatigable worker, Wesley Clair Mitchell, who almost singlehandedly developed a new type of economic analysis based on statistical methods. Professor Arthur F. Burns, former Chairman of the Council of Economic Advisors to the President of the United States, said of Mitchell's book *Business Cycles* (1913), "No other work between Marshall's *Principles* and Keynes's *General Theory* has had as big an influence on economic thought of the Western World." In this book, Mitchell departed from previous deductive methods and offered "an analytic description of the complicated process by which seasons of business prosperity, crises, depression, and revival came about in the modern world."

Mitchell's early life was a hard one. He was born in Rushville, Illinois, August 5, 1874. His father was a physician who later saw service in the Civil War as an army surgeon. Wesley Clair was the second child and first son born to the family which soon consisted of seven children. The family had very little money and the father's continued illnesses forced Wesley Clair to take on adult responsibilities far too early in life. However, he managed to complete high school and enroll, in 1892, at the newly founded University of Chicago. Despite the fact that he worked hard on the family farm in the summers, and was forced to pinch pennies during the winters, Mitchell found college to be a "shining opportunity, not a dull duty." He was a bright and eager student and soon attracted the attention of his professors. He received the A.B. degree in 1896, spent one year in Vienna studying with Karl Menger, and with the financial help of Professors J. Lawrence Laughlin and John Dewey, obtained the doctorate in 1899 *summa cum laude*.

At Chicago, Mitchell had the good fortune to study under two extraordinary men who left their indelible marks on a wide range of intellectual disciplines in the United States: Thorstein Veblen and John Dewey. Although Dewey taught philosophy and Veblen taught economics, they both emphasized the importance of group behavior as an evolutionary influence in social development. Under their tutelage, Mitchell studied ethnology, anthropology, and psychology.

From Dewey he acquired the new concepts of pragmatism built upon modern psychology. It was Dewey's pragmatic view that no idea or concept has any meaning unless it can be applied in some way to something that our senses can detect.

From Veblen, who was then mounting his attack upon the formal systems of existing economic theory, Mitchell acquired ideas concerning the influence of custom and convention upon economic behavior. Veblen held that many of the accepted theories that were supposed to explain economic movements were themselves arbitrarily accepted ideas that needed investigation and analysis. Veblen made a profound impression on Mitchell and he continued his association with Veblen until the latter's death in 1929. Mitchell, along with John R. Commons, became one of the leading exponents of Veblen's type of "institutional economics," which emphasized the dominant role of evolving institutions on social and economic conduct.

The foremost economist at Chicago during Mitchell's stay was Professor J. Lawrence Laughlin, whose primary interest was in currency questions and monetary problems. Laughlin urged Mitchell to pursue economic studies for the purpose of recasting the prevalent subjective economic theories of the classical school. His doctoral dissertation, written under Laughlin's direction, was the *History of the Greenbacks,* which today is still the standard reference work on a very important period in the monetary history of the United States.

Upon the completion of his doctorate in 1899, Mitchell worked for one year at the Census Bureau and then obtained his first teaching position at the University of Chicago. Three years later he moved to the University of California, where he met and married Lucy Sprague, the talented and attractive Dean of Women.

In the early 1900's, he published the second volume dealing with the greenbacks, *Gold, Prices, and Wages under the Greenback Standard.* The community of economists immediately recognized this work as a great contribution for its discussion in detail of a vital, formative period in American history, that is, from 1862 to 1878.

In doing the research for the two volumes on the greenback problem, Mitchell became aware of the fact that the knowledge and information he obtained concerning economic fluctuations "suggest more problems than they solve." For example, Mitchell wanted to know what relationship there was between the money economy and the fluctuations of business, between the changes in the value of money and economic behavior, and between the making and spending of money incomes.

As Mitchell thought about the importance of money to a proper understanding of economic life, he resolved to investigate further all price movements in those countries that had highly developed monetary economies, such as England, France, Germany, and the United States. Where statistical data concerning the interaction of various stock, bond, commodity, and labor prices, and the money supply were lacking or incomplete, Mitchell computed his own. Finally, in 1913, after three years of intensive work, he published the six-hundred-page volume of *Business Cycles,* a masterpiece in economic literature. Shortly after its publication, Mitchell was invited to join the faculty of Columbia University where he became outstanding as a teacher and researcher. With the exception of the three-year period beginning in 1918, when he, Charles Beard, Alvin Johnson, and James H. Robinson organized and staffed the New School for Social Research, Mitchell remained at Columbia until his retirement in 1944.

One of the most important contributions made by Mitchell was his work from 1920 to 1945 in helping to organize and direct the National Bureau of Economic Research, whose reports in the fields of national income, business cycles, housing, banking, and transportation are read and highly respected wherever economics is studied. The emphasis in the work of the Bureau was to be on empirical research and verification, with no attempt to exert influence on public policy via recommendations or judgments. Mitchell himself wrote many of the studies published by the Bureau, the most notable being *Business Cycles: The Problem and Its Setting* (1927) and *What Happens during Business Cycles*, published posthumously in 1951.

More important than the actual output of books and studies developed within the Bureau was Mitchell's concept that an organization devoted to pure scientific research and analysis, consisting of gifted investigators from diverse fields, and free of political pressures could contribute to human welfare. It was this concept and his guiding spirit that has made the National Bureau of Economic Research an outstanding scientific research institution.

In addition to writing many of the Bureau's *Annual Reports, Bulletins,* and *Occasional Papers,* Mitchell coauthored several important volumes, including *Income in the United States* (1921), *Business Cycles and Unemployment* (1923), *Recent Economic Changes* (1929), and *Economic Research and the Development of Economic Science and Public Policy* (1946).

Mitchell died in 1948, at the age of seventy-four, after a full and satisfying life, in which he saw many of his ideas concerning the validity and importance of empirical verification accepted by competing groups in the economy.

During his lifetime Mitchell was honored by a great many academic institutions and learned societies. He was president of several associations in his field, and, in 1947, he was the first recipient of the Francis A. Walker medal, awarded by the

American Economic Association only once in every five years to an American who during his lifetime has "made a contribution of the highest distinction to economics."

Mitchell's lifework can be said to have centered around his detailed analysis of the nature and causes of business cycles. The study of panics, depressions, and crises had received the attention of economists before Mitchell's studies. However, most of the theories developed were closely related to orthodox banking and monetary ideas, dealing with a surplus or deficit in the quantity of money in circulation. Furthermore, there was no general agreement as to why there were recurring rounds or cycles of instability in the levels of business activity. All the theories advanced—including those of Veblen, Sombart, and Aftalion—were logically constructed, but lacked any systematic foundation of factual material.

When Mitchell indicated that very little of value in this area could be obtained by the use of logic based on limited facts, his entire approach was considered "novel and, in a degree, revolutionary." Mitchell was convinced that the only way to attack the entire problem of business cycles was to learn everything possible about them through "the collection and analysis of elaborate records of business experience in quantitative form." Furthermore, he believed that these records should be collected and analyzed without reference to any set of theories already in existence, but instead should be made to yield whatever theories they held within themselves.

The only concession that Mitchell was willing to make to this postulate was his statement concerning the framework from which the data had to be viewed. Thus he adopted a theoretical position concerning the operation of the entire economy which emphasizes the extreme importance of the price mechanism. At one point Mitchell stated that "money prices, in brief, are the formal basis on which the economic relations of individuals in modern society are organized and the formal mechanism by which economic processes are carried on." He was saying, in effect, that modern economic life is built around a "money economy" and that an extremely important aspect of this economy is "not the use of money as a medium of exchange, but the fact that economic activity takes the form of making and spending money incomes." The welfare of the nation depends upon the amount of available goods and services, but the welfare of the individual depends upon his control of a sufficient amount of money income.

Mitchell reasoned further that the output of useful goods and services is determined by the possibility of profits, so that the complicated system of making and distributing the various types of goods is simply a subsidiary activity to the profit-making process. This was an important concept because Mitchell was to open a new orientation by showing that business cycles or the fluctuations in the levels of business activity are actually related to the changing prospects for profit-making.

Mitchell then developed his systematic method for tracing the movements and relationships of purchase prices and sale prices for commodities, services, securities, and bank credits. Retail prices, in turn, are very closely connected to prices charged by the wholesaler and manufacturer, and less closely to one another. In visualizing the system of prices as an "endless chain," without "any logical beginning or end," Mitchell was trying to trace realistically the various directions in which the economy moved. He considered inaccurate the prevailing view that the capitalist was able to direct economic activity by supplying the needed capital, taking the required risks, and reaping all the profits. In fact, Mitchell saw very little coordination in the overall operation of the economy, which, it seemed to him, indicated that only potential profits determine which goods are to be produced in the society.

Another major defect that Mitchell saw was the great amount of uncertainty which the economy generated and which was sure to get increasingly worse as new technology and growing competition made systematic planning more difficult. Everything, therefore, seems to be subordinate to money-making and profit-making. He asserted that "the ebb and flow of economic activity is brought into dependence upon the profits of business enterprises. Profits, in their turn, depend upon the margins between buying and selling prices, and upon the volume of transactions." These factors, taken together, said Mitchell, contained the true explanation of the violent fluctuation of the economic system.

The emphasis on money, profit, physical production, and output did not obscure in Mitchell's mind the underlying motivating causes that are part of the institutional culture and framework of modern society. Thus Mitchell, following in the footsteps of his friend and teacher Thorstein Veblen, viewed the economy as a process of evolution in which each phase of economic activity is instrumental in bringing about a succeeding phase, causing unending economic changes in the society.

Mitchell originally had started out to gather only facts and not to develop any position in economic theory, yet his work has achieved an important place in the field of theory. He was the first to reject the subjective position of the orthodox economists and to develop a method leading to a fuller understanding of the complexities of economic life by emphasizing a thorough utilization and investigation of all the available facts. His extensive exploration of business cycles showed economic and political leaders the interrelationships between other economic problems and business cycles, as he had described them. Perhaps most important of all was the stimulation he afforded others in their research projects—and the acceptance by all scientific investigators of his emphasis on the importance of quantitative data.

At heart, Mitchell was a firm believer in the democratic process and in the importance of human welfare. He hoped to make his contribution to those ends by improving economic science so that it would afford a clearer picture of how an economy actually operates. The work that he started has helped develop forecasting and control devices that assist in stabilizing the economy.

FURTHER READING

Azres, C. E. and others. *Institutional Economics: Veblen, Commons and Mitchell Reconsidered.*
Burns, A. E. *Wesley Clair Mitchell: The Economic Scientist.*
Mitchell, L. S. *Two Lives.*

───Martin Buber───
[1878–1965]

THIS WAS A STAGE upon which symphony orchestras and grand-opera performers had appeared. The "sold out" sign usually appeared only for the royalty of the entertainment world. But on this night of April 6, 1952, the "sold out" sign was up for a seventy-four-year-old philosopher. More than 2,500 people of all denominations had gathered in New York City's Carnegie Hall to hear him talk.

Few had ever seen him before and most had never even read his books. Martin Buber was surely not an imposing figure as he walked to the rostrum—far below average in height, about five feet two inches tall, bald-headed except for two white patches of hair, and with a long white beard. As he began to speak with a continental accent, the audience was quiet out of curiosity and politeness, but as he proceeded, his dark brown eyes flashed and his message came through with a moving clarity which held the audience spellbound. It was as though one were in an ancient temple listening to an inspired prophet who talked of a living God, a prophet whose words revived faith in goodness and a desire to combat evil, a prophet who gave new values to existence.

The ideas that he uttered that night had been developed through a lifetime of reading, thoughtful contemplation, writing, and discussion. Martin Buber had been trained to be a scholar; he had become a philosopher and a teacher.

Born in Vienna, he had spent much of his childhood at the home of his grandfather, Salomon Buber, a leading Hebrew scholar, in Galicia (present Poland), then a center of Hebrew learning. It was in this environment that Martin was introduced to the Haskalah (meaning Enlightenment or Cultivation of the Mind), a reform movement in Judaism that sought

550

to substitute reason for faith, that stressed the importance of
the individual, and favored a softening of orthodoxy in favor
of western European ideas and culture. Here, too, he became
acquainted with the Hasidic rabbis, who were the elite among
the pious, whose creed was a mystic spiritualism, who were
recognized as leaders of the community, and who inspired
faith and love of God, charity, humaneness, and righteous
living.

When Buber was eighteen, he entered the University of
Vienna. Here and at Berlin and Zurich during the next three
years he studied Western culture, philosophy, logic, history,
and the arts. In his memoir, *My Road to Hasidism* (1943), he
describes this period as one of searching and confusion of
values, one when he was assailed by doubts about the rationalism and orientation toward western European culture of the
Hebrew Haskalah and about other aspects of Judaism. In
1899 he joined the Zionist movement led by Theodor Herzl,
who advocated Jewish nationalism and a homeland in Palestine. In 1901 Buber became the editor of the Zionist magazine
Die Welt.

In 1904 he found his religious orientation and, for some
five years, he gave himself to concentrated study of Hasidism.
The Hasidic movement as developed in the eighteenth century by Baal Shem Tov had been a reaction against earlier
rationalism and had later drawn upon the Zohar, one of the
great books of Judaism, attributed to Rabbi Simon bar Yohais
of the second century A.D. The keynote of the Hasidic rabbis
was the nearness of the individual to God. The way to spiritual
satisfaction and salvation was not so much by obedience to
Jewish law as through prayer in which each man could mys-
tically receive his own revelation. The Hasidic teachers had
revived faith in the immanence of the deity as a force against
evil and they had a more fervent belief in the future appearance of a Messiah who would redeem the universe from evil.
It was this faith that took hold of Martin Buber and led him
to consider how it might be revived and turned to the benefit
of all mankind.

From 1916 to 1924 he edited *Der Jude,* a prominent magazine of German Jewry. From 1926 to 1930, Buber joined with
a Catholic writer and a Protestant writer to edit a magazine
called *Die Kreatur.* He was also a professor of comparative
religion at the university at Frankfort. When the Nazis forced

the resignation of Jews from German universities, Buber went
to Hebrew University in Palestine, where he was professor of
Jewish Philosophy from 1938 to 1951.

In 1931 he began publishing the fruits of his research on
the Hasidic movement with his *Legends of Baalshem*, about
the Hasidic leaders. His translated Hasidic tales were published in 1947 and 1948, and *The Origin and Meaning of
Hasidism* in 1960.

Aside from his research on and translations of ancient
Hasidic literature and his exegeses of Biblical works, Buber's
contribution to religious philosophy has been called a religious existentialism which has influenced religious thought in
Catholic and Protestant circles. He enunciated this philosophy
in his book *I and Thou* (1937), in which he urged man to
live in an I-and-Thou relationship with God and the universe,
a personal, reverential relationship, rather than the more common I-and-It relationship which the excessive analysis of rationalist philosophers had created. "Each of us is encased in
an armour which we soon, out of familiarity, no longer notice," Buber wrote; and in the latter situation, a man treats
other men, the universe, and indeed the concept of God, as
objects to be manipulated, rather than as a totality that includes the man in which there are reverential relationships. He
gave an example of this "reverential relationship":

> In the deadly crush of an air-raid shelter the glances of
> two strangers suddenly meet for a second in astonishing
> and unrelated mutuality; when the All Clear sounds it
> is forgotten; and yet it did happen, in a realm which
> existed only for that moment.

I and Thou contains Buber's conception, based on what the
early Hasidic rabbis had envisioned, of a more direct communion or dialogue between God and man. In *Between Man
and Man* (1947), he wrote about man's condition:

> This condition is characterized by the union of cosmic
> and social homelessness, dread of the universe and dread
> of life, resulting in an existential constitution of solitude
> such as has probably never existed before to the same
> extent. The human person feels himself to be a man ex-
> posed by nature—as an unwanted child is exposed—
> and at the same time a person isolated in the midst of the

tumultuous human world. The first reaction of the spirit to the awareness of this new and uncanny position is modern individualism, the second is modern collectivism.

He said further that:

Individualism sees man only in relation to himself, but collectivism does not see *man* at all, it sees only "society." With the former man's face is distorted, with the latter it is masked.

The book goes on to show how the "I-Thou" conception in the relationship between man and man leads to man's humanity to man, an existence of mutual respect and compassion, and beyond this to a love for all God's creatures.

In *The Prophetic Faith* (1949) and *Moses* (1946), Buber applied I-Thou to the Biblical relationship between God and the people of Israel as a dialogical communion between God and man. This directness of encounter, this immediacy and spontaneity of relationship between man and his divinity, forms a religious basis for existentialism, the philosophy which emphasizes the importance of man, the freedom of his will, and the dignity of his efforts.

In *Paths to Utopia* (1950), Buber applied his theological principle to government. He opposed Soviet collectivism but favored a type of socialism, if individuals could be persuaded to adopt his I-Thou ideals. He showed the application of those ideals in some of the small communities of the new state of Israel, which was his home. In *Good and Evil* (1953), Buber stressed the necessity of an orientation to God and action on behalf of the good, declaring that inaction and lack of direction promote evil.

Martin Buber died in 1965. The scholar who filled Carnegie Hall has had an audience many times 2,500, including leaders of diverse faiths. Many contemporary scholars believe that his I-Thou concept is one of the most stimulating and influential theories of our time.

FURTHER READING

Brown, James. *Kierkegaard, Heidegger, Buber, and Barth.*
Diamond, Malcom L. *Martin Buber, Jewish Existentialist.*
Smith, R. G. *Martin Buber.*
Friedman, Maurice. *Martin Buber.*

———Oswald Spengler———
[1880–1936]

JUST BEFORE THE OUTBREAK of the First World War, an obscure German schoolteacher completed the first draft of a manuscript he called *Der Untergang des Abendlandes (Decline of the West)*. Working completely alone, he had spent the three years from 1911 to 1914 in writing this work. However, because of the war, it was not until July of 1917 that he was able to publish the first volume of his study as a limited edition of fifteen hundred copies. Almost overnight the author was acclaimed as "one of the most influential thinkers of his generation." In spite of the pessimistic nature of the work, it sold more than ninety thousand copies in a relatively short time, created a huge amount of controversy over its merits and implications, and was translated into many languages. In the dark atmosphere of defeat and pessimism of postwar Germany, Spengler's views of the impending doom of Western civilization seemed to appeal to the masses as a kind of explanation for their defeat and humiliation.

The main idea that Spengler expressed in *Decline of the West*, subtitled *Outlines of a Morphology of World History*, is that there are definite, discernible laws of growth in world history, laws from which the birth and death of all known cultures can be determined. Going one step further, he stated that history is predictable and that in point of time and stage of development, Western cultures had already entered a declining phase, or as he put it, had changed from a "culture" to a "civilization," which, according to Spengler, is a major step in the decline. This cycle is similar to the one that people must undergo. That is, they are born, develop in their youth, mature, decline with old age, and finally die. As he put it: "Western Civilization is the latest but not the last of the recurring cycles which advance and recede like the tides of the sea."

Oswald Spengler had prepared himself well before writing his masterpiece. He was born at Blankenburg, in the Harz mountains in Germany, May 29, 1880. His father came from a long line of mining technicians, but had been forced to give up the family trade because of the exhaustion of the Harz mines. At the time of Spengler's birth, his father was a postal official with a deep interest in mathematics and science. From his mother's side of the family the children inherited some artistic talent. His oldest sister, of whom he was very fond, was a recognized painter. Unfortunately, she committed suicide in 1917, at the age of thirty-five. With the exception of his maternal grandmother, who was a Catholic, both sides of the family followed the Protestant faith.

As a student Spengler worked hard, studying mathematics, natural science, history, and art at the universities at Munich, Berlin, and Halle. It was at Halle in 1904, after failing the oral examination the previous fall, that he obtained his doctoral degree with a dissertation on Heraclitus, a philosopher in the pre-Socratic period. From then until 1911 he worked as a schoolmaster in Hamburg and Munich. He taught a variety of subjects including German, history, and geography. His students recall that he was a good teacher who had an "intuitive" style and who maintained firm discipline in the classroom.

In 1911 Spengler inherited a sum of money sufficient to allow him to resign his position and devote his full time to research and writing. During this period he also experimented with various forms of creative writing, including poems, dramas, sketches, and stories. Several of these were published after his death by his niece.

After the publication of *Decline of the West* had brought him recognition, Spengler tried to call attention to forthcoming political changes in the world. He believed he saw great world conflicts developing, and in a book called *The Hour of Decision* (1934) he advocated power politics in Germany, which some observers felt undermined liberal and progressive institutions in that country. In that book Spengler advocated both revolutionary measures to preserve the power of Germany's ruling classes and the use of war to achieve world hegemony under Germany's leadership. Much of Spengler's earlier writings also had racial overtones, especially his emphasis on the peril posed by the "colored" races. After Hitler came into power, Spengler protested that this was not the type of leadership he had in mind for Germany. But it was too late: though the Nazis did not molest Spengler during the last three years of his life, he was under an official boycott, which reduced his influence.

In addition to works already listed above, Spengler published the following works: *Man and Technics: A Contribution to a Philosophy of Life* (1932); *Prussianism and Socialism* (1919); *Reconstruction of the German Reich* (1924); and *A Contribution to the World History of the Second Millennium before Christ* (1935). After his death many of his notes and articles were published by his niece under the title *Thoughts* (1941). All these works were either elaborations of details or additional views on the main theme presented in the *Decline of the West.*

There are probably as many different ways of viewing history as there are historians. A few special viewpoints have predominated in historical writings in modern times. For example, the economic interpretation of history developed fully by Marx stated that history is determined according to what is produced, how it is produced, and for whom it is produced. Some political scientists view history as a power struggle between various kings, rulers, dynasties, and ideologies. The Greeks believed that geography, including soil, climate, and physical topography, strongly influences the formation of character, which in turn changes the traits and behavior of a people and thus affects their historical development. Others have stated that history is a series of unrelated happenings or an unstructured conglomeration of dates, wars, and names from which nothing of lasting value can be abstracted. Henry Ford's statement that "history is bunk" falls in this category. Other viewpoints have emphasized "great men," religion, or psychocultural hostilities as the motivating forces that determine history.

The philosophical interpretation of history is the method adopted by Spengler to explain historical evolution. Other famous thinkers who have used the same approach include the German philosopher Georg Friedrich Hegel and the English historian Arnold Toynbee. Basically, these three writers believed that history consists of a series of events that are interrelated and possess continuity, and that civilization does follow a predictable pattern.

Spengler was critical of historians who divided the past into ancient, medieval, and modern periods and regarded Western culture as the best. Instead, Spengler developed a "Copernican system" in which no culture had a privileged position and in which full attention was given to the "high cultures" of India, Babylon, Mexico, China, Egypt, and the Arabs. He saw a number of great cultures developing "with primitive strength from the soil of a mother-region to which each remains firmly bound throughout its whole life-cycle; each stamping its material, its mankind in its *own* image; each having its *own* idea, its *own* passion, its *own* life, will and feeling, its *own* death."

Thus, continued Spengler, when a culture is born, it develops its own form, makes progress, and breaks into full bloom when it becomes sure of its own power. At that stage "every individual trait of expression is deliberate, strict, measured, marvelous in its ease and self-confidence." Then a period approaches when the spirit and fire in the soul of the culture die down. This is the beginning of the last phase, the change from culture to civilization.

The characteristics of civilization are many: in place of "home," "race," and "fatherland," the emphasis is on cosmopolitanism and the sprawling megalopolis; in place of love of tradition and respect for age, there is only a "cold matter-of-factness"; in place of motherhood, one finds only sex; in place of true religion of the heart, there is scientific "irreligion" or obtuse metaphysics; and in place of unity and quality, there are only class or group struggles, desire for power, and the "cult of bigness." In this last stage of civilization, which Spengler said could continue for hundreds or thousands of years, individuals will attempt to influence the collective society to return to its prior values and revive the spirit of the earlier high-culture phase, but they will not be successful. In this "Indian summer" period some revival of earlier forms will occur, but it will be too late because all of its creative forces have broken down and petrification has set in. Thus the culture, in the stage of civilization, "loses its desire to be, and, as in Imperial Rome, wishes itself out of the overlong daylight and back in the darkness of protomysticism, in the womb of the mother, in the grave."

Spengler went on to identify and describe in minute detail

seven great cultures: Egyptian, Babylonian, Indian, Chinese, Classical (Greco-Roman), Magian (Arabic, Islamic, Iranian, Jewish, Syrian, Byzantine, Manichaean, and early Christian), and Western. Russian culture was not included in these seven because Spengler believed that Russian culture suffered early in its development a partial suppression from the older civilizations and, therefore, had not yet gone through its life cycle. (Prior to the Russian Revolution, Spengler predicted that a new, powerful Russian culture would develop in that country after the decline of Western culture.)

Each culture has its own basis for existence, or its prime symbol, which differs completely from any other culture. The prime symbol will find expression in all the arts, sciences, and beliefs of the culture. For example, the prime symbol of the Egyptian culture was "stone." Everything in the Egyptian culture was related to stone in some way. It represented timeless, unstirring space, and represented the place of burial. In the Classical culture (Greek), the prime symbol was the "sensuously present individual body as the ideal type" repeated in the nude statues, in paintings, and in medical and religious activities. Spengler worked out this detail for each of the cultures he identified. The prime symbol is what makes each culture unique, shaping its own personality and applying its own meaning and style to science, philosophy, religion, arts, and all aspects of cultural and social behavior. The logical conclusion, therefore, if one accepts Spengler's reasoning, is that there is not one universal science, art, mathematics, philosophy, value, or belief, but rather that all cultures produce their own variations in these areas, different from the others. The best example of this point, Spengler stated, could be found in such an exact area as numbers and mathematics. Spengler denied the existence of numbers as such. He believed that there were as many "number-worlds" as there were cultures. For example, the inner structure of the Euclidean geometry is quite different from that of the Cartesian, and the analysis of Archimedes moves in a different direction from the analysis of Gauss, "not merely in matters of form, intuition and method, but above all in essence, in the intrinsic and obligatory meaning of number."

Spengler further claimed to have discovered "periodicities" of fifty, one hundred, three hundred, and six hundred years in length; that is, "Every one of the Culture's intrinsically necessary stages and periods has a definite duration, always the same, always recurring." Furthermore, the development of the fine arts in all cultures always follows in this time sequence: "architecture—sculpture—painting—music."

Spengler suffered a heart attack and died in 1936. His last years were ones of frustration and despair. Whatever influence he had had was eliminated officially by the Nazis, who considered him too pessimistic and reactionary. Abroad, he was blamed for preparing the groundwork for the downfall of German democracy. Professional historians scoffed at his thesis and the unscientific nature of his work. He belonged to no formal academic or literary groups, and had very few friends. He was never offered a university position, and was too proud and independent to ask for one. He never married and remained a lonely figure, believing to the end that he had painted the only true picture of historical development.

A closer examination of Spengler's life indicates that he accomplished a great deal in his relatively short lifespan. He was a trained classical scholar and a good mathematician, with a grasp of all the natural sciences. He had a broad knowledge of art and music, and was versed in literature, economics, and philosophy. In addition to his native German, he had mastered Latin, Greek, French, and English, and had a working knowledge of Italian, Spanish, and Russian. In person his "vast forehead and bald dome," huge bulk, and forceful and forbidding countenance belied the intense sensitivity that was contained therein.

Since the end of the Second World War, Spengler's thesis has been revived by a new group of historians, philosophers, and sociologists who favor the cyclical interpretation of history. Outstanding among these are the British historian Arnold Toynbee, the Russian-born Harvard sociologist Pitirim Sorokin, and the late German philosopher and missionary Albert Schweitzer. They differ from Spengler in emphasis and conclusion, but closely follow his structural concepts of history.

Oswald Spengler's works have been criticized as being more intuitive literature than historical research, and he himself has been called the "Jeremiah of Munich," yet one authority has called the *Decline of the West* the "key to our times. It formulates . . . comprehensively the modern *malaise* that so many feel and so few can express. It has become the classic summary of the now familiar pessimism of the twentieth-century West with regard to its own historical future."

FURTHER READING

Hughes, H. Stuart. *Oswald Spengler.*
Sorokin, Pitirim A. *Modern Historical and Social Philosophies.*

——John Maynard Keynes——
[1883–1946]

THE YEAR 1929 ushered in the Great Depression. Most of the leading nations of the world were devastated by it, and in the United States it seemed as though capitalism was about to perish. The Depression touched every area of American life. A year after the stock-market crash of 1929, six million men walked the streets looking for work. By 1932, the physical output of manufacturing was off 54 percent from the 1929 figure. Farming communities, which had seen little of the prosperity of the 1920's, were further depressed by the loss of what remained of foreign markets. American foreign trade declined from $10 billion in 1929 to $3 billion in 1932. In the cities, breadlines and relief rolls lengthened. The hungry stood for hours on lines to get a bowl of broth from charity "soup kitchens." Young people were graduated from colleges and universities without the slightest chance of finding a job. The collapse of European banks, the defaulting on war debts and reparations, and the demand for gold by Europeans undermined the banking structure of the United States. Bank failures in the United States multiplied, creating an atmosphere of panic. In 1931, 2,294 banks failed, and, by the fall of that year, a billion dollars had been taken from banks and put in safe-deposit boxes or stuffed in old mattresses.

In the midst of the confusion and general economic chaos some people called upon the country to adopt fascism; others pointed to communism as a way out. Above the cries of distress, however, a calm British voice offered a plan that would help to steady the economic props under capitalism—this was the voice of John Maynard Keynes. His plan involved government action to provide jobs for the unemployed, public-works projects to stimulate investment, and loans to farmers and businessmen.

Had Keynes been born during the renaissance, he would have been a wonderful representative of the man of many accomplishments considered so desirable at that time. He was at various times an economist, a writer, a teacher, a diplomat, a speculator, and an art collector. It is for his contributions to economic theory, however, that Keynes is best known. As the eldest son of John Neville Keynes, an economist of the classical school, Keynes could almost be said to have been born into the subject. At the age of four and a half he was trying to solve the economic meaning of interest, and not long afterward he was able to talk intelligently upon a variety of economic subjects. As a teenager at Eton he achieved a brilliant record, which was further enhanced by his work at Kings College at Cambridge. At the age of twenty-two, after graduation from college, Keynes entered the India Office of the Civil Service. After two monotonous years he resigned and in 1909 he returned to Cambridge as a teaching fellow in economics.

But Keynes had not wasted his two years in the India Office. From what he learned he wrote a book called *Indian Currency and Finance,* a solid and substantial work which was favorably received by his professional colleagues. Using a straightforward classical analysis, Keynes argued for a managed currency. He asked that a central bank be set up in India to centralize the gold reserves so that extraordinary monetary drains could be met in times of crisis. It was his opinion that this plan would give the Indian currency system greater stability.

About the time that his book on Indian currency appeared, Keynes was given the editorship of the *Economic Journal,* Britain's most influential economic publication. For this position, he had the backing of Alfred Marshall, a leading economist who had been his teacher.

Called to the Treasury during the First World War, he was

assigned to work on Britain's overseas finances. At the close of the war he attended the peace conference at Paris as deputy for the Chancellor of the Exchequer on the Supreme Economic Council. Although Keynes could offer advice, he was not in a position to influence decisions directly.

The course that the conference took distressed Keynes. He felt that the peace settlement was "outrageous and impossible" and could bring "nothing but misfortune behind it." Resigning his position at the Paris conference, Keynes wrote a sensationally successful book, *The Economic Consequences of the Peace* (1919), attacking the terms of the settlement. In a principal section of the book he noted that the Allies called for impossibly high reparations from Germany while depriving the defeated nation of the means of making foreign payments. He also noted that the war had dealt the delicate mechanism of prewar capitalism a terrible blow. In Keynes's words, "It was the task of the Peace Conference . . . to reestablish life and to heal wounds." It did not do this. He concluded that the settlement "was one of the most serious acts of unwisdom for which our statesmen have ever been responsible." Not long after the publication of this book, Keynes became known as an economist of extraordinary foresight, for when the Dawes Plan, in 1924, began the long process of undoing the mistakes of 1919, his prophesy was confirmed.

Following the war, Keynes became a man of many interests. In the 1920's, while retaining his editorship of the *Economic Journal* and his teaching position at Cambridge, he successfully speculated in the international markets, making himself financially independent. He bought the British weekly the *Nation,* merged it with the *New Statesman,* and wrote for the *Manchester Guardian.* In addition, Keynes collected paintings and subsidized the ballet, capping his interest in that art form by courting and marrying Lydia Lopokova, a charming dancer of the Russian ballet.

The question of whether England should return to the gold standard at the prewar gold value of the pound was very much in the news in the early 1920's. The issue involved price stability, which would act as a stimulus to business activity. To Keynes, gold had failed to remain stable in terms of purchasing power.

In 1923, he wrote a *Tract on Monetary Reform* pointing

out that there was nothing sacred about a gold standard. He would have the Bank of England quote a weekly buying and selling price for gold rather than establish a set price. The bank's weekly price would fluctuate as conditions warranted. He asked, Why should British labor be made to endure misery for an abstraction like the gold standard? It would be much better to devalue the pound than to try to reach a precarious balance through the route of painful price adjustments. Keynes argued further that "in the modern world of paper currency and bank credit there is no escape from a 'managed currency,' whether we wish it or not;—convertibility into gold will not alter the fact that the value of gold itself depends on the policy of the Central Banks."

Despite Keynes's plea, however, in 1925 England returned to the gold standard at the prewar gold value of the pound. In 1931 the failure of the great central banks in Vienna, Berlin, and Basel, to which the Bank of England had made loans, led foreign depositors to withdraw their funds from their English banks. These withdrawals were largely in gold. Since the Bank of England could not call in its continental loans and since the drain of gold from England was becoming very serious, the British government, on September 21, 1931, suspended the right to demand gold for notes. In other words, Britain went off the gold standard. Again, Keynes's foresight was confirmed.

Classical economic doctrine assumes a competitive marketplace in which price is determined by the bids of buyers and sellers. In 1930, Keynes published a two-volume *Treatise on Money*, which used classical economic reasoning. In place of buyers, Keynes refers to savings, or what is left after buying, and, in place of sellers, he refers to investment, which helps to create the goods offered by sellers. The whole aim of the *Treatise* was to tell us how to keep prices stable—or, what is the same, to keep savings and investment equal. Keynes felt that this balance or equilibrium between savings and investment could be accomplished by deliberate manipulation of the rate of interest. Thus, if the rate of interest were lowered, loans would be more plentiful and businessmen would invest more readily; if the rate of interest were raised, savings would be encouraged.

But manipulation of interest rates was a far cry from what was needed to deal with the realities of the Depression. By the summer of 1932, unemployment in the United States had reached 12,840,000—almost 25 percent of the working force—farm prices had fallen 60 percent below the low level of 1929, and bank failures were multiplying at an alarming rate. It was the practical measures devised by the New Deal to cure these real economic ills that underscored Keynes's major work, *The General Theory of Employment, Interest and Money* (1936). Keynes now discarded such classical doctrines as the virtue of thrift and the need for free trade. He began to advocate, instead, increased consumer spending, a protective tariff, a "Buy British" campaign, and public-works expenditures. He believed that the spending of money and the purchasing of goods would lead businessmen to invest money in expanding their plants. The effect would be to raise national income, a concomitant of which is employment; they go up and down together. With full employment, national income must be high. But when you subtract "effective demand"—the demand of people who have both the money and a willingness to buy—from income, you find you have a gap, or withdrawal from the purchasing market, caused by savings. Keynes wanted these savings to be put to work to overcome this gap. Investment in new buildings and machines would accomplish this. New jobs and new income would thereby be created and, in turn, there would be new effective demand. Moreover, Keynes believed that investment of this kind had a sort of multiplier effect of about three times. Thus, in order to close a gap of $55 billion, we would need real investments of only $18 billion.

In his *General Theory,* Keynes systematically organized the changes in his thinking to answer the question of how an economy could remain in a state of depression for a prolonged period. His analysis shed new light on the classic conception of business cycles with periodic fluctuations, and indicated that an economy need not necessarily move upward or downward—that it was possible for it to stand still in either depression or prosperity. He pointed out, for example, that as income contracted during a depression, savings were squeezed out. Without a surplus of savings there would be no downward pressure on interest rates to encourage businessmen to borrow for investment. And if there were no surplus of investment, there would be no impetus for expansion. Thus, during the Depression there actually was no built-in safeguard, as some economists believed, that would reverse the trend and swing the economy to full production again.

This rather bleak outlook was reinforced when the Keynesian proposition was turned around; for just as savings contracted when the economy contracted, so they would expand when the economy expanded. Every boom period was, therefore, threatened with collapse; for, if at any time investment were suddenly slowed down, the cycle of buying and selling would be broken and the process of contraction would begin. In the final analysis, therefore, declared Keynes, the economy was dependent on the amount of investment by business. When investment was low, the economy shrank in size; when it was high, it pulled the nation up with it; if investment failed to remain high, it permitted the process of contraction to begin again. Wealth and poverty, boom and slump, all depended on the willingness of business to invest.

The major problem was how to keep the economy constantly in high gear by maintaining investments and business enterprise at a high level. Keynes recognized that the investor was unlikely to invest during hard times, just when the economy needed new investments badly. To expand investment opportunities, methods of increasing effective demand had to be put forward. Keynes's prescription centered on government action. He called on the government to keep interest rates as low as possible so that investors could profit from the use of borrowed money. Also, the government should deliberately invest its money from taxes where it was most needed.

The New Deal program in the United States had this pattern and was in full swing at the time of the publication of the *General Theory*. The book, however, gave the program respectability and an economic rationale. Elaborating on the Keynesian idea, it was pointed out that if investment could not be directly stimulated, the problem might be tackled through building up consumption, which provided the foundation for economic activity. Thus, the WPA projects were designed to tackle the problem from two sides: by directly helping to keep up purchasing power among the unemployed and by stimulating a resumption of private business activity. In more recent times the government has continued to use the Keynesian formula by putting into effect tax cuts designed to increase purchasing power and stimulate investment. Keynes saw the government program as a balancing force that served only to supplement the behavior of individual capitalists.

There are those who condemn the practical reform measures of the Keynesian economists, saying that the result will be socialism. What they do not see is that the Keynesian reforms do not infringe momentously on the rights of private individuals to own the means of production. The socialist approach visualizes the state, as representative of the people, as the major entrepreneur. The Keynesian policy, on the other hand, aims to conserve free-enterprise capitalism.

The receptiveness for the Keynesian theory was, in large measure, created by the Great Depression. While some economists considered Keynes a mischievous meddler, none could gainsay his aim—the creation of a capitalist economy in which unemployment, the single greatest and gravest threat to its continuance, would be forever eliminated. Stated more completely, Keynes's objective was full employment in an expanding economy with a rising standard of living and a stable dollar. Those taking issue with Keynes, however, pointed out that he assumed a state of perfect competition and that his proposals did not take into account the problems created by the enormous growth of monopoly power and advertising techniques. There was a real question as to whether the consumer was still king. Also, it was pointed out that the Keynesian formula might result in overinvestment. The effect of overinvestment would be that investors, through their corporations, would reach out for materials that would already be in short supply and for labor that would already be fully employed. This would raise prices and wages and would therefore be violently inflationary.

Nevertheless, in spite of certain weaknesses, the Keynesian doctrine has now triumphed to the point where no responsible government will allow or risk allowing the economy to run down as it did in the 1930's. The advent of the "welfare state" has helped to maintain a high level of demand. The "built-in stabilizers" that have been developed can be interpreted as corrective agents that compensate for those developments that might throw an economy off balance.

In 1937, Keynes was partially immobilized by a heart attack. When war came again, however, he was once more called to the Treasury. Soon there was another book, *How To Pay for the War*. In this instance, Keynes urged a system of compulsory saving. A portion of every pay envelope would automatically be invested in government bonds to be redeemed after the war was over. The problem was now that too much money was available for purchasing goods and investment, and its consequence was inflation. Now savings were far short of what was needed to balance out the flow of income. Keynes noted that his scheme would also serve to broaden the distribution of wealth. Compulsory saving, however, did not enlist much support; instead, voluntary savings drives were relied upon, together with taxation and rationing.

Between 1941 and 1946 Keynes made six trips to the United States. He headed the British delegation to the Bretton Woods monetary conference in 1944 and became coauthor of the plan for an international monetary fund and a world bank to avoid, in the future, the international financial rivalry that had contributed to physical warfare. Honors now poured in upon Keynes from all parts of the world. He became Lord Keynes, Baron of Tilton. Then, on Easter Sunday, April 21, 1946, his heart stopped and a brilliant mind was stilled.

While certain aspects of Keynesian doctrine are still controversial, it was his great contribution that he found serious flaws in the classical explanation of the business cycle, successfully challenged timeworn but fallacious assumptions, and suggested practical solutions to the vexing problems of unemployment and business depressions in modern times. The framework of his proposals has provided governments with a useful tool for aiding the citizenry. The result has been more intelligent government planning to lessen the fluctuations of the business cycle, and, in general, a greater flexibility in the approach to economic problems.

FURTHER READING

Dillard, Dudley. *The Economics of John Maynard Keynes.*
Harrod, R. F. *Life of John Maynard Keynes.*
Keynes, John M. *Essays in Persuasion.*

———Karl Barth———

[1886–   ]

KARL BARTH once likened himself to a man groping his way through the dark bell tower of a church. The man reaches out to grasp something by which to steady himself and he is startled to hear the great bell of the church begin to ring. He has inadvertently grasped the bell rope, rung the bell, and wakened the town.

The "darkness" in which Karl Barth had felt himself was centered on his task, as a minister, of preaching a sermon every week. On the one hand he saw his congregation, people in search of meanings for their lives, in search of God; on the other hand he saw the Bible, the book out of which he was expected to provide for the people the word of God. But he was in the dark because the traditional way of interpreting the Bible no longer seemed to him to speak to the people's need; worse, it did not seem to convey the word of *God*.

The groping for something by which to steady himself was in Barth's case a prolonged study (with many notes taken) of St. Paul's Epistle to the Romans. It was the publication of his findings in *Der Römerbrief (Epistle to the Romans)* in 1919 that "rang the bell." All over German-speaking Europe pastors and theology professors knew that a major thinker had arrived.

Karl Barth was born on May 10, 1886, in Basel, Switzerland. His father, Fritz Barth, was a minister of the Swiss Reformed (Calvinist) Church and professor of the New Testament at Basel's Reformed Church theological seminary. Young Karl attended the University of Berne and then, as a prospective minister, continued his studies at a number of universities at which he could hear the leading theologians of the time. At Berlin he studied under Adolf Harnack, the great church historian and

568

historian of dogma; at Marburg he was an eager disciple of
Wilhelm Herrmann in systematic theology. Both these teachers
were representatives of the liberal, almost humanistic theology
that was dominant in German Protestantism at the time; under
them Barth became a militant liberal.

Ordained to the gospel ministry in 1908, Barth spent a year
on the staff of *Die Christliche Welt*, a German-language
religious paper, and then two years as assistant pastor of a
church in Geneva. In 1911 in the Swiss town of Safenwil he
began the ten-year pastorate in the course of which he
agonized about what to preach and achieved his widely hailed
solution.

Safenwil, besides being a rural town counting many farmers
among its residents, was also the site of some textile factories.
Barth's congregation included both owners and managers, on
one hand, and wage earners, on the other. He felt that the
owner-management group wanted a pastoral leadership that
would help the wage earners to be content with what they
had; he knew the wage earners hoped for a pastoral leadership
that would support their demands for higher wages and better
working conditions.

In this period of his life Barth joined the Social Democratic
party and he helped to organize the workers. He was deeply
occupied with the proposals of various pastors who felt that
their service to the Kingdom of God should be rendered not
only through preaching but also through political efforts to
secure greater economic justice for their poor parishioners.

Barth was disillusioned in many respects by World War I.
On the one hand, he was let down by the fact that none of
his German theological mentors raised his voice to protest
the support of the German churches for the Kaiser's war aims.
This fact called into question the whole system of Christianity
which he had been taught in the universities. On the other
hand, he was equally disappointed that none of his internationally minded religious socialist associates was able to
rise above the nationalistic hostility of the war years. It
was in this period that he felt his frustration about what to
preach and joined forces with a good friend from student days,
Edward Thurneysen, who served a neighboring parish. Together they put political and ecclesiastical questions away and
began intensive study of the Bible and of theology, especially
St. Paul's Epistle to the Romans.

The nature of Barth's second edition of his commentary
on Romans is characterized by its emphasis on God as the
"Wholly Other." That is, Barth was rebelling against pictures
of God as merely human goodness "writ large." He stressed
Sören Kierkegaard's "infinite qualitative difference" between
eternity and time, that is, between God and man. As he
saw it, ordinary religion was man's way to God, that is, the
expression of an effort to get God to support ordinary human
aspirations. In contrast with that, for Barth the biblical
revelation indicated God's approach to man in Jesus Christ,
according to which man, in all his works and all his pre-
tensions, was judged to be a sinner; man was also forgiven in
Christ, but the new life into which forgiven man was invited,
a life in which man waited upon God and volunteered to
serve God's grand purposes, was thought of as entirely futur-
istic, that is, dependent on a future resurrection from the dead.

Not all German-speaking European clergy welcomed Barth's
proclamation; his old teachers were largely offended. But he
had also come to be much in demand as a lecturer to pastors'
groups in the period in which these newer views of his were
being worked out. His book *The Word of God and the Word
of Man* is a sampler of his addresses in that period.

In 1921, Barth began a new career as professor of Calvinist
theology in the previously all-Lutheran faculty of theology
of the University of Göttingen, Germany. About a year later,
Barth joined forces with some like-minded theologians in
launching a magazine, *Between the Times,* dedicated to a
revival of biblical and reformation-type theology and opposed
to the optimistic and humanistic liberal theology.

In 1925, Barth moved to the University of Münster, Germany, and in 1927 he began the publication of his *magnum
opus* with Volume I, *The Doctrine of the Word of God:
Prolegomena to Christian Dogmatics.* In contrast with his
commentary on Romans, Barth here allows for at least a beginning of the redemption of mankind in this life, that is, a
foretaste on earth of the ultimate redemption of man in the
resurrection from the dead.

Barth's masterwork has subsequently grown through the
years to embrace twelve thick books; and it is unfinished, with
Volume V on redemption still to be written. It is, in essence,
an attempt to restate the whole of Christian doctrine from
Barth's standpoint. Barth's position, meanwhile, has been

undergoing modifications while the work has been in progress. For example, the title of the whole has been changed from *Christian Dogmatics* to *Church Dogmatics*, emphasizing that the point of view is located within the "circle of the church." Even more important, Barth completely rewrote the opening volume in 1932, in order to abandon the attempt to ground Christian doctrine on any nonbiblical statement about mankind's condition or need. He has endeavored to let the work as a whole presuppose nothing beyond the Christian faith itself, as it is evoked by the conviction that it is *God* with whom one has to do in the biblical revelation. Barth is here expressing his rejection of all forms of "natural theology," the attempt to base any statements about God on observations of nature or of history or on any foundation other than the Bible.

In the meantime, in 1930, Barth moved to the University of Bonn, and it was while he was there that he fell out with the government headed by Adolf Hitler. In May 1934, Barth was one of the prime movers of the Barmen declaration, in which about two hundred clergy who had been active in the organization of the (Protestant) Confessing Church in Germany declared against the Hitler-sponsored "German Christianity," that the loyalty and obedience of the Christian church belonged and was offered to Jesus Christ alone and that the church could not accept the state as a master. Barth was now a German (as well as a Swiss) citizen and as a university professor he was required to sign the civil servant's oath of loyalty to Hitler. This he refused to do without permission to specify that under all circumstances he owed a higher loyalty to God. Consequently he was dismissed from the University of Bonn in 1935. From 1935 to 1962, Barth taught theology at the University of Basel, his native city, in Switzerland.

Barth has been called the most famous Protestant theologian of the twentieth century. He has also drawn a remarkable amount of attention and published study of his thought by Roman Catholic theologians. The theology he has taught has been variously known as "neo-orthodox," as the "theology of crisis," the "dialectical theology," and the "theology of the Word of God." As a label, "neo-orthodox" points to the recovery of biblical and reformation ways of thinking. The phrase "theology of crisis" indicates the emphasis, in the earliest phase, on the "otherness" of God and on God's *judgment* against all human claims to adequacy in a culture that was

doomed to revolution and war. "Dialectical theology" points to
the Barthian delight in paradox, the placing against each
other of the divine and the human, time and eternity, good
and evil, and the counterbalancing of assertions made from
different viewpoints in such a way as to suggest the complexity
of the whole truth. "Theology of the Word of God" points to
Barth's concern to subordinate everything in theology to the
"Christological principle," the idea that the one sure revelation
of God's nature is given in the earthly existence of Jesus Christ.

Karl Barth visited the United States in 1962. When he was
given an honorary degree of doctor of divinity by the University of Chicago, the citation read in part (and it is an
excellent summary of his work): "Barth's concern was to assert
the centrality of God over and against the centrality of man in
the method and message of theology."

FURTHER READING

Barth, Karl. *Church Dogmatics: A Selection.*
Brown, James. *Kierkegaard, Heidegger, Buber, and Barth.*
Casalis, Georges. *Portrait of Karl Barth.*
Come, Arnold B. *An Introduction to Barth's Dogmatics for
    Preachers.*
Hartwell, Herbert. *The Theology of Karl Barth.*

———Ludwig Wittgenstein———
[1889–1951]

LUDWIG WITTGENSTEIN, the Austrian-born mathematician and philosopher, once counseled with his philosophy
professor, Bertrand Russell, the great English mathematician
and philosopher, about becoming a pilot or a philosopher.
Russell told him to write something during his vacation and to

submit it for evaluation upon completion. Upon receiving the manuscript and reading "only one sentence," Russell said, "No, you must not become an aeronaut [pilot]."

G. E. Moore, an English philosopher and a contemporary of Wittgenstein, said of him: "When I did get to know him, I soon came to feel that he was much cleverer at philosophy than I was, and not only cleverer, but also much more profound, and with a much better insight into the sort of inquiry which was really important and best worth pursuing. . . ."

Wittgenstein, who influenced many philosophers of the twentieth century, was born in Vienna in 1889, the youngest of five brothers and three sisters. The family was of Jewish descent, even though the grandfather was converted to Protestantism and Ludwig was baptized a Catholic, the religion of his mother. His father, a prominent engineer, and his mother were artistically and intellectually inclined. In fact, because of their intense interest in music, Johannes Brahms, the great German composer, was a close friend of the family. However, tragedy was to stalk Ludwig's life, for three of his brothers committed suicide, and Ludwig himself lived on the "border of mental illness."

After being educated at home until the age of fourteen, Wittgenstein attended school in Linz in upper Austria and a technical school in Berlin, where he studied engineering. At the age of sixteen Ludwig read Schopenhauer, the German philosopher. The youth was influenced by Schopenhauer and accepted his "world as an idea" but not his "world as will." Schopenhauer launched Wittgenstein's philosophical bark.

After registering in 1908 as a research student in engineering at the University of Manchester in England, Wittgenstein was engaged in studying aerodynamics. Becoming perplexed about the philosophical and logical basis of mathematics, he read Russell's *Principles of Mathematics* and the writings on symbolic logic by the German mathematician Frege. These were the "gateways" by which Wittgenstein entered philosophy. Apparently on the advice of Frege, Wittgenstein in 1912 entered the University of Cambridge to study philosophy under Russell.

During World War I, he served in the Austrian Army, and when the Austrian Army surrendered in 1918, he became a prisoner of the Italians. When captured, he had in his knapsack the manuscript for his only book that was published in his lifetime, *Tractatus Logico-Philosophicus*. While reading a magazine in a trench, Wittgenstein conceived of the idea of language being but a tool to picture reality. Through the aid of his friend John Maynard Keynes, the English economist, Wittgenstein sent copies of his manuscript to Russell and Frege, even though Wittgenstein was still a prisoner. Russell wrote an introduction to *Tractatus*, and the book was finally published in 1921.

Tractatus Logico-Philosophicus, written first in German and later inaccurately translated into English, is a classic in philosophy, but its aphoristic style has caused difficulties in interpretation. Wittgenstein often gives no examples for important ideas and metaphors. Moreover, he compressed his ideas almost to the point of obscurity.

The *Tractatus* presents the roles of language and the purposes of philosophy. It is often called the bible of "logical atomism"—a philosophy which maintains that perplexities can be clarified by an ideal language in which each object or quality has a definite symbol. Wittgenstein introduced this work with a metaphysical concept of the world. The world consists of elementary or "atomic facts." They are so called because they cannot be analyzed into simpler propositions. Nonetheless, atomic facts—models of reality—consist of "objects"—things or entities which are unanalyzable. Yet Wittgenstein gave no examples of atomic facts, so Russell in his introduction to the book presented a proposition that might serve as an atomic fact: "Socrates is wise." This proposition, which cannot be further analyzed into a simpler proposition, has two objects, "Socrates" and "wise." Objects in combination form atomic facts; the latter constitute the world.

Wittgenstein maintained that language, the vessel of thought, pictures facts in "logical space," a typical metaphor Wittgenstein was fond of using, and concerning which he gave insufficient insight. However, logical space is comparable to the world of the thinking mind.

A proposition, then, pictures the *possibilities* of facts in logical space. In the proposition "Plato is human" the picture of the fact shown through language is a logical picture, in Wittgenstein's concept, and not a *sensory* one. "Plato" pictures the object Plato; "human" pictures of the object "humanity."

Similarly a map of Los Angeles pictures the structure of the city of Los Angeles. Language pictures anything that is think-able. If something is thinkable, it is logical; if it is not, it is "unlogical."

What does Wittgenstein call language that does not present a picture of facts? "Nonsense!" He declared that trying to portray a picture showing the relationship between proposition and fact is absurd. A map can represent a city, but another map drawn to represent the representation between the map and a city is nonsensical. The original map *shows* the repre-sentation. In philosophy, nonsense abounds. Wittgenstein classified *Tractatus* as nonsense because it attempts to picture the pictorial representation between language and fact. No proposition can say anything about itself. Wittgenstein com-mented that "Most of the propositions and questions . . . in philosophical works are . . . nonsensical. . . .[They] arise from our failure to understand the logic of the language." Wittgenstein's own use of language was not to convey literal truths of philosophy but to serve as steps whereby an individ-ual could develop his own insights.

The purpose of philosophy according to the *Tractatus* is to make logical clarification of all propositions. Wittgenstein criticized all philosophical systems, saying that philosophy is not a theory but an *activity* which elucidates theories and propositions. Since philosophy is not a body of doctrines, it does not discover new facts. The natural scientists add new facts to knowledge. If the natural scientists discover a new theory, the philosopher plays the role of stating what the theories mean. The philosopher examines the wording to see if all words make sense and if the theory contains nonsense. "Philosophy," said Wittgenstein, "settles controversies about the limits of natural science."

To aid philosophy, Wittgenstein suggested that a scientific language be employed with the sole job of describing the world. He hoped to devise a symbolism which would follow the concepts of logical grammar. The verb "to be," for example, may denote a state of being, or be an intransitive verb. Wittgenstein's symbolism would make a distinction among the various uses of the verb "to be." Thus, language would be more precise and accurate. With such a scientific language, philosophy's purposes would be complete.

The *Tractatus* greatly influenced the movement known as "logical positivism." Logical positivism contained a "thorough-going empiricism," relied heavily on concepts of modern logic, respected some of the findings of modern science, and rejected metaphysics on logical bases. Logical positivism was originated by a group of philosophers known as the "Vienna Circle," Moritz Schlick being the leader. The logical positivists needed a theory of meaning for propositions, and the *Tractatus* performed this constructively. Wittgenstein's concepts of logical atomism, portrayed in *Tractatus*, influenced Russell in his work "The Philosophy of Logical Atomism."

After being released as a prisoner, Wittgenstein, surmising that he had completed his task in philosophy as he would have finished an engineering project, became a schoolmaster in Austria from 1920 to 1926 and an architect in Vienna from 1926 to 1928. Through these years Wittgenstein was philosophically unproductive and might have remained so except for the impetus of some friends.

In 1928, Wittgenstein heard a lecture on the foundations of mathematics by the Dutch mathematician L. E. J. Brouwer; the lecture again sparked Wittgenstein's interest in philosophy. In 1929 he returned to Cambridge, where he received his Ph.D. This latter period saw a change in his thinking. A biographer of Wittgenstein wrote that Wittgenstein was "fighting his way out of the *Tractatus*."

After 1933, Wittgenstein "lost confidence" in the main theses of the *Tractatus*—such as that the world is composed of facts—and striving to clarify his thinking, he turned to philosophical linguistics.

In 1937, Wittgenstein became a Professor of Philosophy at Cambridge, and took the Chair of Philosophy, vacated by G. E. Moore, in 1939. Wittgenstein resigned his position in 1947, and died of cancer in Cambridge on April 29, 1951.

Wittgenstein's second work, *Philosophical Investigations,* published posthumously in 1953, germinated from a collection of notes dictated to his class (1933–1934) in Cambridge. In 1947 he revised the manuscript. The *Investigations* portrays his new, more flexible concepts of language, the nature of philosophical puzzlement, and the communication of mental states.

In the *Investigations,* Wittgenstein employed two metaphors that help to unravel his new thinking about language. The first, language as "tools," is best explained by Wittgenstein himself: "Think of the tools in a tool-box: there is a hammer, pliers, a saw, a screw-driver. . . . The functions of words are as diverse as the functions of these objects." Words, then, in contrast to their function in the *Tractatus,* have many uses; words do not have only one meaning.

The second metaphor—somewhat more complex—depicts language as "language games." The metaphor, according to Wittgenstein, "is meant to bring into prominence the fact that the language then becomes a game that a speaker plays when using words and referring to things." Such various "language games" are as follows: "giving orders and obeying them," "describing the appearance of an object," "reporting an event," "forming and testing a hypothesis," "making up a story," and "asking, thanking, greeting, praying."

Wittgenstein portrays a typical language game. (The following employs his knowledge of engineering and architecture.)

A is building with building-stones: there are blocks, pillars, slabs and beams. B has to pass the stones, and that in the order in which A needs them. For this purpose they use a language consisting of the words "block," "pillar," "slab," "beam." A calls them out: B brings the stone which he has learnt to bring at such-and-such a call.

Language games, then, as activities, involve linguistic form ("stone") and nonlinguistic behavior ("passing the stones").

As a result, Wittgenstein contended that the only way to make language intelligible is to evaluate it as it is actually used in its many ways. Thus a word becomes like an action, and meaning must be deduced from the action.

Wittgenstein concluded that philosophical puzzlement or confusion occurs when the users of the language confuse basic concepts about language. One type of philosophical puzzlement occurs when one looks for the common feature of all things called by the same name. The two sentences "He described his room" and "He described his state of mind" would cause confusion if one looked for the common feature in the idea related by "described." In the first usage, "described" pertains to the reporting of physical objects which can be perceived by the senses; in the second, "described" pertains to an evaluation or classification of the psychological processes of the mind. Thus the two usages of the word "described" do not have one common feature but a wide spectrum of features, some of which overlap and crisscross. "Described" in the two sentences is involved in different language games.

In the *Investigations,* Wittgenstein also discusses the way man communicates his mental states. Man does not have an internal vocabulary by which he communicates his feeling. If a person says "I understand," one does not know whether a person does understand. Wittgenstein maintained that the only way a person knows whether one understands is if he applies that which he says he understands. If a person experiences a certain sensation, how does he hope to identify it since the mental word used to identify the first sensation may not apply to a second similar sensation?

Wittgenstein, in the *Philosophical Investigations,* gave his aim of philosophy in this metaphor: "To shew [show] the fly the way out of the bottle." Philosophy prescribes the language to end the intellectual confusion of man—to give him precision of thought and communication outside the constriction of confused language. The philosopher does this by looking at words as tools that can be used in various ways, by refusing to admit that language has only one function, and by rejecting a single-meaning concept of words. "Philosophy," wrote Wittgenstein, "simply puts everything before us, and neither explains nor deduces anything. —Since everything lies open to view there is nothing to explain. . . ." The work of the philosopher, as likewise propounded in the *Tractatus,* is to clarify, unravel, and describe the language.

The philosopher John Wisdom expounded on Wittgenstein's philosophy in his *Other Minds* (1952) and *Philosophy and Psychoanalysis* (1953). For years these were some of the few sources that philosophers could consult to discover Wittgenstein.

Philosophical Investigations gave impetus to Oxford's linguistic philosophy from 1945 to 1960. Wittgenstein's latter work, Gilbert Ryle's *Concept of Mind* (1949), and G. E. Moore's *Philosophical Papers* (1959) were the exponents of the "Oxford philosophy," the clarification of the meaning of language as the undertaking of philosophy. Along with Bertrand Russell, Wittgenstein helped to lead a devastating attack on traditional academic philosophy and, quoting Gilbert Ryle, "has made our generation of philosophers self-conscious

about philosophy itself." As a result philosophy has a new aim
or goal to achieve, and there is a better understanding of the
tools of philosophy, namely, language and logic.

FURTHER READING

Anscombe, Gertrude. *An Introduction to Wittgenstein's Trac-
tatus.*
Malcolm, Norman. *Ludwig Wittgenstein: A Memoir.*
Pitcher, George. *The Philosophy of Wittgenstein.*
Pole, David. *Later Philosophy of Wittgenstein.*

——Reinhold Niebuhr——

[1892–   ]

DURING REINHOLD NIEBUHR'S LIFETIME many utopian reforms and plans have been advanced by individuals
and political leaders to ameliorate the lot of the common man.
However, Niebuhr is one of the few who realized that although these plans might contribute to material satisfaction,
they could not help mankind to achieve greater happiness because they offered solutions outside man himself. With brilliance of logic and forcefulness of oral delivery, Niebuhr focused attention upon the inner man in relationship to social
forces and the flow of history. He was the prototype of the
clergyman who refuses to stand aloof from civil movements,
fighting in the temporal arena for social justice while convey-
ing to his parishioners disturbing truths concerning their religious faith. Niebuhr has been outstanding in clarifying the
relationship of Christian faith to social dynamics.

Reinhold Niebuhr was born in Wright City, Missouri, on
June 21, 1892, the son of a recent immigrant from Germany,

the Reverend Gustav Niebuhr, then a pastor of the Evangelical Synod of North America. Young Niebuhr attended schools of his denomination, and completed his formal education at Yale University Divinity School with a Bachelor of Divinity degree in 1914 and Master of Arts in 1915. He has described himself as being shy and awkward at the time and uncritically conformed to the prevailing liberal outlook in theology.

Rather satiated with academic life, Niebuhr began, in 1915, a career as a parish pastor at Bethel Evangelical Church in Detroit. Under the leadership of its energetic young pastor, this congregation grew from forty members to over eight hundred in the course of his thirteen-year pastorate.

Many of Niebuhr's parishioners were workers in automobile factories, and he not only found himself drawn into identification with them in their economic problems, but he became their ardent champion against the employment policies of the automobile industry. Henry Ford's five-dollar-a-day wage seemed to many at the time to represent industrial enlightenment and progressivism, but Niebuhr was in a position to observe the uncertainty of steady employment, the lengthy lay-offs, and the low annual wage, as well as the other problems workers faced in connection with efforts to organize unions. He became widely known as a speaker at labor and Socialist party forums. In one of his early books, *Moral Man and Immoral Society,* he brilliantly recorded his observation that loyalty to their group, for example their economic class, repeatedly betrayed reasonably moral persons into becoming instruments of the ruthless collective assertiveness of their group in its struggle with other groups.

In 1928, Niebuhr was called to Union Theological Seminary in New York City (affiliated with Columbia University), as associate professor of philosophy of religion, and in 1930 he was appointed professor of applied Christianity. Throughout his tenure at the Seminary he was also constantly in demand as a preacher to college and university audiences, and he was honored repeatedly by leading American and foreign colleges and universities with honorary degrees.

In 1939, Niebuhr became the fifth American scholar to be invited to deliver the prestigious Gifford Lectures at the University of Edinburgh, Scotland. These lectures were subsequently published in the United States as *The Nature and*

Destiny of Man (2 vols., 1941, 1943) and are Niebuhr's major works. In them he compares the biblical idea of mankind's nature and destiny with classical and other philosophic views, always with the intention of showing the 'superior realism of the biblical views, properly understood.

It is in this work that Niebuhr's doctrine of sin is most completely set forth. In contrast with liberal theology, which seemed to him to exaggerate the pervasiveness of human virtue and reasonableness, Niebuhr asserted the biblical view that sin (that is, human pride and egotism) corrupts all human decision-making and action. Human reason, far from being able to control and inhibit selfishness, according to Niebuhr's analysis, cannot escape its own becoming an instrument of selfishness. And at every level of civilization or of attainment of social and personal discipline, selfishness finds new and more sophisticated ways of asserting itself. Thus even those who love their neighbors may not be too sure that they know all that needs to be known about what is best for the neighbor. And there are no human beings so good that they can be trusted with unlimited power over others. Thus the liberal, complacent, nineteenth-century doctrine of inevitable human progress was seen as refuted, with abundant and obvious evidence supplied both by the various current class struggles and by international wars and threats of war.

Niebuhr's provisional pessimism and pragmatism about the virtue and prudence of human behavior did not prevent him from also being a creative pragmatist. That is, while recognizing the prevalence of tendencies toward evil, he preached a restoration of faith and resolute efforts to transcend evil. He was also very much of an activist in reference to America's political affairs. (In fact, he has been sharply critical of Karl Barth, to whom he has sometimes been compared, for what Niebuhr has characterized as "transcendental irresponsibility" in not addressing himself to postwar political problems.)

Niebuhr was, in the 1930's, a leading member of the Socialist party in the United States and an editor of its paper, *The World Tomorrow*. In 1935, he became one of the founders of the Fellowship of Socialist Christians and editor of its quarterly journal, *Radical Religion*. He was also, during this period, a leading member and sometime national chairman of the Fellowship of Reconciliation, a society of chiefly Christian pacifists who totally rejected violence as a method both in the class

struggle and in international affairs. But in 1940, when World
War II was about to break out in Europe, Niebuhr resigned
both from the pacifist movement and from the Socialist party,
which was following a pacifist line. He simply could not go
along with the judgment that war was a greater evil than submission to tyranny. Only a sentimentalized Christianity, he asserted, could prefer slavery to war. And he was embarrassed
by the temporary alliance of moralistic pacifism with such iso-
lationist and, as he saw it, internationally irresponsible movements as the America First committee.

In 1941, Niebuhr became one of the founders and editor
of *Christianity and Crisis,* a biweekly paper dedicated to advocating what he thought was a more responsible Christian
attitude toward World War II. He also became chairman of
the Union for Democratic Action, a committee of ex-pacifist
liberals who were now ready to go to war with Hitler. Niebuhr
did not, however, propose active United States participation
in the war, on the ground that the American people were too
divided about the issue to undertake the national risks involved in being at war. (This dividedness passed, of course,
with the Japanese attack on Pearl Harbor in December 1941.)
During the war years, Niebuhr was active in the Liberal party,
and in 1944 he was elected vice-chairman of that party.

Reinhold Niebuhr has been repeatedly hailed as the most
influential modern American Protestant theologian and the
major postliberal theologian of the English-speaking world. He
has modestly demurred at the title "theologian," for he regards himself as chiefly a student of applied Christianity
(Christian ethics, especially Christian social ethics) and of
apologetics (the work of defending Christianity against skepticism). There is no doubt, however, that he has been the most
powerful single factor in the shaping of current American
Protestant theology.

Niebuhr conceived of justice and love as synonymous. The
spirit of love leads to justice. Justice embodies love in the
social structure of society. The chief foundations of his thought
are to be found in the theology of the Protestant reformation,
that is, in Luther and Calvin. For this reason, he has been
classified, along with Karl Barth and Emil Brunner, as "neo-
orthodox." This term must not be understood as meaning "neo-
fundamentalist." Niebuhr is not a literalist in his reading of
the Bible, nor is he uncritically conformed to the thought of

Luther and Calvin. He fully accepts modern historical-critical
interpretations of the Bible and the findings of modern science.
It is simply that he is convinced, on the evidence of such experience as all persons may share, that man's pride and self-
centeredness (as the Bible indicates) corrupt his behavior
both as an individual and as a member of his various groups
and at all levels of moral attainment. Thus human achievements are always ambiguous in value; for example, modern
science produces both victory over disease and the nuclear
bomb. The only answer to this ambiguity lies in the grace of
God from "beyond history" (the title of another of Niebuhr's
books), which awakes true repentance in men and inspires
them to good works that are unspoiled by pride.

Thus Niebuhr is disillusioned in advance about the promises contained in all utopian or perfectionist schemes of social
reform; yet to him it is still the human calling to work for
social betterment, even without receiving any support from
the illusions that such work will produce a perfect society.
The balance of his thought is well expressed in his frequently
quoted observation on democracy: "Man's capacity for justice
makes democracy possible; but his inclination to injustice
makes democracy necessary."

FURTHER READING

Harland, Gordon. *The Thought of Reinhold Niebuhr*.
Scott, Nathan A., Jr. *Reinhold Niebuhr*.
Tillich, Paul; Bennett, John C., and Morgenthau, Hans J.
   Reinhold Niebuhr: A Prophetic Voice in Our Time.

——Jean Paul Sartre——

[1905–   ]

IN 1965 the world's most honored literary prize was awarded to the French philosopher-writer Jean Paul Sartre. The Nobel Prize for Literature was his. But he chose to reject it, as he had forewarned the prize commission before their decision. Sartre felt that his works and thoughts must be judged on their own merit, and not according to the prizes accorded them: "A writer must refuse to allow himself to be transformed into an institution, even if it takes place in the most honorable form. . . . It is not the same thing if I sign Jean Paul Sartre or if I sign Jean Paul Sartre, Nobel Prize winner." Elaborating further, he objected to the fact that the Nobel Prize was awarded only to Westerners or "to rebels of the East"; but although he stressed that his "sympathies go undeniably to socialism and what is called the Eastern bloc," he did not want to be an institution in either the East or the West.

In a similar manner, Sartre, a second cousin of Dr. Albert Schweitzer, had refused the French *Légion d'Honneur* in 1945 for his efforts in the French Resistance, efforts that cost him nine months in a German prison. The cause of freedom might well be honored, but to honor one man would be to suggest that he was more important than the cause itself.

Sartre's contribution to modern thought lies in his fresh approach to the nature of man and man's relationship to the world. Sartre is the foremost modern exponent of existentialism, a philosophy that has been offered as an alternative to idealism. Although the seeds of existentialism can be traced to early Hebraic literature, especially Job, Sartre has been influenced most by Hegel's dialectical process of reasoning,

584

Nietzsche's early existentialism, and the social consciousness and analysis of history of Marx.

Sartre commences his analysis from a consideration of Descartes's initial subjective assertions, "I think, therefore I am." But contrary to Descartes and Kant, Sartre maintains that there must be an object of thought, and not just an infinite inward progression of consciousness of the state of consciousness. Thus Sartre starts from the premise of the *act* of thinking, rather than from the *awareness* of the act of thinking. To Sartre, "Consciousness requires the given objective world." Whereas Descartes starts from an awareness of the self and attempts to rationally construct the material universe according to a priori principles of logic, Sartre begins with an awareness of self in relation to an existing material world. Similarly, on a social level, the establishment of the self comes only with the realization and establishment of relations with others. As we shall see, this relationship of man to his fellow man plays a major part in Sartre's views of personal ethics and morality.

The objective world to which Sartre refers is the biological, economic, political, and cultural world in which man finds himself; it is man's human subjectivity that enables him to discover this environment and to relate himself to it. Sartre refers to man's consciousness as *être-pour-soi* (being-for-itself), and to the object of consciousness as *être-en-soi* (being-in-itself). These are the two modes of being, reminiscent of a host of earlier dualisms in philosophy that stemmed from the division between mind (soul) and body. To Sartre, man must attempt to overcome this dualism. As soon as he reflects on the objective world, he makes it part of his consciousness: the *en-soi* becomes *pour-soi*. Man must then constantly attempt to combine his experiences and his consciousness of these experiences into a unified whole, the actual man. In other words, the *en-soi* is constantly hindered by the reflective consciousness, the *pour-soi*; it is man's goal to merge awareness itself and the awareness of objects. Indeed, it is this idea that lies at the foundation of Sartre's existential psychoanalysis.

The basic characteristic of all existential philosophy lies in the assertion that "existence precedes essence." That is to say, there are no Platonic Forms (pure essence) of which man and all else is a temporal manifestation (existence), but man *is* (existence), and by the nature of his existence determines *what* he is (essence).

Essential to the existential view of man is the basic assumption of man's freedom. According to this view, one cannot say that a certain man is innately a coward; one can only say that he acts in a cowardly manner, and by his actions attains the attributes (essence) of cowardliness. Man is free at all times to change the nature of his acts; he is not bound by a rigid "essentialistic" framework, but determines his own essence by his own actions. Similarly, "there is no love apart from the deeds of love; no potentiality of love other than that which is manifested in loving."

There are various very important consequences to Sartre's view of man as a completely free being.

If man is free to be what he makes of himself, he is necessarily responsible for his actions. Good or bad, he himself must answer for the consequences of his actions to others and to himself. There is no outside or higher power to whom he can go for refuge or excuse, no one to redeem him for being other than he has been. Responsibility lies squarely upon man's own shoulders.

Thus when Sartre speaks of the "anguish" of the human predicament, he refers to the responsibility from which man cannot escape; he refers to the anguish of total responsibility. And when Sartre says that man is "condemned" to be free, he means that man is alone, without recourse, in determining his own nature. "Each and every individual man must commit himself and act upon his commitment. Man cannot know what is to be; he only knows what is in his power to make things so. Beyond that, he can count on nothing."

Just as man must choose a commitment and act upon it, man is committed to choosing, for even not to choose is itself a choice—the choice of abstention. Indeed, Sartre's philosophy has often wrongly been called negativistic due to his assertion that man's freedom is contained in the ability to say "No"— as when he refused the Nobel Prize. Since man is free and has no recourse other than the actions he himself takes, to hesitate is in itself a decision apparent in the subsequent act of hesitation.

While there are no a priori values for Sartre, there are values—the values that man determines by his choice and actions. There is no good other than that which man creates. The same holds true for society. "In reality, things will be such as men have decided they shall be." Thus man is not only responsible for himself, but he is responsible for all men, "for in effect, of all the actions a man may take in order to create himself as he wills to be, there is not one which is not creative, at the same time, of an image of man such as he believes he ought to be. To choose between this and that is at the same time to affirm the value of that which is chosen." The image man creates for himself, he asserts for all men. There cannot be freedom for one unless there is freedom for all. To claim freedom to oppress others is not itself freedom, but license for oppression.

Jean Paul Sartre was born in 1905, and as he says in the first volume of his autobiography, *The Words*, "I began my life as I shall doubtless end it; amidst books." But Sartre is hardly the epitome of the ivory-tower philosopher. His philosophy is a philosophy of life, and Sartre himself has demonstrated his ideas by his actions.

So Sartre takes on the struggle of the poor and claims for himself "the thinking of the oppressed insofar as they rebel against oppression." Although financially independent with the income from his works, he lives quite modestly and with constant awareness of the world about him. While France was undergoing the throes of the Algerian revolution, Sartre joined other writers in condemning French colonialism and spoke for Algerian independence, signing a manifesto defending the right of French youths to refuse to serve with the French military in Algeria. For this act, a commitment that grew out of his sense of freedom for himself and others, his apartment was bombed twice by right-wing terrorists. Advisers to President Charles de Gaulle asked the French leader to jail Sartre for his urging Frenchmen not to bear arms against the Algerians. But Charles de Gaulle responded, "Sartre is also France." In a similar manner, in 1965, Sartre refused to accept a speaking engagement in the United States, stating that his refusal came as a condemnation of the American people's choice of consenting to their government's military policy in Vietnam. Under these circumstances, he asserted, there can be no intelligent dialogue.

Sartre is also in the tradition of great French writer-philosophers, such as Voltaire, who have articulated their philosophic concepts in literary works that have achieved recognition for their artistic merit as well as for their substantial philosophic statements. He has written a philosophic biography *(Saint*

Genet), plays, novels, essays, philosophic treatises, short
stories, and introductions to the works of others.

In 1942, while Paris was under the heels of the German in-
vaders, he wrote his first play, *The Flies*, a retelling of the
Orestes story, that brought him his first recognition. In this
play man is pictured as right and noble in defying the gods,
and his freedom is shown to come from discovering and realizing his individuality. Four years earlier, as an obscure philosophy teacher, he had written *L'Être et le Néant (Being and
Nothingness)*, his first major philosophic work, which appeared
in 1943. Many of his later plays, including *No Exit*, have appeared on the stage throughout the world and he has adapted
many of his plays for the screen.

After the liberation, Sartre gave up teaching to devote all
his time to writing. His tetralogy, *Roads to Freedom*, which
consists so far of the novels *Age of Reason, The Reprieve,* and
Troubled Sleep, documents the crimes of passivity in the face
of crisis and the personal irresponsibility of Frenchmen just
prior to and during the Nazi occupation of France. Since the
end of the war he has edited a literary monthly, *Les Temps
Modernes*, to which he has periodically contributed articles
and in which he has engaged his critics in debate. His best-
known philosophic work, "Existentialism Is a Humanism"
(often entitled "Existentialism"), was delivered as a lecture
in 1946 in answer to the misunderstanding of his ideas by
many critics who saw in his philosophy a resignation, despair,
and "nothingness."

Sartre is the major exponent of atheistic existentialism. He
goes beyond the nihilistic existentialism of Kafka and Camus,
who despair of the world as "absurd," to present a positive
ethic to which man can aspire and which he can achieve by
his own committed actions. The religious existentialists, Kierkegaard and Tillich, assert that the ideal life can be achieved
by seeking God, whereas Sartre maintains that the sole hope
of man lies within himself, in effect imparting to man the
deity traditionally attributed in defeat to a transcendent supreme being.

Sartre's contribution to modern thought has been to fully
face modern man's vision of an "absurd" situation with a philosophy of integrity and action. As he himself includes in his
"Existentialism Is a Humanism," atheistic existentialism declares that "even if God existed, that would make no differ-

ence." If there is to be social justice and peace on earth, man himself must make it so, or it shall not be.

FURTHER READING

Cranston, Maurice. *Sartre.*
Cumming, Robert, ed. *The Philosophy of Jean Paul Sartre.*
Greene, Norman N. *Jean Paul Sartre: The Existentialist Ethic.*
Kaufmann, Walter, ed. "Existentialism Is a Humanism," *Existentialism from Dostoevsky to Sartre.*
Murdoch, Iris. *Sartre: Romantic Rationalist.*
Stern, A. *Sartre.*

Glossary

———Glossary———

abolitionist—One who during the American Civil War period advocated the immediate abolition of slavery without compensation.

aesthetics—The study of the nature and qualities of beauty.

agnostic—One who believes that neither truth, nor the nature of being, nor divine will is knowable.

anarchist—One who favors a society without government.

a posteriori—Reasoning from observations to generalizations; inductive method.

a priori—Reasoning from self-evident propositions to conclusions about a particular subject; deductive reasoning.

atomism—The belief that the universe is composed of minute, indivisible particles.

business cycle—A complete phase of a succession of economic conditions (depression, recovery, and the steps in between).

capitalism—An economic system in which there is private ownership of the means of production and distribution.

communism—In Marxist theory, the societal development to follow socialism. A society in which the state has withered away and in which goods and work are distributed "from each according to his ability, to each according to his *need*." A classless society. See SOCIALISM.

company union—A labor union formed by employees of one company who are not affiliated with other unions; usually dominated by the employer.

cosmology—The study of the origin and nature of the world.

deductive reasoning—The method of reasoning from the general to the specific.

deist—One who believes in God as the creator and final judge of man, and who bases his faith on human reason rather than on revelation.

delegated powers—Powers specifically granted to the federal government by the Constitution.

determinism—The doctrine that all acts are determined by causes beyond an individual's control.

dialectic—As introduced by Socrates, the art or practice of logically

593

examining opinions or ideas by the method of question and answer to determine their validity. As used by Hegel, a process of
reasoning in which an initial premise (thesis) and its opposite
(antithesis) logically suggest a new premise (synthesis) that
unites and transcends the opposite assertions, and that thereby
offers a new thesis (e.g., being, nonbeing, becoming).

diminishing productivity—The principle that each successive additional unit influences the total product less than the preceding
one.

dogma—A formal doctrine of belief proclaimed by a church.

Donatism—A heretical movement of the fourth century that held
that sanctity is essential for the administration of sacraments and
church membership.

dualism—A philosophy that regards the universe as composed of
two irreducible and opposed elements, e.g., good and evil, form
and matter, mind and matter.

ecumenical—Relating to the whole Christian church.

empiricism—The belief that all knowledge is derived from experience and observation. Opposite of RATIONALISM, the belief that
all knowledge is derived from reason.

Epicureanism—The belief that intellectual pleasure and serenity
are the highest good.

epistemology—The study of the origin, processes, and validity of
knowledge.

esthetics—See AESTHETICS.

ethics—The study of morality, or of the right and wrong of human
behavior.

existentialism—A philosophy based on the assertion that existence
(act) precedes essence (idea); opposed to idealism. A philosophy stressing the importance of man's Being through individual
freedom of choice, commitment and action. The universe is irrational rather than an organized system.

fatalism—The belief that a person's life is preordained and cannot
be altered.

free will—The belief that an individual can make conscious and
effective choices in his life.

fundamentalist—One who believes in the infallibility of the Bible
as divinely inspired, literal truth.

gold standard—Governmental policy of redeeming all money in
gold.

grace—The gift of divine favor and faith that are necessary for
salvation.

guild socialism—An economic system in which industry is run by
the men working in the industry.

hedonism—The belief that pursuit of pleasure is the sole motivation
for behavior.

Hegelian idealism—The belief that the only true reality pertains to
ideas, spirit, or life existing in man's mind. Whatever man conceives in his mind is reality.

humanism—A renaissance movement characterized by a revolt against medieval religious authority and a return to the study of and agreement with the Greek and Latin classics.

humanitarianism—The practice of kindness and charity toward the less fortunate; the active concern for the human welfare of all people.

idealism—The belief that underlying reality exists only in ideas and ideal forms, that there is an absolute, ideational representation of reality. Opposite of MATERIALISM. See HEGELIAN IDEALISM.

indirect tax—A tax on merchandise paid by the producer, usually added to the price and indirectly paid by the consumer.

inductive reasoning—The method of reasoning by first finding the facts and by then generalizing from them. Opposite of DEDUCTIVE REASONING.

intuitionism—The belief that intuition rather than reason is the proper guide to truth.

logic—The study of reasoning.

logical atomism—A philosophy maintaining that problems can be clarified by a language in which each object or property has a definite symbol.

Manichaeism—A dualistic religion spiritualizing light and dark as the struggle between good and evil.

marginal unit of capital and labor—The unit that produces just enough income to pay for itself.

marginal utility—The added amount of satisfaction or usefulness derived from an additional unit of an economic goods.

materialism—The belief that the physical universe of matter and motion is the true reality, and that natural laws within the understanding of reason determine or describe, without divine guidance or intervention, all processes and phenomena.

mercantilism—An economic system based on a favorable balance of trade, the development of a merchant marine, the development of agriculture and manufacturing, and the development of foreign-trade monopolies as sources of raw materials and markets for manufactured goods.

metaphysics—The study of ultimate reality, the nature of being, and the existence of God.

monolatry—Worship of one god without denying the existence of other gods.

nationalism—The spirit of unity existing within a country because of common backgrounds or aspirations of its people.

naturalism—The belief that "laws of nature" govern all reality and human conduct and that reality is within man's grasp without benefit of revelation or of supernatural control.

neutral monism—The belief that there is no difference between mind and matter or between what is physical and what is mental.

nirvana—A state of bliss in Hindu philosophy arising out of the cessation of all desire.

noumenon—The term used by Kant to describe ultimate reality, the "thing-in-itself," which cannot be perceived but exists in the mind.

ontology—The study of the nature and essential properties of being.

orthodoxy—The adherence to traditional or commonly held beliefs.

pantheism—The belief that the universe, as a whole, is God; that there is no God except the forces and laws of the universe.

Pelagianism—A Christian heretical sect denying predestination and original sin and believing that anyone could enter Heaven.

physiocracy—A school of economic thought asserting the "rule of nature" in economic and social affairs.

pluralism—The belief that the world is not unitary in structure and form but composed of separate elements and forces; opposed to ATOMISM.

positivism—The belief that philosophy should be and can be limited to problems solvable by scientific methods and logical analysis. Also known as "logical positivism."

pragmatism—The belief that whatever works well in practice is good.

rationalism—The belief that truth may be achieved by reasoning, not by faith or strict empiricism.

realism—The belief that the external world exists independently of human perception and that the nature of its appearance is substantially what we perceive.

reformation—A revolution of thought in western Europe originally urging reforms in the Catholic Church and eventually evolving doctrines of Protestantism.

scholasticism—A medieval theological philosophy of reasoning by speculation and the use of authority rather than by experimentation.

socialism—In Marxist theory a society in which the means of production are in the hands of the state and in which goods and work are distributed "from each according to his ability, to each according to his ability." See COMMUNISM.

stoicism—A philosophy asserting that all reality is material and that man should live according to nature, justly, and without excesses.

suffrage—The right to vote.

technological unemployment—Unemployment caused by displacement of workers by machines.

Torah—The fundamental laws governing Jewish life as divinely revealed to Moses; the Pentateuch or the Five Books of Moses.

totalitarianism—A system of highly centralized government which permits no public control of government and in which individual freedoms are suppressed.

utilitarianism—The belief that human actions should be judged on the basis of their efficacy in bringing about the greatest good for the greatest number.

Vienna circle—A group of philosophers following logical positivism in the first half of the twentieth century. Leaders were Moritz Schlick and A. J. Ayer.

voluntarism—The belief that the will is the potent factor in human behavior.

welfare state—A society in which there is partial state control and ownership of social services and of some of the means of production.

Supplementary List
of
Great Thinkers

Supplementary List
—of Great Thinkers—————

ADAMS, HENRY (1838–1918). American historian and writer. Pessimistic view of democratic society as corrupt, excessively complex, lacking in unity, materialistic. Favored unity and stable faith of medieval times. Wrote autobiography, *The Education of Henry Adams.*

ADLER, FELIX (1851–1933). American educator and reformer. Founder of Society for Ethical Culture, a society for spiritual fellowship outside the orthodox church. Influenced educational methods and social reforms.

ANAXAGORAS (c. 500–428 B.C.). Greek philosopher. Asserted that the mind operates on matter to produce visible objects, and that matter is composed of atoms possessing all qualities. Banished from Athens for alleged impiety.

ANAXIMANDER (c. 611–c. 547 B.C.). Greek philosopher and astronomer. Taught that matter is composed of a primary substance, infinite, indescribable, and in motion. Made first geographic maps.

ANAXIMENES (c. 550 B.C.). Greek philosopher, from Miletus. Taught that the primary substance is air, of which everything else is formed.

APULEIUS, LUCIUS (2d century A.D.). Greek philosopher and author. Wrote *Metamorphoses,* or *The Golden Ass,* comments on life viewed from transformation as an ass.

AUSTIN, JOHN (1790–1859). English jurist. Believed that authority rather than ethics is the basis of law.

AVERROËS (1126–1198). ibn-Rushd. Muslim philosopher and physician. Major commentator on Aristotle. Reason over faith, anti-theological views.

AYER, ALFRED JULES (1910–   ). English philosopher. Logical positivist. Believed major purpose of philosophy to be logical clarification of thoughts. Wrote *Problems of Knowledge.*

BAAL SCHEM TOV (c. 1700–1760). Israel ben Eliezer. Founded modern Hasidism. Taught disciples with oral sayings and parables. Opposed formal asceticism. Believed formal prayer and learning not necessary for religious feeling and participation.

602 SUPPLEMENTARY LIST OF GREAT THINKERS

BANCROFT, GEORGE (1800–1891). American historian. Favored rationalist approach to history as fulfillment of divine intentions. Featured democratic movement.

BAYLE, PIERRE (1647–1706). French philosopher. Defended liberty of thought and religious toleration. Removed from professorship at Rotterdam because of skepticism. Called founder of eighteenth-century rationalism.

BEARD, CHARLES (1874–1948). American political theorist. Economic factors decisive in history; i.e., struggle between debtors and creditors, between planters and industrialists, desires of merchants, munition makers, etc.

BEDE, SAINT (673–735). Baeda, Beda, or "the venerable Bede." English theologian. A Doctor of the Church. Taught at Jarrow. Wrote an ecclesiastical history of England and De natura rerum, on physical science.

BLACKSTONE, SIR WILLIAM (1723–1780). English jurist. His Commentaries on the Laws of England influenced jurisprudence throughout the world.

BOLIVAR, SIMÓN (1783–1830). South American statesman and general. Responsible for liberation of five republics from Spain. Wanted to unite them, but failed.

BRADFORD, WILLIAM (1590–1657). American historian. Christian interpretation of history as epic of man's progress to redemption.

BRADLEY, FRANCIS H. (1846–1924). English philosopher. Idealist. Believed true reality to be eternal and perfect.

BRUNO, GIORDANO (1548–1600). Italian philosopher. Espoused Copernican cosmology and opposed Aristotelian deductive logic. Arrested by Inquisition and executed. Influenced Leibniz, Spinoza, Hegel.

BURCKHARDT, JACOB (1818–1897). Swiss political theorist. Foresaw decay of democracy to mediocrity and lack of interest in freedom, and rise of a dictator in Germany who would trample on individual rights. Longed for harmony and creative energy of the renaissance. Wrote Force and Freedom (1871).

BURKE, EDMUND (1729–1797). English statesman and orator. Advocated liberal treatment of American colonies against King George in Conciliation with America (1775). Opposed slave trade. Favored constitutional government. Opposed extremism of French Revolution.

CHEN LI-FU (1889–). Chinese philosopher. Expounded dynamic Confucianism as the basis for the Kuomintang ideals. Opposed agrarian reform. Philosophy of Life (1948).

CHUANG-TZU (c. 369–c. 286 B.C.). Chuang Chou. Chinese mystic philosopher. Expounded and extended the Taoist teachings of Lao-tzu. Idealized nature; deplored the character-eroding influence of social and governmental institutions.

COMMAGER, HENRY STEELE (1902–). American historian. Wrote sourcebook Documents of American History (1934). Has been called a Jeffersonian democrat with liberal views. Tried to stimulate thought in *Living Ideas in America* (1951) and *Freedom, Loyalty, Dissent* (1954).

COMTE, AUGUSTE (1798–1857). French philosopher and mathematician. Founded school of positivism. Favored orderly rules for life and government with everyone acting properly from a sense of duty. Advocated a rational society.

CONDORCET, MARQUIS DE (1743–1794). Marie Jean Antoine Nicholas de Caritat. French philosopher and social reformer. Believed that knowledge led to progress. Saw his era as one of advancement in education, science, the emancipation of man, respect for human rights. Died in prison during the French Revolution.

COPERNICUS, NICOLAUS (1473–1543). Polish astronomer. Overthrew Ptolemaic view of astronomy with view of heliocentric solar system—that the planets revolve around the sun. Placed man within the natural order—considered man no longer the center of the solar system.

DANTE ALIGHIERI (1265–1321). Italian poet. Formulated a plan for the unity of religion and politics in which church and empire functioned separately, giving purpose and direction to man's destiny. *Divine Comedy* and political writings.

DARWIN, CHARLES (1809–1882). English naturalist. Documented theory of biological evolution by natural selection and survival of the fittest in *The Origin of Species*. Placed man within the evolutionary development of the animals.

DEBS, EUGENE VICTOR (1855–1926). American labor leader. Favored industrial unionization over craft unions. One of founders of Socialist party.

DEMOCRITUS (c. 460–c. 362 B.C.). Greek philosopher. Expounded and extended atomistic theory of Leucippus. Believed that reality is composed of the void and atoms, and that all perceptions consist of atoms in constant motion. His philosophy also called materialistic. Referred to concepts as "idols," or as pictures of objects received in the mind.

DIDEROT, DENIS (1713–1784). French political theorist and author. His *Encyclopédie* urged more political and religious freedom, influenced French Revolution.

DIOGENES (c. 412–323 B.C.). Greek philosopher. Cynic school. Satirized social conventions. Walked through streets with a lantern looking in vain for an honest man.

DOUGLASS, FREDERICK (c. 1817–1895). Negro abolitionist and author. An escaped slave, he lectured and worked in Massachusetts for abolition of slavery. Wrote autobiographical narrative and purchased his freedom. Founded abolitionist newspaper *North Star*. Recruited Negro regiments and advised Lincoln in Civil War.

DU BOIS, WILLIAM EDWARD BURGHARDT (1868–1963). American historian and Negro leader. Received doctorate of philosophy from Harvard University. Re-examined role of Negro in American history. One of the founders of the National Association for the Advancement of Colored People; exerted more militant position than Booker T. Washington in Negroes' struggle for human rights.

EDWARDS, JONATHAN (1703–1758). American Calvinist preacher. His *Freedom of the Will* argued for determinism.

EINSTEIN, ALBERT (1879–1955). American (German-born) physicist. Original formulator of the theory of relativity and of the unity of gravitation, magnetism, and electricity. Formulated equation of the relation of matter and energy: $E=mc^2$.

EMPEDOCLES (c. 493–433 B.C.). Greek philosopher. Disciple of Pythagoras. Believed world composed of four elements: earth, air, fire, and water. Accepted permanency of change as well as of objects. Recognized contending forces of strife and love. Believed wisdom could rule human behavior. Had idea of survival of the fittest.

EUCLID (c. 300 B.C.). Greek mathematician. Called "father of geometry." His *Elements,* the basis for all later texts in geometry, was the first unified collation of axioms, theorems, and proofs. Established the deductive method of science.

FEUERBACH, LUDWIG A. (1804–1872). German philosopher. Pupil of Hegel. Renounced Hegelian idealism in favor of naturalistic materialism. Attacked orthodox religion and idea of immortality. Regarded God as a projection of man's inner beliefs.

FRANCIS OF ASSISI, SAINT (1182–1226). Italian friar. Founded Franciscan order under rules requiring poverty and strict religious devotion.

FRANKLIN, BENJAMIN (1706–1790). American statesman and scientist. Clarified understanding of the nature of lightning and electricity. Supported the Declaration of Independence and helped frame the Constitution. Invented bifocal glasses, the lightning rod, and the Franklin stove.

FREGE, FRIEDRICH LUDWIG GOTTLOB (1848–1925). German philosopher. Founded modern mathematical logic. Analyzed meaning within the dual areas of image and association, and the difference between the sense and reference of a word. Developed logical symbolism. Influenced Wittgenstein.

FRIEDMAN, MILTON (1912–   ). American economist. Leading exponent of the "Chicago school" of economic thought and policy, which emphasizes conservatism and reliance on automatic stabilizing devices as opposed to government intervention. Critical of the Federal Reserve System and monetary authorities in general.

FROMM, ERICH (1900–   ). American (German-born) psychoanalyst. Leader of neo-Freudian group opposing Freud's emphasis on sex factor and the death instinct. Analyzed individual drives and societal factors of totalitarianism and democracy. Wrote *Escape from Freedom* and *Man for Himself.*

GALILEO (1564–1642). Galileo Galilei. Italian astronomer. Supported the Copernican theory of the solar system. Experimented with falling objects and the pendulum. Advanced the principles of experimentation and observation in science. First to use telescope extensively in astronomy.

GIBBON, EDWARD (1737–1794). English historiographer. Rationalistic approach to history. Espoused material and social progress through rationality. Wrote *The Decline and Fall of the Roman Empire*.

GILSON, ÉTIENNE (1884–   ). French philosopher. His *The Spirit of Medieval Philosophy* (1932) renewed interest in Descartes, Aquinas, and other medievalists.

HAN FEI-TZU (c. 283–233 B.C.). Chinese philosopher. Exponent of legalist school, that law should replace morality or religious principles in setting standards for human behavior. Favored replacing loose feudal relationships with strictly enforced laws.

HANSEN, ALVIN H. (1887–   ). American economist. Often called "the American Keynes" because of his espousal of New Deal policies, which called for government intervention in economic affairs. Believed "stagnation" inevitable unless governments intervened. Wrote *Business Cycles Theory* (1927), a systematic attempt to analyze all factors influencing modern economic and business cycles.

HEIDEGGER, MARTIN (1889–   ). German philosopher. Existentialist; man's anguish can be resolved not by religion but by questioning existence and by "resolute decision." Influenced Sartre.

HERACLITUS (c. 500 B.C.). Greek philosopher. Known as the "dark" philosopher because of his pessimism. One of first metaphysicians, sought to discover universal law.

HERZL, THEODOR (1860–1904). Austrian (Hungarian-born) founder of modern Zionism. Advocated creation of a Jewish state in *Der Judenstaat*.

HILLEL (c. 60 B.C.–c. A.D. 10). Founded influential Jewish school. A leader of the influential Sanhedrin. Set seven rules of Bible interpretation. Believed in leniency in applying Jewish laws.

HIPPOCRATES (c. 460–c. 370 B.C.). Greek physician. Originated oath of professional ethics in medicine used today. Held that physicians should study the patient, not only the illness; applied knowledge of diet, environment, and personal factors to treatment of disease.

HOFSTADTER, RICHARD (1916–   ). American historian. Intellectual patterns and motivations are decisive in history.

HOLMES, OLIVER WENDELL (1841–1935). American jurist. Responsible for interpreting the First Amendment to be valid in all cases in which there is no "clear and present danger" directed against the government.

HSÜN TZÜ (4th century B.C.). Hsün K'uang or Hsün Ch'ing. Chinese eclectic philosopher. Combined the best of Taoism, Moism, and Confucianism in his teachings. Deplored degeneracy of his time. Believed man was evil by nature but could be improved by a salutary government and proper rulers.

HU SHIH (1891–1962). Chinese philosopher and diplomat. Favored pragmatic school. Influenced by John Dewey, William James, and Aldous Huxley.

HUSS, JOHN (c. 1369–1415). Jan Hus. Czech religious reformer. Attacked abuses of clergy. Condemned and executed as a heretic.

HUSSERL, EDMUND (1859–1938). German philosopher. Expounded on relationship of mind and matter. Influenced existentialist thought.

JASPERS, KARL (1883–   ). German philosopher. Asserted a non-rational subjective philosophy; stressed the distinction between facts and an individual's attitude toward facts.

JEROME, SAINT (c. 340–420). Latin church father. Doctor of the Church. Secretary to Pope Damasus. Translated the Bible from Greek into Latin (called the Vulgate). Also wrote ecclesiastic history.

KAPLAN, MORDECAI M. (1881–   ). American (Lithuanian-born) rabbi and philosopher. Founded the reconstructionist movement in Jewish life, including the concept of a Jewish center in the community.

KING, MARTIN LUTHER, JR. (1929–   ). American civil rights leader. Pastor of Baptist church in Montgomery, Alabama. Led Negro boycott of Montgomery buses ended by Supreme Court decision against segregation on buses. Advocate of nonviolent resistance by Negroes to attain civil rights. Head of Southern Christian Leadership Conference. Awarded Nobel Peace Prize in 1964.

KNOX, JOHN (c. 1505–1572). Leader of Scottish reformation. Founded Scottish Presbyterianism. Sought to abolish pope's authority in Scotland and vigorously opposed other creeds.

KUNG, HANS (1928–   ). Swiss theologian. Professor of fundamental theology in the Catholic Theological Faculty of the University of Tübingen. Major role in interpreting objectives of the Second Vatican Council; sometimes called the "theologian of ecumenism"; believes reunion of Catholicism and Protestantism requires renewal and reform.

LASSWELL, HAROLD (1902–   ). American political theorist. Accepts behaviorists' empirical methods but wishes to stress use of history to solve present problems.

LEUCIPPUS (c. 450 B.C.). Greek philosopher. Atomistic theory. Studied under Zeno; taught Democritus.

LIBERMAN, EVSEI (1897–   ). U.S.S.R. economist. Advocated reforms involving introduction of the profit incentive and bonuses to stimulate production; decentralized planning of factory production, more consumer goods.

LONERGAN, BERNARD J. (1904–   ). Canadian philosopher. Entered Society of Jesus at age seventeen. Member of the Pontifical Gregorian University's faculty. Chief intellectual work in analysis of the nature of knowing, and of the intellectual method. Thinking reflects Aristotle and Thomas Aquinas, with modifications deriving from Kant and Freud. His speculations and studies point to a transcultural philosophy.

LOYOLA, SAINT IGNATIUS OF (1491–1556). Spanish ecclesiastic and soldier. Founded Jesuit order after renouncing military career. Order to live ascetic life, seek conversions, and refute the charges of Protestant reform movement.

LUCRETIUS (c. 96–55 B.C.). Titus Lucretius Carus. Roman philosopher and poet. Expounded Epicurianism in his poem *De rerum natura:* the gods are not concerned with mankind and there is no punishment after death; therefore live in peace and happiness.

MACH, ERNST (1838–1916). Austrian physicist and philosopher. Extreme positivist; relied on senses and empiricism to reveal scientific truths. Influenced Vienna circle of logical positivists.

MAHAVIRA, VARDHAMANA JNATIPUTRA (6th century B.C.). Indian religious leader. Founded religion of Jainism; asceticism and self-denial.

MALEBRANCHE, NICOLAS DE (1638–1715). French philosopher. Founded Malebranchism: mind cannot know anything outside itself except through its relation to God.

MAO TSE-TUNG (1893–   ). Chinese political theorist, revolutionary, and poet. One of the founders of the Chinese Communist party, chairman of the Central Council of the People's Republic of China. Foremost spokesman and theoretician of techniques of guerrilla warfare and wars of national liberation.

MARITAIN, JACQUES (1882–   ). French philosopher. Converted from Protestantism to Roman Catholicism (1906). Stressed kinship of the democratic ideal and belief in God. Pointed out distinction between the individualism advocated by Luther and the necessary spiritual orientation of the total person.

MAZZINI, GIUSEPPE (1805–1872). Italian patriot and political theorist. Favored liberal republican nationalism. Believed sovereignty resides in people; religious, optimistic about democratic future. Fought for liberation and unification of Italy.

MENGER, KARL (1840–1921). Austrian economist. Cofounder of school of marginal utility. Opposed historical method in economics and favored analysis by cause and effect. Held theory of value an individual phenomenon, subjective and dependent on individual wants, not on rules of society.

MERRIAM, CHARLES (1874–1953). American political theorist. "The Chicago movement." Approached political science as a behavioral science. Used statistical techniques, sociological and psychological analysis. Wrote *New Aspects of Politics.*

MILLS, C. WRIGHT (1916–1962). American sociologist. Analyzed power and politics in American society both in terms of national and international issues. Wrote *White Collar, The Power Elite,* and *The Causes of World War Three.*

MIRANDA, FRANCISCO (c. 1750–1816). Venezuelan political reformer. Called the precursor of Latin American independence. Fought in the American and French Revolutions. Led revolution against Spain resulting in Declaration of Independence of Venezuela in 1811. Believed in emancipation of slaves and in republican government. Captured by Spain, he died in prison.

MOORE, GEORGE EDWARD (1873–1958). English philosopher. Main fields: philosophic method, ethics, and perception. Accepted "common-sense" beliefs as valid basis for philosophical reasoning.

MORAZÁN, FRANCISCO (1799–1842). Central American statesman. Unsuccessfully sought to hold together the federation of Central American countries and to give them social, religious, and economic reforms.

MO TI (c. 470–c. 385 B.C.). Mo-tzŭ. Chinese artisan and philosopher. Founded the school of Moism as result of dissatisfaction with Confucianism. Described the ideal society based upon utilitarianism and brotherly love.

MÜLLER, ADAM (1779–1829). German political economist of romantic school. Opposed rationalism and individualism. Strong German nationalist convictions. Urged domination of state over individuals.

NEMCHINOV, VASILY S. (1894–1964). Russian economist. Called dean of Soviet economists. Favored modification of central controls over production by contracts to enterprise groups. Responsible for favorable reception given to Liberman.

NEVINS, ALLAN (1890–   ). American historian. Widened history to include findings of anthropologists, psychologists, sociologists.

OCKHAM, WILLIAM OF (c. 1300–c. 1349). William of Occam. Also known as "the Invincible Doctor" and "Venerabilis Inceptor." English scholastic philosopher. Advocated civil rule separate from church. Established nominalist doctrine that universals have no real existence but are only abstract terms, that the real is always individual. Argued that in reasoning one should not seek unknown entities as theories or proofs until the possibilities of known entities or proofs are thoroughly explored.

O'HIGGINS, BERNARDO (1776–1842). South American statesman and soldier. Obtained independence of Chile and set up republican government. Sought social, educational, and religious reform.

ORTEGA Y GASSET, JOSÉ (1883–1955). Spanish philosopher, writer, and statesman. Explained philosophic views in essays. Social analyst signaling the rise of the masses against elite minorities. Precursor of existentialist social thought.

OWEN, ROBERT (1771–1858). Welsh industrialist, philanthropist, and social reformer. Turned his New Lanark mill into a successful financial and social venture with the practice of advanced ideas of social reform. Founded several socialist or cooperative communities, including one at New Harmony, Indiana. Believed man's character determined entirely by environment. Father of cooperative movement.

PARETO, VILFREDO (1848–1923). Italian economist. Used mathematical analysis for societal problems. Favored rule by elite and deprecated democracy, pacifism, and international brotherhood. Wrote *The Mind and Society* (1916). Ideology of Italian fascism is based upon his theories.

PARKMAN, FRANCIS (1823–1893). American political theorist. Romantic approach to history. Romanticized heroes.

PARMENIDES OF ELEA (c. 515–c. 440 B.C.). Greek philosopher. Founded Eleatic school. Wrote in verse. Based his philosophy, which he called "way of truth," on logical deduction. Being and thought are one.

PATANJALI (c. 2d century B.C.). Indian Yoga philosopher. Religious discipline leads to highest consciousness and supersensuous state, thus to achievement of final release from physical life.

PEANO, GIUSEPPE (1858–1932). Italian mathematician and logician. Translated mathematics into symbols of logic. Devised an international language (Interlingua) based on Latin, German, French, and English.

PEIRCE, CHARLES SANDERS (1839–1914). American philosopher and logician. Stressed importance of language and the understanding of the nature of man. Founder of pragmatism. Wrote *Illustrations of the Logic of Science* (1878). Now regarded as greatest logician of his time.

PERLMAN, SELIG (1888–1959). Naturalized American economist. Foremost disciple of J. R. Commons. Wrote *A Theory of the Labor Movement* (1928) to illustrate the changing role of unionism in the United States from an idealistic to a pragmatic approach.

PHILO OF ALEXANDRIA (20 B.C.–A.D. 54). Philo Judaeus. Jewish philosopher. Sought to bridge and harmonize the religious philosophy of Aristotle, Plato, and other Greeks with Jewish scriptures. Represented Jews in a mission to Roman Emperor asking him not to demand his deification by Jews.

PIGOU, ARTHUR C. (1877–1959). English economist. Successor to Alfred Marshall's economics chair at Cambridge. His book *Economics of Welfare* was dedicated to the proposition that it was society's obligation to create the greatest good for the greatest number.

PROTAGORAS (c. 450 B.C.). Greek philosopher. First of the sophists. Banished from Athens for questioning the existence of the gods. Believed that man is the measure of all things. Systematized study of grammar.

PROUDHON, PIERRE JOSEPH (1809–1865). French economist and social reformer. Spokesman for small farmer; urged equality, rule of law, and end to privilege. Opposed strong central government, capitalists, and financiers. Favored credit unions and cooperatives. Opposed trade unions but favored improvement of lot of workers by peaceful, legal means. Predicted that Marxian socialism would lead to serfdom of the masses.

PYTHAGORAS (c. 530 B.C.). Greek philosopher and mathematician. Known as "the Samian sage." First to consider philosophy as a way of life, almost a religion. Believed in transmigration of soul. Founded Pythagorean school, known for expounding mystical qualities of numbers.

RAHNER, KARL S. J. (1904–   ). Austrian. Jesuit theologian. "Theologian of Innsbruck." Respected for ability to uncover new vistas in basic problems. Stimulated study of theology for its personal as well as academic value. Has questioned previous approaches and has pointed out the gaps in existing theological compendiums. Penetrating analyst of contemporary problems as the phenomenological and existential examination of the real. Author of *Theological Investigations*.

RAMANUJA (c. 1017–1137). Indian philosopher second to Sankara. Whereas the latter believed knowledge is self-luminous and absolute, Ramanuja believed knowledge is relative, nearer to man's reach. Made distinction between subject and object of thought.

RANDALL, JAMES G. (1881–1953). American historian. Held that psychological factors of individuals determine history.

RANKE, LEOPOLD VON (1795–1886). German historian. Founded school of modern history which urged objective writing based on source material and facts rather than on traditions. Extolled Prussia in historical writing.

RASHI (1040–1105). Rabbi Solomon Yitzhaki ben Isaac. French rabbinical scholar. Wrote influential, scholarly, lucid commentary on Pentateuch and the Babylonian Talmud.

ROBINSON, JOAN (1903–   ). English economist. Wrote *Economics of Imperfect Competition* (1933), in which she demonstrated that "monopolistic competition" or competition between producers of differentiated products was the rule rather than the exception. Recognized as an outstanding authority on Marxian economics.

ROYCE, JOSIAH (1855–1916). American idealist philosopher. Believed matter exists only as human minds know it. The individual mind is part of the world mind.

RYLE, GILBERT (1900–   ). English philosopher. Analyzed nature of meaning, philosophy of logic, linguistics. Believed role of philosophy to be the clarification of our conceptual processes. Wrote *The Concept of Mind*.

SAINT-SIMON, COUNT CLAUDE HENRI DE (1760–1825). French philosopher and social reformer. French volunteer with Americans in American Revolution. Founded French socialism to improve lot of the workers, but held the social order should be directed by the best educated and trained. Examined social problems by scientific or "positive" approach. Recognized need for religious belief.

SANKARA ACHARYA (c. 800). Samkara. Shankara. Indian philosopher. One of greatest commentators on Vedanta sutras and Upanishads. Taught that Brahma—the absolute existence, knowledge and bliss—is real but the universe is not real.

SAN MARTÍN, JOSÉ DE (1778–1850). South American statesman and general. Won independence from Spain of Argentina, Chile, and Peru. Desired a limited monarchy and foresaw evils of fractionalizing South America.

SAY, JEAN BAPTISTE (1767–1832). French economist. Popularizer of the work of Adam Smith. His *Treatise of Political Economy* (1803) was a standard textbook in the United States for a quarter of a century. He is best known for his "law of markets," which states that supply, in effect, creates its own demand.

SCHECHTER, SOLOMON (1850–1915). Rumanian-born Jewish scholar. Founded conservative Judaism. Strong force in developing the Jewish Theological Seminary and United Synagogue of America.

SCHILLEBEECK, EDWARD (1914–   ). Belgian theologian. Professor of dogmatic theology at University of Nijmegen; theological expert for Dutch bishops at Second Vatican Council. One of the leading thinkers in "new" personalist emphasis in the current renewal of theology, especially concerned with man's individual encounter with God in the community of men and women who live in and for Christ.

SCHLESINGER, ARTHUR M., JR. (1917–   ). American historian. Opposes revisionism and urges moral judgments by historians and the study of mental atmosphere of historical periods.

SCHLESINGER, ARTHUR M., SR. (1888–1965). American historian. Stressed social-cultural history of people.

SCHLICK, MORITZ (1882–1936). Austrian physicist and philosopher. Leader of Vienna circle of logical positivists—appliers of the inductive methods of science to philosophy.

SCHMOLLER, GUSTAV (1838–1917). German economist. Developed a systematic approach to economics by using ideas and materials from history, psychology, anthropology, biology, and geology. Founder of socialist-type *Verein;* believed in the duty of economists to involve themselves in reform programs.

SCHUMPETER, JOSEPH A. (1883–1950). German economist. On Harvard faculty from 1932. Wrote *Business Cycles* (1939). His *Capitalism, Socialism, and Democracy* (1942) discussed strengths and weaknesses of these two economic systems.

SCHWEITZER, ALBERT (1875–1965). Alsatian-born humanitarian, theologian, philosopher, physician, and musician. Founded a hospital in Lambarene, Africa; devoted life to helping the African people. Wrote *Life of Jesus* and several books revealing his philosophy of life, epitomized as "reverence for life."

SENECA, LUCIUS ANNAEUS (c. 4 B.C.–A.D. 65). Roman stoic philosopher. Taught that philosophy was the means to living a more virtuous life. Tutor to Emperor Nero; committed suicide at Nero's order. Wrote several tragedies, including *Oedipus.*

SHAW, GEORGE BERNARD (1856–1950). Irish playwright, essayist, social critic, and Fabian socialist. Used the drama as a medium to produce evolutionary social change; believed poverty the greatest sin. Made the English middle class the target of his scathing wit.

SMITH, JOSEPH (1805–1844). American religious leader. Founded Mormon Church. *The Book of Mormon* (1830). Founded Church of Jesus Christ of Latter-Day Saints at Fayette, New York. Internal schism and public disapproval of polygamy led to open conflict and his death by shooting.

SOLON (c. 638–c. 559 B.C.). Greek lawgiver. Instituted economic and constitutional reforms in Athens. Reorganized senate, assembly, voting, and laws.

SPANN, OTHMAR (1878–1950). Austrian economist and sociologist. Individual subordinate to nation. Rejected classical economics as "atomistic individualism."

STRAUSS, LEO (1899–   ). American (German-born) political theorist. Opposes scientific, behavioral approach to history. Favors political scientists as philosophers, and common-sense analysis of history.

SUMNER, CHARLES (1811–1874). American statesman. Bitter foe of slavery. First prominent statesman to urge emancipation. Urged more authority for freedmen in reconstruction.

T'AI HSÜ FA-SHIH (1890–1947). Chinese philosopher. Spokesman for liberal Buddhists. Harmonized philosophy and science.

TAUSSIG, FRANK WILLIAM (1859–1940). American economist. Combined practical affairs and theoretical works. First chairman of the United States Tariff Commission. Wrote *Tariff History of the United States* (1888).

TAWNEY, RICHARD HENRY (1880–1963). English economic historian. Stressed role of ethics in economic life. His *Religion and the Rise of Capitalism* (1926) criticized the social framework of society that sanctioned greed and profit over morality. Greatly influenced the British Labour party and the Fabians.

THALES OF MILETUS (c. 640–c. 546 B.C.). Greek philosopher and scientist. Father of philosophy. Taught that water was the prime element from which everything else is created. Founder of geometry and astronomy.

THERESA OF AVILA, SAINT (1515–1582). Spanish Carmelite nun. Had divine visitations. Founded a new order of Carmelite nuns, called Descalzos ("barefoot ones"), to abide by the original discipline of the Carmelite. Despite difficulties, established sixteen convents and fourteen monasteries. Canonized 1622.

THÜNEN, JOHANN H. VON (1783–1850). German economist. Applied deductive method and statistical investigation to economics. Careful analysis of wages, interest, and the idea of marginal productivity.

TILLICH, PAUL JOHANNES (1886–1965). American (German-born) theologian. Re-examined Christian faith in the light of modern philosophy. Spoke of "courage-to-be" and faith in a self-revealing God.

TOCQUEVILLE, ALEXIS DE (1805–1859). French political theorist. An aristocrat who accepted the French Revolution. Visited America (1831) and expressed approval in his book *Democracy in America*, but cautioned that democracy might prove despotic and materialistic and lead to mediocre leadership. Favored decentralization of government.

TOYNBEE, ARNOLD J. (1889–   ). English historian. Wrote monumental *A Study of History* (1934–1954). Has emphasized importance of religious spirit in history. Opposes militarism and nationalism. Believes there is a form and purpose in society.

TREITSCHKE, HEINRICH VON (1834–1896). German historian and political theorist. Supported both Prussian expansion under kaisers and anti-British feeling.

TROTSKY, LEON (1879–1940). Real name Lev Bronstein. Russian revolutionary leader. Foreign minister of first Soviet government. First formulated theory of permanent revolution. Exiled from Russia after Stalin was chosen Lenin's successor; attacked Stalinist government in various political writings, although continued to advocate socialism. Assassinated at his home in Mexico.

TURNER, FREDERICK JACKSON (1861–1932). American historian. Believed in scientific approach to analyzing history. Regarded American history as a series of evolutions from simple frontier to complex. Frontier was necessary outlet for discontented. Creditor-debtor struggle as background of history.

UNAMUNO Y JUGO, MIGUEL DE (1864–1936). Spanish philosopher, essayist, poet, dramatist, and novelist. Attempted to resolve conflict between reason and faith; pleaded for passion over rationality, and for faith over reason. Precursor of existentialist thought.

WANG YANG-MING (1472–1529). Wang Shou-jên. Chinese philosopher. Expounder of Confucianism. Taught integrity of thought and action in *Instructions for Practical Living*. "To do is easy; to know is difficult."

WEBB, BEATRICE (1858–1943), and husband, SIDNEY WEBB (1859–1947). British social and economic reformers. Helped form British Labour party; advocated socialism.

WEBB, WALTER P. (1888–   ). American historian. Positivist or scientific approach to history. Each region develops own cultural adaptation to circumstances.

WEBER, MAX (1864–1920). German philosopher and political theorist. Studied relationships among ideology, religions, social structure, and material values. Analyzed political and economic institutions such as monarchy, capitalism, technology, and bureaucracy. Stressed need for objectivity in examining social problems. Wrote *The Protestant Ethic and the Spirit of Capitalism*.

WELDON, T. D. (1896–1958). English political theorist. Applied logical positivism and linguistics to political theory. Wrote *The

Vocabulary of Politics (1953) on the use and abuse of language in the making of political theories, declaring that in politics we discuss second-order not first-order questions, and that no political theory can be proved best.

WHITEHEAD, ALFRED NORTH (1861–1947). English mathematician. Professor of philosophy at Harvard. Worked with Bertrand Russell on the logical foundations of mathematics. Viewed life as a continuance of interrelations: man, the world, God, society. Tried to establish a comprehensive system including physical sciences, religion, morality, and metaphysics. Urged more attention to aesthetics and less to "groove thinking." Regarded science as revolt against rationalism of the Middle Ages.

WISDOM, A. JOHN T. D. (1904–   ). English philosopher. Pupil of Wittgenstein. Clarified role of philosopher. Willing to accept metaphysical surmises and unconventional approaches without inductive proof. Wrote *Philosophy and Psychoanalysis* (1953).

WISE, ISAAC MAYER (1819–1900). Father of Reform Judaism. Departed from traditions of orthodox beliefs. Founded Hebrew Union College and the Union of American Hebrew Congregations.

WOODSON, CARTER G. (1875–1950). American historian. Authoritative research on Reconstruction and Negro history. Founded *The Journal of Negro History*.

WYCLIFFE, JOHN (c. 1320–1384). English theologian. Favored limitation of civil powers of Church. Attacked worldliness and abuses of medieval Church officials. Challenged various Church doctrines and the authority of the pope. Advocated inner religion, fewer formalities. Accused of heresy and forbidden to teach at Oxford. Translated Bible into English to reach people directly. Called precursor of the reformation.

XENOPHANES (6th century B.C.). Greek philosopher. Criticized mythological ideas of gods. His belief was pantheistic.

YANG CHU (c. 300 B.C.). Chinese philosopher. Founded materialistic school of Taoism. Believed world created by chance; had a fatalistic concept of destiny and death, and a nonmoral view of life in which sensual delights were the goal (hedonism). He deprecated social institutions.

YOUNG, BRIGHAM (1801–1877). American Mormon leader. Directed Mormon settlement in Nauvoo, Illinois (1838), and supervised mass migration of Mormons to Great Salt Lake Valley in Utah. Succeeded Joseph Smith as head of the Mormon Church. First governor of Utah (1849–1857).

ZENO (c. 336–c. 264 B.C.). Greek philosopher, from Citium. Founded stoic school of philosophy—named after the *stoa* where he lectured.

ZUNZ, LEOPOLD (1794–1886). German-Jewish scholar. Scientific biography in Jewish studies. Influential history of Jewish homiletics. Middle position between Reform and Orthodox Judaism.

Indices

INDEX OF 100 GREAT THINKERS
ACCORDING TO FIELD OF ENDEAVOR

Religion

Akhenaton
Akibah ben Joseph
Anselm
Aquinas
Barth
Boethius
Buber
Buddha
Calvin
Duns Scotus
Eddy
Erasmus
Fox
Gandhi
Gregory the Great
Isaiah

Jeremiah
Jesus
Lao-tzu
Luther
Moses
Muhammad
Nanak
Newman
Niebuhr
Ramakrishna
St. Augustine
St. Paul
Spinoza
Wesley
Zoroaster

Philosophy

Abelard
Aristotle
Bacon
Bentham
Bergson

Berkeley
Confucius
Croce
Descartes
Dewey

Political Theory

Economics

ALPHABETICAL INDEX OF 100 GREAT THINKERS

This book is a production of
Heron Books, London

This book was printed in England
and bound by Hazell Watson & Viney Ltd,
Aylesbury, Bucks